D1485347

House of Commons Library
54056001315446

DIVORCE IN ENGLAND

DIVORCE IN ENGLAND

A Centenary Study

O. R. McGregor

HEINEMANN

MELBOURNE LONDON TORONTO

William Heinemann Ltd
LONDON MELBOURNE TORONTO
CAPE TOWN AUCKLAND
THE HAGUE

First Published 1957

Printed by Morrison and Gibb Ltd
London and Edinburgh

CONTENTS

LIST OF TABLES

The deep damnation of his taking-off

Macbeth

PREFACE

PUBLIC and private discussions of divorce are very much out of harmony. The Press reflects the prurience as well as the uncertainties of ordinary people, and marital unhappiness is "news." The pulpit speaks with many voices in an embarrassed endeavour to reconcile dogma and reality. Divorce lawyers are floundering in a morass of inherited legal and moral attitudes which have led them into chicaneries, loss of status in their profession and public contempt. Is it any wonder that parliament hesitates to legislate?

The appointment of the Morton Commission in 1951 raised hopes that these urgent issues would be squarely faced. But the Commission neither related the personal, legal and social problems posed by its terms of reference nor attempted to investigate the social reality which divorce law seeks to regulate. Its *Report* cannot therefore serve as a basis for informed discussion or for legislation. We have now practised civil divorce for a hundred years and the only voice that has not yet been heard on this experience is that of the social scientist. This book is the comment of a historically minded social scientist. It examines the claims of those religious leaders, lawyers and moralists who assert their right to tell other people, especially working people, how to behave. It does not claim to be impartial (whatever that may mean); it does claim to be candid because throughout it attempts to distinguish between fact and opinion. If it seems to handle the social thinking and statistical projections of ecclesiastical dignitaries and their secular counterparts somewhat roughly, there is no intention of impugning their sincerity. They all, like the rest of us, find it hard to reconcile belief and conduct. But there can be no excuse for unscientific explanations of such data as exist or for the substitution of dogma for empirical knowledge in this crucial area of human behaviour.

It is not the purpose of this book to offer suggestions for comprehensive divorce law reform. Legislative schemes abound : they cover the possible range of legal expedients from complete abolition of divorce to the establishment of divorce by consent. The Morton Commission made no attempt to secure the social evidence by which alone the merits of these schemes can be judged or their consequences predicted. In this situation, the only worthwhile procedure is to assemble available information, to define the areas of knowledge and of ignorance, and to distinguish scrupulously between fact and opinion. In tackling social problems the most constructive attitude is often the recognition that awareness of ignorance is the beginning of wisdom. Meanwhile, life will not wait upon the social sciences nor will human beings model their behaviour upon principles laid down by backward looking Royal Commissions. In our own as in all similar societies divorce is now an urgent issue. This not because marriage and the family have broken down, not because religion has yet lost all its sanctions, but because in democratic industrial societies freedom of choice is replacing compulsion. If people are free to base their political and personal loyalties on choice, they will get into the habit of exercising choice. The art of successful choosing takes much learning especially in societies which have been and still are conditioned by social inequality. Prevailing attitudes towards divorce as reflected in the *Report* of the Morton Commission are defensive if not atavistic. The essence of democratic living is the rational exercise of choice. Choice necessarily implies change and fear of change has never been a successful guardian of morality. Free men and women ought not to tolerate barriers erected as safeguards against their assumed irresponsibility. And, in any case, they won't.

I cannot acknowledge my obligation to all those friends and colleagues who, in their different ways, have helped me to an understanding of my subject matter. I have benefited greatly from access to the admirable collection of the Women's Service Library and from the bibliographical erudition and kindness of its Librarian, Miss Vera Douie. Mrs. Marjorie McIntosh and Mr. A. R. Ilersic kindly read and improved parts of the text. Mr. N. H. Carrier and Miss Griselda Rowntree generously read and commented on the chapter dealing with the statistics of divorce. Mr. Alan Hill read the manuscript and made valuable suggestions for its improvement. Mr. Morris Finer patiently and unprotestingly endured an endless stream of legal queries.

I am especially grateful to Dr. Barbara Wootton who read the manuscript and gave me much help and advice. I have been too long and too deeply in debt to Mr. H. L. Beales to be able here to make adequate acknowledgment. My wife did not inspire me to begin this book but it would never have been finished without her critical and continuous assistance.

It is the convention that authors should, when petitioning the public in prefaces, absolve the persons named from final responsibility. This I gladly do, but I think they all would admit to some measure of collusion, connivance and condonation.

Department of Sociology,
Bedford College,
University of London.

CHAPTER I

THE HISTORY OF DIVORCE IN ENGLAND

By the middle of the twelfth century the previously uncertain beliefs and jurisdiction of the Roman Church, dominating Western Christendom, had hardened into settled doctrine. From then until the Reformation the law of marriage was embodied in the law of the Church, the canon law, administered by the Church in its own Courts Christian. The civil law in England and Scotland had neither doctrine concerning nor jurisdiction over marriage and divorce. The law enforced by the Church derived its principles from the prevailing Christian fear of the pleasures of copulation. The medieval Church, regarding copulation in much the same way as Victorian temperance reformers thought of drink, accordingly followed St. Paul's advice to the Corinthians and recommended marriage as the only means by which the concupiscent generality of men and women might escape the sinful consequences of their incontinence. Consequently the Church held marriage to be a formidable barrier to the attainment of spiritual purity because it exposed husbands and wives to the risks of sexual pleasure. The law of the Church therefore imposed celibacy on the clergy, encouraged the establishment of celibate communities, and extolled the virtues of virginity. Only an inferior sort of sanctity was possible for married people. "I praise marriage," St. Jerome had said, "because it produces virgins for me." Copulation within marriage, provided it was limited to the occasions necessary for procreation and conducted without anticipated or actual enjoyment, was permissible, though no one could hope to escape some measure of defilement. Without the sacramental protection of marriage, copulation was translated into the deadly sins of fornication and adultery.

"The law that springs from this source," remark the greatest historians of English law, "is not pleasant to read."[1] Marriage became the most formless of all contracts. It could be celebrated openly *in facie ecclesiae* according to the rites of the Church after the due publication of banns, or clandestinely. A clandestine marriage was contracted *per verba de futuro* if a couple prefaced their copulation with a verbal declaration of their intention to be man and wife; or *per verba de praesenti* if a couple simply announced "we are now man and wife." Canon law permitted children above the age of seven to contract marriage without their parents' consent. The canon law thus established the principle that marriage required nothing more than the free consent of the parties. Only marriages *in facie ecclesiae* were deemed "regular" marriages, nevertheless irregular marriages were perfectly valid and thus indissoluble.[2] Irregular, or clandestine marriages were as popular amongst the poor who thereby escaped the payment of fees, as they were disliked by the Church. Parties to them were liable to ecclesiastical censure, but the canon law continued to recognise their validity until the middle of the sixteenth century. If the Church made the form of the contract so elastic that, in the extreme case, an existing marriage could be both valid and unprovable, it also made the terms so rigid that no validly contracted Christian marriage could be dissolved. A consummated marriage had the immutable character of divine law and was held, by God's own ordinance, absolutely indissoluble. A marriage law that asserted both the validity and indissolubility of clandestine marriages was a practical absurdity which could be

[1] F. Pollock and F. W. Maitland, *The History of English Law*, 2nd. ed. (1898), vol. II, p. 385.

[2] There is a very clear account in the book of James Bryce, *Studies in History and Jurisprudence* (1901), vol. II, p. 416 *et. seq.*

sustained only by exercising the full range of canonical casuistry. The resulting doctrine of nullity was the tribute exacted from medieval theology by the realities of the world it attempted to control.

The Church had abolished divorce *a vinculo matrimonii*, (a divorce which dissolved the bond of marriage and gave one or both of the parties the right to marry another), by elevating marriage to the status of a sacrament. If a spouse were guilty of adultery, cruelty, or heresy and apostasy, the ecclesiastical court would only pass sentence of divorce *a mensa et thoro* (a divorce from bed and board), which had the effect of a modern judicial separation. The harsh realities of this theory were never pushed so far in practice as to bring the will of God into implacable conflict with the waywardness of the medieval laity. By a series of elegant if ingenuous sophistries canon law maintained the indissolubility of marriage and yet gave the practical consequences of a wide freedom of divorce. Only a valid marriage was indissoluble. If it could be shown that an impediment to the validity of a marriage had existed at the time it was contracted, then that marriage was held never to have existed even though it had lasted *de facto* for thirty years and produced a quiverful of children. The impediments to the formation of a valid marriage were extensive and sophisticated. Marriages between persons within the fourth degree of consanguinity were forbidden after the beginning of the thirteenth century. Nor was blood relationship the only impediment. The Church held that copulation made man and woman one flesh and, with inexorable logic, established the rule that such connection created a relationship of affinity. The blood kinswomen of a man's mistresses were for this reason connected with him by way of affinity to the fourth degree. Affinities so acquired were impediments to marriage as dire as blood relationships. As sexual union created one flesh so also, the Church insisted, baptism created a new birth and with it, through the relations of godparents, spiritual affinities which also impeded the validity of marriage. The table of consanguinity together with the carnal and spiritual affinities turned the law of marriage into "a maze of flighty fancies and misapplied logic"[1] so tortuous that, in England, "spouses who had quarrelled began to investigate their pedigrees and were unlucky if they could discover no *impedimentum dirimens*."[2] English common law met the inevitable complications of this system for the legitimacy of children by the invention of a doctrine of possessory marriage under which men and women could, and frequently did, marry twice and had two legitimate families. In a small country like Scotland, the upper classes could scarcely contract a marriage outside the intricate web of the canon lawyers' tables of consanguinity and affinity.

Occasionally the absurdity and uncertainty which characterised the Christian doctrine of marriage in this period creep into the histories of an age in which marriage and diplomacy went hand in hand. After the death of James IV of Scotland, his widow, Margaret Tudor, married the Earl of Angus. In 1524, by collusion with her husband, she secured a sentence of nullity from the ecclesiastical court and married Lord Methven. By a further ecclesiastical suit she again freed herself upon evidence that Methven was cousin, eight degrees removed, to her former husband Angus. The marriage of the great Elizabeth's mother, Anne Boleyn, to Henry VIII was annulled by the ecclesiastical court on the double grounds of her earlier pre-contract with Northumberland and the affinity created by Henry's sexual intercourse with her sister. These are late examples, familiar nowadays to all Scots and English schoolchildren from their history lessons, of the flimsy grounds on which the rich and powerful obtained dissolution of their marriages in

[1] Pollock and Maitland, *op. cit.* II, p. 389.
[2] *ibid.*, p. 393, fn. 5.

the period from the twelfth century to Tudor times. When the Roman Church extirpated some of the scandalous and profitable abuses of its canon law of marriage by the provisions of the Council of Trent (1545–1563), the papal authority in Britain had been broken. A new settlement of the relation between church and state was being hammered out in which " the Church no longer ran the country : the country ruled the church." [1]

With the Reformation divorce takes a new aspect. Most reformers rejected outright the doctrines of the medieval church. They regarded marriage as a civil contract to be regulated by the state. They rejected both the safety-valve and sacramental conceptions and re-established marriage as desirable and normal for all human beings, including the clergy. They argued that marriage was dissoluble though differing widely as to the grounds on which divorces should be allowed. These protestant ideas were quickly accepted in Scotland. John Knox had followed Luther in permitting divorce for adultery.

> Marriage once it is lauchfullie contracted may not be dissolved at manis pleasour, as oure Maister, Jesus Christ, doth witness, onles adulterie be commited ; which being sufficientlie proven in presence of the civil magistrate, the innocent (yf thei so requyre) ought to be pronounced frie, and the offendor ought to suffer the death as God hath commanded.[2]

From 1557 the Commissary Court which took over the jurisdiction of the ecclesiastical courts of the Roman Church, gave absolute divorce for adultery and malicious [3] desertion for four years. By 1573 these (without Knox's penalty for the offendor) had become, and have since

[1] A. L. Rowse, *The England of Elizabeth* (1950), p. 391. In chs. X and XI Mr. Rowse admirably describes the Elizabethan Settlement and the attitudes of Puritans and Catholics.

[2] Works, vol. II, p. 248.

[3] In English usage, malicious means wilful.

remained, grounds for divorce in Scotland. For Scots protestants, they have been justified for nearly four hundred years alike by scriptural warrant and public policy. The extravagant medieval doctrine of nullity disappeared from Scotland with the Reformation though the pre-contract survived. The law of Scotland continued to recognise the three types of marriage sanctioned by the old canon law. Until the twentieth century a valid marriage could be contracted *in facie ecclesiae* or according to the forms for civil marriage, or *per verba de praesenti*, or *per verba de futuro subsequente copula*. In Scotland the reception of the Reformation was swift, its consequences for marriage and divorce were clear and certain. The reformed Church in Scotland early achieved a clarity of thought and certainty of doctrine about divorce which have always eluded its sister Church of England. But Scotland, as Lord Campbell once remarked to an English audience, " is a small country of peculiar habits and very religious notions and what will serve there will not do here."

The effects of the Reformation on the law relating to marriage and divorce in England are obscure and confusing. In the century before the Civil War there was great perplexity as to the principles which ought to be enforced and the laws actually in force. The evils of the canon law of marriage were vigorously recited and abolished by a statute [1] of 1540 " for marriages to stand notwithstanding pre-contracts."

> Whereas heretofore the usurped power of the Bishop of Rome hath always intangled and troubled the mere jurisdiction of this realm of England, and also unquieted much the subjects of the same, by his usurped power in them, as by making that unlawful which by God's word is lawful, both in marriage, and in other things . . . marriages have been brought into such an incertainty thereby, that no marriage can be so surely knit and

[1] 32 Henry VIII c. 38.

bounden, but that it should lie in either of the parties' power and arbiter, casting away the fear of God, by means and compasses to prove a precontract, a kindred and alliance or a carnal knowledge, to defeat the same, and so in the pretence of these allegations aforerehearsed, to live all the days of their lives in detestable adultery, to the utter destruction of their own souls, and the provocation of the terrible wrath of God upon the places where such abominations were suffered and used. . . . Be it therefore enacted . . . that no reservation or prohibition, God's law except, shall trouble or impeach any marriage without the Levitical degrees ; and that no person of what estate degree or condition soever he or she be, shall . . . be admitted in any of the Spiritual Courts within this the King's realm, or any of his Grace's other lands and dominions, to any process, plea or allegation, contrary to this foresaid Act.

This Act abolished pre-contract and closely circumscribed the doctrine of nullity by substituting the Levitical degrees within which marriage was forbidden for the canon lawyers' tables of consanguinity and affinity. The new certainties were short-lived ; the Act was repealed in 1548. For another two hundred years the English ecclesiastical courts, their ultimate authority transferred from Pope to Crown, continued to enforce the medieval law of marriage and the restricted survivals of the law of nullity.

The necessity for the introduction of new principles of divorce was widely recognised. Statutes were passed in the reigns of Henry VIII and Edward VI delegating to Commissioners the duty of reforming all the laws of England relating to ecclesiastical matters. The resulting *Reformatio Legum Ecclesiasticarum* of 1552, prepared largely by Peter Martyr, Professor of Divinity in the University of Oxford, under the eye of Archbishop Cranmer, contained a section entitled *De Adulteriis et Divortiis*. This proposed to grant divorce for adultery, desertion, cruelty and deadly hostility, and to subject matrimonial offenders to the condign penalties of perpetual banishment or life imprisonment and expropriation of property. Divorce *a mensa et thoro* was to be abolished as contrary to Holy Scripture. The *Reformatio Legum* never became law in England. It was a victim of troubled times and the papist reaction under Mary who came to the throne in 1553. Its general theological outlook pleased neither Puritan nor moderate opinion, and the severity of its divorce code was repugnant to the laity. However, the preparation of the *Reformatio Legum* poses the question whether the section on divorce represented Church of England opinion in the decades following the Reformation. The answer is much disputed. For if the Church of England accepted absolute divorce in the early days of its establishment, then assertions now being made by the doctrinally dominant section that the Church has never deviated from the medieval doctrine of indissoluble marriage, have no historical warrant. In a document remarkable for its omissions and historical refinement the Church of England explained to the Morton Commission in 1952 that the section on divorce of the *Reformatio Legum* did not represent the settled mind of the Church. "The code," it explained, "was the work of extremists, and largely of foreign protestant refugees (Laski, Martyr), and their 'fellow-travellers' or sympathisers, such as Cranmer and Hooper." [1] The dislike of the modern Church of England for its protestant origins is not, perhaps, surprising, although the evident anxiety of established Christians to judge the soundness of theological opinions according to the nationality of their advocates is a disturbing sign of the modernity of their outlook. In this instance the Church's argument is not only repugnant but historically unsound. No less an authority than Sir Lewis Dibdin was certain that the *Reformatio Legum* "is merely a literary relic," but he also thought

[1] Minutes of Evidence, Royal Commission on Marriage and Divorce, 6th Day, p. 163.

"the opinion that adultery was on biblical grounds a valid reason for the complete dissolution of marriage seems to have been widely . . . even generally, held by English divines in the latter half of the sixteenth century."[1] The attitude of most protestants in the second half of the sixteenth century was elegantly summarised by Henry Smith in his *Preparative to Marriage*, published in 1591.

> Divorcement, which is the rod of marriage, and divideth them which were of one flesh, as if the bodie and soul were parted asunder, but because all performe not wedlocke vowes therefore He which appointed marriage hath appointed divorcement as it were, taking our privilege from us when we abuse it. As God hath ordained remedies for every disease, so He hath ordained a remedie for the disease of marriage. The disease of marriage is adulterie, and the medicine thereof is divorcement . . . thus, He which made marriage did not make it inseparable, for then marriage would be a servitude.[2]

Protestant doctrines of divorce, widely accepted in England, were never legally recognised during the Reformation, though there is clear evidence[3] that the laity obtained divorce with the right of subsequent marriage in the second half of the sixteenth century. By the beginning of the next century, however, the Church of England publicly affirmed its belief in the absolute indissolubility of marriage relieved only by divorces *a mensa et thoro* granted for adultery, cruelty and the like. By a curious irony the leading protestant

[1] Minutes of Evidence, Royal Commission on Divorce and Matrimonial Causes, vol. III (Cd.6481), 1912, p. 52. The Gorell Commission obtained elaborate memoranda discussing, *inter alia*, the doctrinal position of the Church of England regarding divorce during the sixteenth century from Sir Lewis Dibdin, Sir John Macdonell and Lord Gorell.

[2] pp. 90, 92.

[3] It is set out in Appendix I, p. 15 *et. seq.*, Appendices to Minutes of Evidence and Report of Royal Commission on Divorce and Matrimonial Causes (Cd. 6482), 1912.

country in Europe maintained the jurisdiction of ecclesiastical courts over marriage and divorce, the formless and uncertain marriage contract, and the rigorous theory of indissolubility prevalent in medieval times. The only effect of the Reformation on marriage in England was the abolition of the very evasions, fictions and loopholes which had made the medieval system tolerable in practice. The Church of England did, however, go so far as to reject sacerdotal celibacy.

After the Restoration the ecclesiastical courts would not give an absolute divorce and the civil courts had no jurisdiction. As the only authority in England competent to overrule divine law was Parliament, those who wished to be divorced had to secure a Private Act for the purpose. The pressures for relief and the grounds on which it was accorded clearly emerge from the early instances. In 1697 the Earl of Macclesfield who had earlier failed to persuade the ecclesiastical court to grant him a divorce *a mensa et thoro*, successfully petitioned the House of Lords for a Private Act giving him an absolute divorce on the grounds

> that it would be a most unreasonable hardship upon him, that the standing law which is designed to do every man right, should, by the rigour of the letter, be to him the cause of the greatest wrong : and that for his wife's fault he should be deprived of the common privilege of every freeman in the world, to have an heir of his own body to inherit what he possessed either of honour or estate, or that his own brother should lose his claim to both, and have his birthright sacrificed to the Lady Macclesfield's irregular life.[1]

In 1700 the Duke of Norfolk, likewise unsuccessful in securing a divorce *a mensa et thoro* in the ecclesiastical court, obtained " An Act to dissolve the Duke of Norfolk's marriage with the Lady Mary Mordant and to enable

[1] First Report of Royal Commission (on) The Law of Divorce (1604), 1853, p. 12, fn. 6.

him to marry again." The Act alleged the Duchess's adultery and continued :

> Forasmuch as the said Henry, Duke of Norfolk, hath no issue nor can have any probable expectation of posterity to succeed him in his honours, dignities, and estates, unless the said marriage be declared void by authority of Parliament ; and the said Duke be enabled to marry any other woman . . . the King's and Queen's excellent Majesties, having taken the premises into their Royal consideration, for divers weighty reasons are pleased that it be enacted . . .[1]

These Acts were passed to safeguard the inheritance of property and family succession endangered by a wife's adultery. They established a precedent followed until 1857. There were five such Acts before 1715 ; they averaged one a year between 1715 and 1775, and three a year thereafter. In 1798 these judicial proceedings by legislative process were standardised by standing orders of the House of Lords which required, *inter alia*, that all applications for divorce in the House of Lords should be supported by a sentence of divorce *a mensa et thoro* from the ecclesiastical court,[2] and by a verdict of damages for criminal conversation secured against the wife's seducer in the Common Law courts. During the first half of the nineteenth century a Divorce Bill could be obtained as a matter of right by an innocent husband against a wife guilty of adultery. During a century and a half there were only four cases in which an Act was passed at the suit of a wife. In each the husband was proved guilty not only of adultery but of aggravating enormities such as bigamy and incest. For practical purposes the Private Act procedure could be invoked only by men whose wives were adulterous.

[1] First Report of Royal Commission (on) The Law of Divorce (1604), 1853, p. 12, fn. 6.

[2] This was a very odd procedure because a decree *a mensa et thoro* pledged the petitioner not to remarry during the lifetime of the spouse from which it separated him.

After the Restoration the consequences of the medieval doctrine of indissoluble marriage were mitigated in England by resort to the procedure of Private Act of Parliament as they had been evaded before the Reformation by the sophistical doctrine of nullity. No Bishop in the House of Lords objected to Private Act divorces on Christian grounds between the beginning of the eighteenth and the second quarter of the nineteenth century [1]; and the Church never refused to re-marry in these cases.[2] But some of the abuses of the canon law of marriage did not survive. The ease with which marriages could be contracted, and the subsequent difficulty of dissolving them, created a situation which scandalised even eighteenth-century opinion. London was plagued by the evils of Fleet marriages vividly described by Lecky.

> A multitude of clergymen, usually prisoners for debt and almost always men of notoriously infamous lives, made it their business to celebrate clandestine marriages in or near the Fleet (Prison). They performed the ceremony without license or question, sometimes without even knowing the names of the persons they united, in public-houses, brothels, or garrets. They acknowledged no ecclesiastical superior. Almost every tavern or brandy shop in the neighbourhood had a Fleet parson in its pay. Notices were placed in windows, and agents went out in every direction to solicit the passers-by. A more pretentious, and perhaps more popular establishment was the Chapel in Curzon Street, where the Rev. Alexander Keith officiated. He was said to have made a "very bishopric of revenue" by clandestine marriages, and the expression can hardly be

[1] Evidence of Sir Frederick Pollock, Q. 42059, vol. III, p. 437, Minutes of Evidence, Royal Commission on Divorce and Matrimonial Causes (Cd. 6481), 1912.

[2] The Archbishop of Canterbury, *Problems of Marriage and Divorce* (1955), p. 14 asserts that "the Church . . . was not in a position to refuse to re-marry in these cases." This is a puzzling use of language. The Church then had the same capacity as it has today to refuse such remarriage. The Archbishop should have said "the Church . . . did not choose to refuse to remarry in these cases."

exaggerated if it be true, as was asserted in Parliament, that he had married on an average 6,000 couples every year. . . . Young and inexperienced heirs fresh from college, or even from school, were thus continually entrapped. A passing frolic, the excitement of drink, an almost momentary passion, the deception or intimidation of a few unprincipled confederates, were often sufficient to drive or inveigle them into sudden marriages, which blasted all the prospects of their lives. In some cases, when men slept off a drunken fit, they heard to their astonishment that, during its continuance, they had gone through the ceremony. When a fleet came in and the sailors flocked on shore to spend their pay in drink and among prostitutes, they were speedily beleaguered, and 200 or 300 marriages constantly took place within a week. Among the more noted instances of clandestine marriages we find that of the Duke of Hamilton with Miss Gunning, that of the Duke of Kingston with Miss Chudleigh, that of Henry Fox with the daughter of the Duke of Richmond, that of the poet Churchill, who at the age of seventeen entered into a marriage which contributed largely to the unhappiness of his life. The state of the law seemed, indeed, ingeniously calculated to promote both the misery and the immorality of the people, for while there was every facility for contracting the most inconsiderate marriages, divorce, except by a special Act of Parliament, was absolutely unattainable. It is not surprising that contracts so lightly entered into should have been as lightly violated. Desertion, conjugal infidelity, bigamy, fictitious marriages, celebrated by sham priests, were the natural and frequent consequences of the system.[1]

Such evils necessitated the revision [2] of the whole marriage law carried through Parliament by the Lord Chancellor in 1753. Lord Hardwicke's Marriage Act "for the better preventing Clandestine Marriages," provided that no

[1] W. E. H. Lecky, *A History of England in the Eighteenth Century*, 3rd. ed. (1883), vol. I, pp. 490–491.

[2] This had earlier been achieved by Cromwell's Civil Marriage Act which was repealed after the Restoration.

marriage in England was to be valid unless celebrated by an ordained priest according to the Anglican Liturgy in a parish church or public chapel of the Established Church. No ceremony could be performed, save by expensive licence from the Archbishop, unless banns had previously been called for three successive Sundays. It enacted that a marriage register book be kept in every church, in which a record of every marriage be entered and confirmed by the signatures of the contracting parties and witnesses, and provided severe penalties, including transportation for life, for neglect of these provisions. This Act established two principles of great importance. Marriage became for the first time a public and certain contract; and secondly, the right to determine what constituted a valid marriage was removed from the Church and assumed by the state. Special arrangements were made only for Jews and Quakers. Other nonconformists were left with considerable grievances by their forced submission to an Anglican ceremony which, if observed, disturbed their consciences and, if ignored, the settlement of their property. These were not remedied until 1836 when a further Marriage Act licensed nonconformist places of worship for the celebration of marriage. It also drew out the logical consequences of Lord Hardwicke's Act by establishing a wholly civil procedure for contracting marriage. Thus, by 1836, the marriage laws of England had been reformed and citizens provided with a voluntary choice of religious or civil marriage. Some consequences of the different marriage laws of England and Scotland for long continued to cause anxiety and indignation south of Gretna Green. William Farr, writing the Introduction to the first volume of the Census of 1851, explained that:

> Seduction and polygamy are greatly facilitated—concubinage is concealed by the appearance of marriage—under the law of Scotland; and in the North of England the bargain to live together, and to marry

> conditionally is very much encouraged by the facility of going into Scotland and being married. The degree in which that takes place in the border counties is incredible. English minors are legally married, without the consent of their guardians, in Scotland; and at Gretna Green, one important object of the English Marriage Act of 1753 is defeated. English parents of property are still afraid . . . to send their eldest sons to the University of Edinburgh, from the justifiable apprehension that they might succumb before the facilities of the law and the charms of the women of Scotland: against which the breasts of their youthful countrymen, alone, are steeled—by habit probably—as it does not frequently happen that Scottish heirs contract irregular marriages.[1]

In 1845 the self-reliant attempt of a labourer, Thomas Hall, to shoulder his parental responsibilities and to shield his many children from the worst consequences of maternal deprivation, brought him to Warwickshire Assizes on a charge of bigamy. The stark conflict between his legal and familial obligations was underlined in the judgment of Mr. Justice Maule.

> Prisoner at the bar, you have been convicted before me of what the law regards as a very grave and serious offence: that of going through the marriage ceremony a second time while your wife was still alive. You plead in mitigation of your conduct that she was given to dissipation and drunkenness, that she proved herself a curse to your household while she remained mistress of it, and that she had latterly deserted you; but I am not permitted to recognise any such plea. You had entered into a solemn engagement to take her for better, for worse, and if you got infinitely more of the latter, as you appear to have done, it was your duty patiently to submit. You say you took another person to become your wife because you were left with several young children who required the care and protection of someone who might act as a substitute for the parent

[1] p. 1

who had deserted them ; but the law makes no allowance for bigamists with large families. Had you taken the other female to live with you as your concubine you would never have been interfered with by the law. But your crime consists in having—to use your own language—preferred to make an honest woman of her. Another of your irrational excuses is that your wife had committed adultery, and so you thought you were relieved from treating her with any further consideration —but you were mistaken. The law in its wisdom points out a means by which you might rid yourself from further association with a woman who had dishonoured you ; but you did not think proper to adopt it. I will tell you what that process is. You ought first to have brought an action against your wife's seducer if you could have discovered him ; that might have cost you money, and you say you are a poor working man, but that is not the fault of the law. You would then be obliged to prove by evidence your wife's criminality in a Court of Justice, and thus obtain a verdict with damages against the defendant, who was not unlikely to turn out a pauper. But so jealous is the law (which you ought to be aware is the perfection of reason) of the sanctity of the marriage tie, that in accomplishing all this you would only have fulfilled the lighter portion of your duty. You must then have gone, with your verdict in your hand, and petitioned the House of Lords for a divorce. It would cost you perhaps five or six hundred pounds, and you do not seem to be worth as many pence. But it is the boast of the law that it is impartial, and makes no difference between the rich and the poor. The wealthiest man in the kingdom would have had to pay no less than that sum for the same luxury ; so that you would have no reason to complain. You would, of course, have to prove your case over again, and at the end of a year, or possibly two, you might obtain a divorce which would enable you legally to do what you have thought proper to do without it. You have thus wilfully rejected the boon the legislature offered you, and it is my duty to pass upon you such sentence as I think your offence deserves, and that sentence is, that you be imprisoned for one day; and in as much as the present assizes are three days old, the result is that you will be immediately discharged.[1]

This Benthamite irony crystallised early Victorian dissatisfactions with the inherited system of divorce by reducing it to an untenable hypocrisy. Politicans were forced to face embarrassing questions which they pushed on to a Royal Commission under the chairmanship of Lord Campbell, in 1850.

The Commissioners surveyed the consequences of the Reformation and reported on the Private Act procedure against the background of half a century's demand for the reform and cheapening of law and the persistent attack by middle-class people on the privileges of aristocracy. They estimated " that the total cost, under the most favourable circumstances, of obtaining a divorce *a vinculo matrimonii* (that is, absolute divorce) can hardly be less than £700 or £800; and when the matter is much litigated, it would probably reach some thousands. In Scotland, the average cost of rescinding a marriage is said to be £30 and that when there is no opposition, £20 will suffice. In Scotland, also, it is not a privilege for the rich, but a right for all. . . ." [2] The necessary inference was inescapable. Divorce by Private Act had either to be abolished or the facility cheapened and generalised.

The Commission's recommendations were largely enacted in 1857 by the Matrimonial Causes Act which made a decisive break with the past and established the basis of present jurisdiction and procedure. The main object of this Act was to create a new Court for Divorce and Matrimonial Causes to which was transferred all jurisdiction at that time exercised in matrimonial matters

[1] Several variants of the unreported judgment in *Regina* v. *Thomas Hall*, alias *Thomas Rollins*, are current. The above is printed in the book of M. I. Cole, *Marriage Past and Present* (1938), p. 55, fn. 1.

[2] First Report of Royal Commission (on) Law of Divorce (1604), 1853, p. 21.

by the ecclesiastical courts in England. It abolished divorces *a mensa et thoro* and substituted decrees for judicial separation. The grounds for such actions in the ecclesiastical courts had been the adultery or cruelty of either spouse; to these the Act added desertion without cause for two years or upwards. The Court was given power to pronounce a decree of divorce *a vinculo matrimonii* for the same causes as had merited relief by Private Act. In a husband's petition, simple adultery sufficed; a wife was required to prove not only adultery but the additional aggravation of desertion, cruelty, incest, rape, sodomy or bestiality. Connivance, collusion, or condonation were to be absolute bars to a petition for divorce. Actions against a wife's seducer for criminal conversation were abolished; in their place a husband could claim damages in the divorce court against a co-respondent. The Act further provided that the court could sit outside London and should have power to enable persons to sue *in forma pauperis*. The former provision was never acted on, the latter remained ineffective.

The main and only important purpose of the Act of 1857 was to make the civil system of divorce established by the House of Lords in 1697, more widely available. It altered the procedure for obtaining divorce, but introduced no new principles. This was repeatedly emphasised during the debates on the Bill in both Houses. The Attorney-General, Sir Richard Bethell, later Lord Westbury, moved the second reading in these terms:

> The Bill had excited great anxiety and even alarm in the country at large. It had been said by some, and believed by others, that the Bill was an attempt to introduce new laws and new principles . . . the Bill only involved long-existing rules and long-established principles, and it was intended to give only a local habitation to doctrines that had been long recognised as part of the law of the land, and for a century and a

> half administered in a judicial manner, although through the medium of a legislative assembly. Its object was to remove the inconvenience of that practice, but in all other respects the law of England upon the subject of divorce would remain what it was now.[1]

This simple but significant point is stressed because this Act has been persistently misrepresented. Lord Justice Denning, for example, recently discussing the importance of religion in family life, wrote: "the principle of indissolubility was the binding force which cemented it. During the last ninety-six years the State has abandoned the principle."[2] The only principle abandoned in 1857 was the propriety of giving legal remedies for matrimonial difficulties to the aristocracy and withholding them from the growing upper middle class.

The cheapened procedure under the Act, which resulted in an immediate increase in the number of divorces from an annual average of 148 in the decade after 1859 to one of 582 in the decade before 1900, was criticised during the remainder of the century on two main grounds. First, that by making divorce easier for men than for women, it sanctioned two standards of morality. Secondly, that the cheaper procedure in the divorce court remained so costly that working people were denied the remedy of divorce for their matrimonial difficulties.

The Commissioners in 1850 recommended that the law should continue to regard a wife's adultery as a more serious offence than a husband's. They quoted as a "just observation" Dr. Johnson's view that "the difference between the adultery of the husband and the

[1] Hansard, 1857, vol. 147, cols. 718–9.

[2] Alfred Denning, *The Changing Law* (1953), p. 121. Similarly, Mr. Arthur Macmillan, a barrister who has written extensively on divorce, wrote in a memorandum submitted to the Morton Commission, "... from 1857, when divorce was introduced ..." (Minutes of Evidence, Royal Commission on Marriage and Divorce, 5th Day, p. 127). In the large pamphlet literature of religious bodies it is frequently assumed that divorce was introduced into England in 1857.

adultery of the wife (socially speaking) is boundless," and asserted in their Report the rule of conduct succinctly summarised by Lord Tennyson in *Idylls of the King*.

> I hold that man the worst of public foes
> Who either for his own or children's sake
> To save his blood from scandal, lets the wife
> Whom he knows false, abide and rule the house.

Lord Lyndhurst's attempt,[1] in the discussions on the Bill in the House of Lords, to secure equality of treatment for women was answered by the Lord Chancellor, Lord Cranworth, who stated the grounds for inequality then generally accepted in England as socially necessary.

> A wife might, without any loss of caste, and possibly with reference to the interests of her children, or even of her husband, condone an act of adultery on the part of the husband ; but a husband could not condone a similar act on the part of a wife. No one would venture to suggest that a husband could possibly do so, and for this, among other reasons . . . that the adultery of the wife might be the means of palming spurious offspring upon the husband, while the adultery of the husband could have no such effect with regard to the wife.[2]

The Lord Chancellor did not explain why nearly three hundred years' experience of legal equality between men and women in Scotland in matters of divorce had not there resulted in the dire consequences with which its adoption was thought to threaten English society. But two generations later, when women had begun to claim equality of rights, and birth control had become a growing habit amongst the affluent, such arguments appeared irrelevant and even dangerous to morality. The new attitudes deriving from changing social habits were thus described by Mrs. Fawcett, the leader of the constitutional section of the organised women's movement.

[1] Hansard, 1857, vol. 145, col. 496 *et. seq.* [2] *ibid.*, col. 813.

> The cause (of divorce) most generally and properly recognised is that of unfaithfulness to the marriage vow, and I hold it to be highly injurious to the moral sense of men and a real degradation to them, to put them on a lower plane than women as regards marital fidelity. As the law of England now stands it sets up two standards, a fairly high one for women, a lower one for men. . . . I urge most strongly that the difference between the sexes which now exists in divorce law should be put an end to. If this be not done, I foresee a special danger in the circumstances in which we now stand. There is a great social and political movement going on making for equality between the sexes. It is visible to every one, whether he sympathises with it or not. In a very large number of matters it begins to be thought that what is good enough for men is good enough for women, and *vice versa.* If in matters of morality you do not level up, you will almost certainly level down. . . . If the law were equalised as between men and women in the matter of divorce, it would tell in the direction of levelling up.[1]

Lord Redesdale was the only member of the Commission of 1850 who dissented from the recommendations of the Report. He held that Christianity imposed indissoluble marriage on its adherents and, logically, proposed the abolition of the Private Act procedure. He pointed to a necessary consequence of the establishment of the divorce court proposed by his colleagues.

> These divorces will thus be opened to another and numerous class, but a still more numerous class will be equally excluded as at present. Once create an appetite for such licence by the proposed change, and the demand to be permitted to satisfy it will become irresistible. The cry for cheap law has of late been universally attended to . . . and must ultimately lead to extreme facility in obtaining such divorces.[2]

[1] Minutes of Evidence, Royal Commission on Divorce and Matrimonial Causes (Cd. 6480), 1912, vol. II, p. 371.

[2] First Report of Royal Commission (on) Law of Divorce (1604), 1853, pp. 28–29.

Lord Redesdale's prediction was borne out by the Report of the County Courts Committee in 1909 which examined the jurisdiction of county courts. It showed that poor people had access to local courts in practically all the emergencies of their lives, except in the case of divorce. By the early twentieth century, the Committee pointed out, the situation had become analogous to that existing before 1858. There was one law for those who could afford to bring a suit for divorce in London and another for those who could not, and the latter were the large majority of the population. "Without doubt," the Committee concluded, "there is a practical denial of justice in this matter to numbers of people . . . who belong to ranks in life in which the relief to be obtained under the Divorce Acts is probably more necessary than in ranks above them." As the divorce court in London was beyond the reach of working people, attempts had to be made to meet their matrimonial difficulties in other ways.

In the early 1870s there was much anxiety about the prevalence of crimes of violence in working-class districts, especially in the case of men against their wives. Evidence accumulated, and was reinforced by lurid newspaper reporting, to show that the law was ineffective to protect women from brutal husbands. One of the worst areas was Liverpool whose "Kicking District" in 1874 supplied the magistrates with some 3,000 charges of crimes of violence and the coroners with 160 verdicts of "Found Dead."[1] A Commission of eminent lawyers reported on the state of the law relating to brutal assaults in 1875. The majority favoured flogging offenders as a solution. Some laymen, however, rejected this simple lawyers' remedy, fearing lest the rod applied in prison would merely be stored in pickle for the wife at home. Frances Power Cobbe's pamphlet of 1878, *Wife Torture*, proposed

[1] The situation in Liverpool is described by Mr. Serjeant Pulling in *Transactions*, 1876, National Association for the Promotion of Social Science.

that the only thing effective was to give an assaulted wife the power of separating herself and her children from her husband.

> Of course in the upper ranks, where people could afford to pay for a suit in the divorce court, the law had for some years opened to the assaulted wife this door of escape. But among the working classes, where the assaults were ten-fold as numerous and twenty times more cruel, no legal means whatever existed of escaping from the husband returning after punishment to beat and torture his wife again. I thought the thing to be desired was the extension of the privilege of rich women to their poorer sisters, to be effected by an Act of Parliament which should give a wife . . . the power to obtain a Separation Order under Summary Jurisdiction.[1]

Miss Cobbe's campaign influenced the drafting of Lord Penzance's Matrimonial Causes Act, 1878, which gave magistrates' courts power to grant a separation order with maintenance to a wife whose husband had been convicted of aggravated assault upon her. An aggrieved wife also became entitled to the custody of any children of the marriage under ten years of age.[2] A series of Acts [3] followed under which the powers of magistrates

[1] Frances Power Cobbe, *Life of F. P. Cobbe* (1894), vol. II, pp. 220–221.

[2] The Act provided that no order for maintenance or custody of children was to be made in favour of a wife who should be proved guilty of adultery, unless such adultery had been condoned.

[3] The Matrimonial Causes Act, 1884, enacted that where a suit for restitution of conjugal rights was brought by a wife the Court might award maintenance. But this Act applied only to proceedings in the divorce court. The Maintenance of Wives (Desertion) Act, 1886, empowered magistrates to order a husband who wilfully refused or neglected to maintain his wife, or who had deserted her, to pay her a sum not exceeding £2 a week. (The amount remained £2 until 1949.) The Summary Jurisdiction (Married Women) Act, 1895, added persistent cruelty and terms of imprisonment exceeding two months as grounds on which magistrates could grant orders. Both the 1886 and 1895 Act contained a provision concerning an adulterous wife similar to that in the Act of 1878. The Licensing Act of 1902 gave both husband and wife the right to apply for an order under the Summary Jurisdiction Act on the ground that their spouse was an habitual drunkard.

to grant maintenance and separation orders were extended and consolidated. Their facilities were immediately and extensively used. In the ten years between 1897 and 1906, magistrates' courts granted over 87,000 separation and maintenance orders.[1]

By the beginning of the twentieth century, there were thus two systems of legal remedy for matrimonial difficulties in England. The affluent used the centralised divorce court and, through it, annually obtained some 600 divorces and 80 judicial separations. The poor, denied the convenience of divorce, went to the magistrates' courts and there obtained some 8,000 separation orders every year. An increasingly organised and articulate working class was no more prepared to accept this particular form of inequality between income groups than the women's movement was willing to tolerate the double standard of morality. These and other [2] dissatisfactions were publicised by a Divorce Union and culminated in the judgment of the President of the Probate, Divorce and Admiralty Division in the

[1] Evidence of R. T. Gates, Minutes of Evidence, Royal Commission on Divorce and Matrimonial Causes, vol. I (Cd. 6479), 1912, p. 217.

[2] On Boxing Day, 1859, Queen Victoria wrote in characteristic vein to the Lord Chancellor. "The Queen wishes to ask the Lord Chancellor whether no steps can be taken to prevent the present publicity of the proceedings before the new divorce court. These cases, which must necessarily increase when the new law becomes more and more known, fill now almost daily a large portion of the newspapers, and are of so scandalous a character that it makes it almost impossible for a paper to be trusted in the hands of a young lady or boy. None of the worst French novels for which careful parents would try to protect their children can be as bad as what is daily brought and laid upon the breakfast-table of every educated family in England, and its effect must be most pernicious to the public morals of the country." (*Letters of Queen Victoria* (1907), vol. III, 1837–1861, p. 482.) The Lord Chancellor replied that he was helpless to prevent the evil. In Scotland cases involving sexual matters were held *in camera*, only the judgment or verdict being made public. The Royal Commission was accordingly charged with the duty of considering means by which freedom of the Press could be reconciled with a prohibition on the publication of salacious details of divorce actions. The problem was ultimately settled in 1926 by the Regulation of Reports Act.

case of *Dodd* v. *Dodd* in 1906. Sir Gorell Barnes, Lord Gorell as he later became, contrived and intended this written judgment as a call to reform in the tradition though not, unfortunately, the literary style of Mr. Justice Maule, sixty years earlier.

> That the present state of the English law of divorce and separation is not satisfactory cannot be doubted. The law is full of inconsistencies, anomalies, and inequalities almost amounting to absurdities ; and it does not produce desirable results in many important respects. Whether any and what remedy should be applied raises extremely difficult questions, the importance of which can hardly be overestimated, for they touch the basis on which society rests, the principle of marriage being the fundamental basis upon which this and other civilised nations have built up their social systems ; it would be most detrimental to the best interests of family life, society and the state to permit of divorce being lightly and easily obtained, or to allow any law which was wide enough to militate by its laxity against the principle of marriage. . . . This judgment brings prominently forward the question whether, assuming that divorce is to be allowed at all . . . any reform would be effective and adequate which did not abolish permanent separation, distinguished from divorce, place the sexes on an equality as regards offence and relief, and prevent a decree from being obtained for such grave causes of offence as render future cohabitation impracticable and frustrate the object of marriage ; and whether such reform would not largely tend to greater propriety and enhance the respect for the sanctity of the marriage tie which is so essential in the best interests of society and the State. It is sufficient at present to say that, from all I have pointed out, there appear to be good reasons for reform, and that probably it should be found to be in the directions above indicated.[1]

[1] This extract from the judgment in *Dodd* v. *Dodd* is printed in the biography of J. E. G. Montmorency, *John Gorell Barnes*, 1848–1913 (1920), pp. 90–91.

The Asquith government responded by the appointment of a Royal Commission on Divorce and Matrimonial Causes in 1909, indicating its attitude by handing the chairmanship to Lord Gorell. The Commission's terms of reference were

> to inquire into the present state of the law and the administration thereof in divorce and matrimonial causes and applications for separation orders, especially with regard to the position of the poorer classes in relation thereto . . . and to report whether any and what amendments should be made in such law, or the administration thereof. . . .

The members were distinguished and commanded a wide range of experience and outlook. They included Cosmo Lang, then Archbishop of York and later of Canterbury; J. A. Spender, the journalist and historian; Sir William Anson, for nearly forty years Warden of All Souls and a lawyer whose political career was characterised by opposition to all major change; Thomas Burt, who had represented the Northumberland miners in Parliament for nearly fifty years, and was Secretary to the Board of Trade in Gladstone's last government; and Mrs. Tennant who, as May Abraham, had helped to extend the work of the Women Inspectorate of Factories.

Their Report [1] is a model of relevance, clarity and the thorough analysis of evidence, and is the last in the great Victorian tradition of investigating Commissions. Within three years this Commission produced four large volumes of evidence which are still essential reading, and a Report of remarkable clarity and intellectual distinction. It defined the questions at issue, sifted and secured evidence relevant to them, clarified opposing points of view, and made straightforward recommendations.

[1] The Secretaries to the Commission prepared a short, useful summary of the Majority and Minority Reports: H. G. Barnes and J. E. G. Montmorency, *The Divorce Commission. The Majority and Minority Reports Summarised* (1912).

The Majority Report met the two main criticisms of the operation of the 1857 Act by proposing that the law should be amended so as to secure the equal treatment of men and women in regard to the grounds on which divorce could be obtained ; and recommended a simplification and decentralisation of procedure by which the High Court could sit and exercise divorce jurisdiction locally, so that none should be excluded from legal relief by poverty. The Majority also recommended an extension of the grounds of divorce. After an exhaustive examination of Christian principles concerning the dissolubility of marriage, they found that opinions were maintained in favour of each of the following principles :

That all marriages are indissoluble.
That Christian marriages are indissoluble.
That marriage is dissoluble on the ground of adultery only.
That marriage is dissoluble on the grounds of (i) adultery, (ii) desertion.
That marriage is dissoluble on other serious grounds based upon the necessities of human life.[1]

In face of such conflict between the opinions of " persons equally learned, equally able, equally pious and honest, equally disinterested and humane, and equally public spirited "[1] the Majority Report was unable to

> find any general consensus of Christian opinion which would exclude any of the questions stated above from being freely considered. In view of the conflict of opinion which has existed in all ages and in all branches of the Christian Church . . . and the fact that the State must deal with all its citizens, whether Christian, nominally Christian, or non-Christian, our conclusion is that we must proceed to recommend the Legislature to act upon an unfettered consideration of what is best for the interest of the state, society, and

[1] Report of the Royal Commission on Divorce and Matrimonial Causes (Cd. 6478), 1912, p. 30.

morality, and for that of parties to suits and their families.[1]

The Majority, impressed by evidence showing separation to be a socially unsatisfactory remedy in cases where married life had become intolerable, accordingly rejected as unrealistic the previously accepted view that adultery should be the only matrimonial offence which merited the legal destruction of a marriage. They therefore recommended that desertion for more than three years, cruelty, incurable insanity, incurable drunkenness, and imprisonment under commuted death sentence should constitute statutory matrimonial offences and be additional grounds of divorce. The Report wished to retain the principle of the matrimonial offence as the basis of divorce law, but applied it to a wider range of behaviour. The recommendations are thus to be regarded as an extension of the old principle rather than the establishment of a new.

The Minority Report, signed by the Archbishop of York, Sir William Anson and Sir Lewis Dibdin agreed in substance with most of the Majority's recommendations, but, whilst accepting additional grounds of nullity,[2] emphatically rejected the proposal to extend the grounds of divorce.

On publication the Report met great hostility. *The Times*, for example, summarised both Majority and Minority Reports, but printed the latter *in extenso*, as a

[1] Report of the Royal Commission on Divorce and Matrimonial Causes (Cd. 6478), 1912, p. 30.

[2] Since the Reformation a marriage could be annulled when the parties (*a*) were incapable of contracting a marriage by reason of nonage, etc., (*b*) were by kindred and affinity within the prohibited degrees, (*c*) were already married, (*d*) had not freely consented to marry, and (*e*) had not observed the due forms and ceremonies. Both the Majority and Minority Reports recommended the following additional grounds of nullity: (1) Where one of the parties exhibits defects of which, at the time of the marriage, the other party was ignorant—(*a*) unsoundness of mind, (*b*) recurrent insanity, (*c*) communicable venereal disease, or (*e*) pregnancy by a man other than the spouse, and (2) wilful refusal to permit intercourse.

free supplement for all its readers. After Lord Gorell's death in 1913, his son introduced a Bill into the House of Lords to give effect to those recommendations upon which majority and minority had agreed. This Bill was withdrawn because it was too late in the session to find time for adequate discussion. Before it could be reintroduced the Kaiser's war had carried discussion of divorce to temporary oblivion and the second Lord Gorell to his death at Ypres.

After the war none of the Gorell Commission's recommendations was hastily enacted. The Matrimonial Causes Act, 1923, sponsored by Lord Buckmaster, placed men and women on an equal footing by empowering a wife to obtain a divorce on the ground of her husband's simple adultery.[1] Thus Lord Lyndhurst's original proposal waited sixty-six years before reaching the statute book. In 1937, the ingenuity and skill of Mr. (now Sir Alan) Herbert, assisted by Mr. Rupert de la Bère, persuaded Parliament to pass a Matrimonial Causes Act. The preamble explained :

> Whereas it is expedient for the true support of marriage, the protection of children, the removal of hardship, the reduction of illicit unions and unseemly litigation . . . and the restoration of due respect for the law, that the Acts relating to marriage and divorce be amended.

This statement is significant evidence of anxieties inside and outside Parliament at that time. Mr. Herbert justified his Bill to the House of Commons by quoting, as representative of public opinion, a speech by the Archdeacon of Coventry to a Diocesan Conference :

> The limitation of the grounds of divorce to the one

[1] Women are now slightly " more equal " than men in this respect. A woman may petition for divorce on the grounds of her husband's unnatural offences. Such partialities in a woman do not constitute a matrimonial offence against her husband unless it can be proved that their indulgence has injured his health and thus constituted cruelty.

ground of adultery had resulted in a state of affairs which was disastrously prejudicial to public morality. As the law stands at present those who wish to bring an end to the marriage were forced to take one of two alternatives—either one must commit adultery or one must commit perjury. The law as it stands is a definite incitement to immorality. It was the duty of the Church to press for and not merely to acquiesce in reform of the existing marriage law ; reform could be found in an extension of the grounds of divorce which did not necessarily mean making divorce more easy.[1]

Mr. Herbert's anxiety to " bring new strength to the institutions which we all value, the Church, the relations between Church and State, the law, marriage and the family " resulted in the first extension of the grounds of divorce in England since 1697. His Act [2] and the earlier legislation were consolidated by the Matrimonial Causes Act, 1950, which contains the present law.[3] A petition for divorce may now be presented to the court either by the husband or the wife on the ground [4] that the respondent

(*a*) has since the celebration of the marriage committed adultery ; or
(*b*) has deserted the petitioner without cause for a period of at least three years immediately preceeding the presentation of the petition ; or
(*c*) has since the celebration of the marriage treated the petitioner with cruelty ; or
(*d*) is incurably of unsound mind and has been continuously under care and treatment for a period of at least five years immediately preceeding the presentation of the petition ;

and by the wife on the ground that her husband has, since the celebration of the marriage, been guilty of rape,

[1] Hansard, 1937, vol. 317, col. 2082.

[2] The circumstances surrounding, and the detailed history of the passing of the Act are entertainingly described in the book of A. P. Herbert, *The " Ayes " Have It.*

[3] For the convenience of readers, this is printed in Appendix I.

[4] Matrimonial Causes Act, 1950 (14–15 Geo. 6, c. 25), sec. 1.

sodomy or bestiality. Save in exceptional circumstances, no petition for divorce may be presented until the marriage has lasted at least three years.[1] New grounds [2] for a decree of nullity of marriage were also created

(*a*) that the marriage has not been consummated owing to the wilful refusal of the respondent to consummate the marriage ; or
(*b*) that either party to the marriage was at the time of the marriage of unsound mind or subject to recurrent fits of insanity or epilepsy ; or
(*c*) that the respondent was at the time of the marriage suffering from venereal disease in a communicable form ; or
(*d*) that the respondent was at the time of the marriage pregnant by some person other than the petitioner.

In cases (*b*), (*c*) and (*d*) proceedings must be instituted within a year of the marriage ; the petitioner must have been ignorant of the facts alleged at the time of marriage ; and there must have been no marital intercourse since the petitioner's discovery of the existence of the grounds for a decree of nullity. The 1912 Commissioners' recommendation that adultery ought not to be the only legally valid cause for dissolving a marriage thus required twenty-five years' consideration before it was enacted.

The outstanding feature in the history of divorce since the Report of 1912 has been reluctance to act on its proposals for facilitating poor people's access to the divorce court. The most influential and, as it has turned out, short-sighted opponents of reform were London practitioners who saw every suggestion for simplifying and decentralising procedure as a threat to their lucrative monopoly. Until 1920 all divorce cases were heard in London.[3] It was then provided that poor persons' and

[1] Matrimonial Causes Act, 1950 (14–15 Geo. 6, c. 25), sec. 2.
[2] *ibid.*, sec. 8.
[3] In the summary that follows I have relied on the succinct account given by R. M. Jackson in his masterly book, *The Machinery of Justice in England*, 2nd ed. (1953), p. 47 *et seq.*

undefended cases could be heard at certain Assize towns. By 1936 nearly half the total of divorce petitions were heard at Assizes, often to the disgust of the judges of the King's Bench. " To what do I owe the advantage of having to deal with this rubbishy case at Lewes? ", Lord Hewart, at that time Lord Chief Justice, is reported to have asked after granting a decree nisi at Sussex Assizes. War-time pressures forced a modification of this capricious and unsatisfactory procedure. In 1943, by Order in Council, judges of the Divorce Division in London were sent on circuit and all classes of divorce cases began to be heard at a limited number of Assize towns. This change merely shifted the location of congestion in divorce work which rapidly increased during and after the war. In 1946 a Committee *On Procedure in Matrimonial Causes* was appointed under the chairmanship of Mr. (now Lord) Justice Denning. The Committee reported that " the existing assize system is a failure " and, whilst stressing the importance of retaining the High Court's jurisdiction, recommended extensive administrative changes. Most important was the proposal that judicial strength should be increased by appointing Special Commissioners, mainly from the ranks of county court judges. This recommendation was accepted and Commissioners, with all the authority of High Court judges, now sit in London and thirty-eight provincial towns to hear divorce petitions. By 1950, 11,099 matrimonial causes were heard in London and 19,402 in the provinces. Of the provincial cases all but 259 were tried before Commissioners.

Behind this piecemeal adjustment of the machinery of justice to social need were the pressures exerted by increasing numbers of poor suitors, assisted by tardy extensions of the system of legal aid for poor persons. None of our social services has a meaner or more squalid history. In no field of social life have democratic attitudes and habits been so difficult to establish. In matters of divorce, at least, the familiar comment of a Victorian judge, Mr. Justice Mathew,[1] " in this country justice is open to all—like the Ritz Hotel," remained true for many years after the Report of 1912 : and matrimonial causes made up the overwhelming proportion of cases for the prosecution of which poor people needed financial help. In the years between the Kaiser's and Hitler's wars a succession of Committees reported. Their helpfulness, and awareness of the need to be met, may be judged by the view of the Committee on Legal Aid for the Poor[2] which rejected, in 1928, the analogy between legal aid and Health Insurance because

> It is manifestly in the interests of the State that its citizens should be healthy, not that they should be litigious.[3]

In this, as in so many other fields of social policy, war dissolved inherited stupidities. The citizen soldier's *morale* became an active public concern and the speedy solution of his matrimonial difficulties a public duty. All three Services set up their own legal aid schemes and arranged litigation through local solicitors or under the Poor Persons' Procedure. Most of these cases were petitions for divorce. Under war-time conditions the old Poor Persons' Procedure was hopelessly inadequate if only because the means test applied would have excluded most service men. The work was handed over to the Law Society which established a Services Divorce Department financed by the Treasury. After this, it

[1] Lord Gorell had been a junior in his Chambers and succeeded to his very large practice when Mathew was elevated to the Bench.

[2] Cd. 3016 (1928).

[3] *ibid.*, para. 17, quoted by R. M. Jackson, *op. cit.* Mr. Jackson comments, p. 271, fn. 2, " It is a Report compounded of ignorance and stupidity." The history of legal aid up to 1945 is described by Robert Egerton in his book, *Legal Aid* (1945). An account of the procedure in this and other countries before Hitler's war is available in the article of E. J. Cohn, " Legal Aid for the Poor, and A Study in Comparative Law and Legal Reform "—*The Law Quarterly Review* (July and October, 1943).

was impossible to go back to the old system, and a Committee, under Lord Rushcliffe, on *Legal Aid and Legal Advice*[1] reported in 1945. Its recommendations led to the Legal Aid and Advice Act, 1949, which achieves a considerable measure of equality before the law. The Legal Aid provisions came into operation in the autumn of 1950; the Legal Advice scheme is still no more than a paper aspiration. It thus required a delay of thirty-eight years before the principle of the Report of 1912 that no person should be denied access by poverty to the divorce court, became a reality.

The history of divorce outlined in this chapter establishes three conclusions. First, Christian beliefs concerning marriage and divorce, and the practices sanctioned by them, show no consistency. They have been confused and often contradictory. Secondly, the obsession of medieval Christianity with the sinfulness of sex persisted through later centuries and determined the character of the civil law of divorce. In England until 1937, adultery was the only type of offence legally recognised as cutting at the root of the marriage relationship and warranting its dissolution. Third, changes in the legal procedure by which divorce might be obtained have been more important for the community as a whole than changes in the grounds on which divorce is permitted. The dominating change since 1857 is not the creation of new grounds for divorce by Herbert's Act in 1937, but the innovations of the legal aid system of 1949, under which all citizens now have a means of access to the divorce court. The next chapter measures the effects of these developments on English experience of divorce during the twentieth century.

[1] Cd. 6641 (1945).

CHAPTER II

THE STATISTICS OF DIVORCE

PRESENT discussions display a striking association of ignorance about the incidence and extent of divorce and confident certainty concerning its causes and social consequences. Indeed, the paucity of statistical information still permits the contradictory assertions of ardent controversialists to masquerade as knowledge. As divorce, in the younger age groups, has become as important a factor as death in the dissolution of marriages, the Royal Commission on Population recommended [1] that additional information should be collected by the Registrar-General. His *Statistical Review of England and Wales, 1946–50* [2] accordingly contained a critical discussion of the old and new material. The account that follows necessarily makes extensive use of the Registrar-General's publications.

The increase in the numbers of petitions for divorce is set out in Table I (*See page* 36).

Petitions for divorce provide a surer indication of the divorce trend during the period than decrees made absolute. They are less liable, remarks the Registrar-General, " to disturbances from changes in procedure designed to clear off accumulated arrears of suits awaiting hearing and from other administrative actions. . . ." [3] The considerable distorting effect of such disturbances is illustrated by Table II (*See page* 37).

In 1945 and 1946 there were substantially more petitions filed than decrees granted, in 1947 and 1948 the position was reversed. In 1946 two administrative changes were made in order to speed divorce suits

[1] Papers of the Royal Commission on Population (1950), vol. II, *Reports . . . of the Statistics Committee*, p. 35, 44.

[2] *Text, Civil*, pp. 54–73.

[3] *ibid.*, p. 54.

TABLE I. NUMBER OF PETITIONS FILED FOR DISSOLUTION AND NULLITY, 1876 TO 1954; ENGLAND AND WALES [1]

Remarks	Quinquennial Period	Number of Petitions Annual averages
Period when working-class people were, in practice, denied access to the divorce court	1876–1880	460
	1881–1885	462
	1886–1890	556
	1891–1895	565
	1896–1900	675
	1901–1905	812
	1906–1910	809
Kaiser's War	1911–1915	1,033
	1916–1920	2,954
	1921–1925	2,848
Poor Persons Rules, 1925 ...	1926–1930	4,052
	1931–1935	4,784
Herbert Act, 1937	1936–1940	7,535
Hitler's War	1941–1945	16,075
Legal Aid Scheme, 1950 ...	1946–1950	38,901
Divorce available to all classes	1951–1954 [2]	33,132

through the courts and to clear off the accumulation of arrears. The Matrimonial Causes (Decrees Absolute) Order reduced the minimum time which must elapse before a decree *nisi* can be made absolute from six months to six weeks, and the Matrimonial Causes (Special Commission) (No. 2) Order provided for the appointment of Special Commissioners to hear divorce petitions. Thus the widely quoted figure of more than 60,000 divorces in 1947 included not only the current cases but also accumulated arrears fortuitously worked off in that year. The many prophecies that the 60,000-odd decrees absolute of 1947 would become the community's normal divorce habit have been falsified. By 1954 the number had more than halved.

The increase in the number of divorce petitions from an annual average of 812 in the years 1901 to 1905 to one

[1] The Registrar-General's *Statistical Review of England and Wales, Text, Civil*, adapted from Table XXVII, p. 55.

[2] Average of four years, the figures are taken from *Annual Abstract of Statistics* (1955), Table 87, p. 80.

TABLE II. PETITIONING FOR DIVORCE AND DECREES ABSOLUTE GRANTED, 1945 TO 1954; ENGLAND AND WALES [1]

Remarks	Year	Divorce petitions filed (including nullity)	Decrees absolute granted (including nullity)
End of Hitler's War	1945	25,711	15,634
Matrimonial Causes (Decrees Absolute) Order; Matrimonial Causes (Special Commission), No. 2 Order	1946	43,163	29,829
	1947	48,501	60,254
	1948	37,919	43,698
	1949	35,191	34,856
Legal Aid provisions of Legal Aid and Advice Act, 1949, brought into operation	1950	29,729	30,870
	1951	38,382	28,767
	1952	34,567	33,922
	1953	30,542	30,326
	1954	29,036	28,027

of more than 33,000 in the years 1951 to 1954 does not reveal the true incidence of divorce during this century. The numbers of petitions must be related, as in Table III, to changes in the size of the married population.

TABLE III. MARRIED POPULATION, PETITIONS [2] FILED AND RATE PER 10,000 MARRIED POPULATION, 1911, 1921, 1937 AND 1950; ENGLAND AND WALES [3]

Year	Number of marriages in existence (thousands)	Number of petitions	Petitions per 10,000 married couples
1911 ...	6,563	902	1·38
1921 ...	7,532	2,907	3·86
1937 ...	9,322	5,903	6·34
1950 ...	11,017	29,729	26·98

[1] Adapted from The Registrar-General's *Statistical Review of England and Wales for 1952, Text,* Table XXXVII, p. 60. Figures for 1953 and 1954 are taken from the *Annual Abstract of Statistics* (1955).

[2] For dissolution and nullity.

[3] *Text, Civil (1946–1950), op. cit.,* Table XXXII, p. 61.

Although the number of divorce petitions was more than thirty times greater in 1950 than in 1911, the rate of petitioning, expressed as a proportion of the married population, was only twenty times greater. This figure would be reduced if it were possible to allow for the lengthened duration of marriage resulting from the increasing expectation of life. However, the Registrar-General makes no estimate by which the numbers of divorce petitions may be corrected for changes in what he describes as the "period of exposure to matrimonial risk."

The sharp rise in the number of divorce petitions has little significance in itself, and the Registrar-General warns against "exaggerated ideas as to the proportion of marriages which ultimately are broken by divorce." [1] His estimate of this proportion is given in Table IV:

TABLE IV. APPROXIMATE PROPORTION OF MARRIAGES TERMINATED BY DIVORCE, 1911 TO 1954; ENGLAND AND WALES [2]

Year	Petitions filed	Average number of marriages contracted annually 5–15 years earlier (thousands)	Petitions per 100 marriages	Percentage of petitions resulting in decrees absolute	Estimated percentage of marriages terminated by divorce
1911 ...	859	257	0·3	75	0·2
1921 ...	2,790	284	1·0	80	0·8
1937 ...	5,750	302	1·9	85	1·6
1950 ...	29,096	369	7·9	90	7·1
1953 ...	29,845	381	7·8	90	7·0
1954 ...	28,347	385	7·4	90	6·7

Before the Kaiser's war, less than half of one per cent. of marriages ended in divorce; before Hitler's war, the proportion was less than two per cent. and, by 1954, it

[1] *Text, Civil (1946–1950), op. cit.*, Table XXXII, p. 61.

[2] Report of Royal Commission on Marriage and Divorce (Cd. 9678), 1956, p. 369, Table 7. It should be noted that nullities have been excluded.

had risen to almost seven per cent. After the first war the proportion doubled, after the second it quadrupled. Today 6·7 per cent. of marriages end in divorce. The meaning of this figure is best understood when stated negatively : only 93·3 of every 100 marriages do *not* end in divorce.

The increasing divorce rate has not been accompanied by an increased unwillingness to marry. A higher proportion of the population is now married than at any time since 1851, and people, especially women, are marrying at younger ages than in the past. Divorced persons fully share this rising enthusiasm for marriage. Indeed, as the Registrar-General emphasises, " at all ages a much higher rate of marriage is shown for divorced men and women than for any other marital conditions." [1] Table V strikingly illustrates the persistent refusal to accept one defeat as final.

TABLE V. PERCENTAGE OF DIVORCED PERSONS WHO RE-MARRIED, 1926 TO 1952 ; ENGLAND AND WALES [2]

1926 to 1930	1931 to 1935	1936 to 1940	1941 to 1945	1946 to 1950	1951	1952
58·3	64·2	69·2	60·4	61·3	76·8	67·9

" It is apparent," remarked the Registrar-General in 1951, " that the re-marriage rate amongst divorced persons has been rising rapidly and/or the bulk of divorce proceedings are instituted with a definite intention of subsequent immediate re-marriage. This latter explanation would imply that a tendency is present not to fly from marriage, but to rectify mistakes in a choice of partner, rather than to perpetuate an unhappy marriage ; and since this phenomenon has been evident to a steadily

[1] *Text, Civil (1946–1950), op. cit.*, p. 72

[2] The Registrar-General's *Statistical Review of England and Wales for 1952, Text Vol.* (1955), p. 62.

increasing extent since 1921–1925, it may reasonably be expected to remain a feature of post-war behaviour."[1]

The demographic, as distinct from the theological, significance of divorce cannot be measured by the numbers of marriages dissolved, but only by the numbers of broken marriages not subsequently reconstituted with new partners. From this point of view, the net loss to the married population as a result of divorce is only a fraction of the total number of marriages terminated by divorce. The figures suggest that the proportion of divorced persons who re-marry is likely to be stabilised in the region of two-thirds to three-quarters. Of the 29,000 couples who divorced in 1954, some 20,000 will die either married or widowed; only some 8,000 will be permanently lost to the estate of matrimony. Unfortunately, no information is available to show the incidence of divorce amongst the subsequent marriages of divorcées and no estimate of the duration or stability of such marriages can be made.

Some further aspects of the situation can be explored by breaking down the general statistics. The trend towards equality of men and women in their use of facilities for divorce between the passing of the Act of 1857 and the appointment of the Gorell Commission is indicated by Table VI.

TABLE VI. PROPORTION OF PETITIONS FOR DISSOLUTION OF MARRIAGE FILED BY HUSBANDS AND WIVES, 1859 TO 1908; ENGLAND AND WALES[2]

	1859 to 1863	1874 to 1878	1884 to 1888	1894 to 1898	1904 to 1908
	(percentages)				
Husbands' petitions	62	60	58	58	56
Wives' petitions ...	38	40	42	42	44

[1] *Statistical Review . . . for 1940–1945, Text*, vol. II, *Civil*, p. 57.

[2] Adapted from Appendix III, Table I, Appendices to the Minutes of Evidence and Report of the Royal Commission on Divorce and Matrimonial Causes (Cd. 6482), 1912, p. 27.

The significant change in this respect during recent years is shown by Table VII.

TABLE VII. PROPORTION OF PETITIONS FOR DISSOLUTION OF MARRIAGE FILED BY HUSBANDS AND WIVES, 1938, AND 1945 TO 1954; ENGLAND AND WALES [1]

	1938	1945	1946	1947	1948	1949	1950	1951	1952	1953	1954
	(percentages)										
Husbands' petitions	47	57	63	61	50	49	46	43	44	44	45
Wives' petitions	53	43	37	39	50	51	54	57	56	56	55

The figures suggest that, in the absence of special factors, the rates of petitioning by husbands and wives are likely to be the same. The immediate aftermath of Hitler's war could be expected to produce a higher proportion of husbands' petitions if only because war-time circumstances made it easier for husbands to obtain evidence against their wives. This trend has been reversed since 1948 largely in consequence of the operation of Legal Aid from the autumn of 1950. It seems likely that more wives than husbands could not afford the facility of divorce in the period before 1950; thus, after 1950, current wives' petitions have been inflated by a number which would have been pursued earlier if the petitioners had not been too poor to obtain access to the divorce court.

Before the Herbert Act of 1937 adultery was the only matrimonial offence which warranted the legal dissolution of marriage. The effect of that Act is shown by Tables VIII, IX and X.

Despite the emphasis placed by the Church of England on nullity and reiterated advice to its members to seek, whenever possible, annulments of marriage rather than divorce, the ratio of nullity to divorce is tending to fall.[2]

[1] Adapted from the *Annual Abstract of Statistics* (1955), Table 87, p. 80. It should be noted that petitions for nullity of marriage have been excluded.

[2] The number of petitions for nullity of marriage has fallen from the peak of 1947 when 1,460 petitions were filed to 689 in 1954.

The additional grounds of nullity under the Herbert Act have stimulated no change in the situation and nullity, though theologically significant, is statistically unimportant.

TABLE VIII. PROPORTION OF PETITIONS FOR DISSOLUTION AND NULLITY, 1933 TO 1954; ENGLAND AND WALES [1]

	1933 to 1937	1938 to 1939	1940 to 1944	1945 to 1949	1950 to 1954
			(percentages)		
Dissolution.	97·1	97·6	97·1	97·2	97·8
Nullity .	2·9	2·4	2·9	2·8	2·2

Tables IX and X show the distribution of divorce petitions by cause and whether filed by husband or wife.

TABLE IX. PERCENTAGE DISTRIBUTION OF PETITIONS FOR DISSOLUTION AND NULLITY BY CAUSE DISTINGUISHING THOSE PETITIONS FOR DISSOLUTION FILED BY HUSBANDS AND THOSE BY WIVES, 1938, 1950 and 1954; ENGLAND AND WALES [2]

Cause	1938 Petitions of Husbands	1938 Petitions of Wives	1950 Petitions of Husbands	1950 Petitions of Wives	1954 [3] Petitions of Husbands	1954 [3] Petitions of Wives
Dissolution						
Adultery ...	51·5	45·9	44·1	36·8	50·1	33·9
Desertion ...	38·8	37·6	49·0	43·9	43·4	40·6
Cruelty ...	0·4	12·6	2·8	16·8	2·5	22·7
Others ...	5·8	2·1	1·4	0·8	1·6	1·2
Total	96·5	98·2	97·3	98·3	97·6	98·4
Nullity						
Total	3·5	1·8	2·7	1·7	2·4	1·6

[1] Adapated from The Registrar-General's *Statistical Review of England and Wales for 1946–1950 Text, Civil* (1954), Table XXX, p. 58 and from the *Annual Abstract of Statistics* (1955), Table 87, p. 80.

[2] The figures for 1938 and 1950 are taken from the Registrar-General's *Text, Civil* (1954), *op. cit.*, Table XXI, p. 60, those for 1954 have been adapted from The Registrar-General's *Statistical Review of England and Wales for 1954, Part II Tables, Civil*, Table PI, p. 76.

[3] It should be noted that, whereas the figures for 1938 and 1950 relate to petitions, those for 1954 relate to decrees made absolute. This is the only form in which the 1954 figures are available; thus they are not strictly comparable.

The matrimonial offences of husbands and wives differ significantly only in respect of cruelty towards their spouses. Wives' petitions on the two grounds of cruelty and adultery together approximately add up to the proportion of husbands' petitions on the ground of adultery. The test of legal cruelty was laid down in *Russell* v. *Russell* (1897) and has not subsequently been altered.[1] It is defined as conduct of such character as to have caused danger to life, limb, or bodily or mental health, or as to give rise to reasonable apprehension of such danger. As such it is largely, though not entirely, a husband's offence. The sharp increase during recent years of petitions alleging cruelty is shown by Table X.

TABLE X. DISTRIBUTION OF ALL PETITIONS FOR DISSOLUTION OF MARRIAGE BY CAUSE, 1945 TO 1954; ENGLAND AND WALES[2]

Cause	1945	1946	1947	1948	1949	1950	1951	1952	1953	1954
	(percentage distribution)									
Adultery ...	68·7	71·0	66·9	54·0	42·5	41·0	37·4	39·4	41·2	42·0
Desertion ...	25·0	23·3	27·0	37·6	47·5	47·2	48·4	44·8	42·5	40·9
Cruelty ...	4·1	4·0	5·5	7·5	8·7	10·6	12·7	14·5	15·1	15·8
Others ...	2·2	1·7	0·6	0·9	1·3	1·2	1·5	1·3	1·2	1·3

This table suggests three conclusions:

(*a*) The statistical insignificance of petitions for nullity of marriage has already been shown in Table VIII. Table X demonstrates that adultery, desertion, and cruelty together account for practically all divorces. Incurable unsoundness of mind and the cruder or more sophisticated matrimonial offences of rape, sodomy, and bestiality, introduced by the Herbert Act, are statistically unimportant.

(*b*) The changing proportions of petitions for adultery and desertion between 1945 and 1954 reflect the working-

[1] *Rayden's Practice and Law in the Divorce Division* (1949), 5th ed., pp. 80–89.

[2] Adapted from the *Annual Abstract of Statistics* (1955), Table 87, p. 80.

out of war-time circumstances when husbands had relatively few opportunities for desertion and wives extended opportunities for adultery. The figures for 1952 onwards suggest that rates for both causes are now becoming stabilised at roughly the same level.

(*c*) The fourfold increase in ten years in the proportion of petitions alleging cruelty is striking. There are several possible explanations. First, that judicial opinion as to the types of marital behaviour that constitute cruelty has changed drastically. Secondly, that there has been either a significant increase in the numbers of cruel husbands or a corresponding decrease in the numbers of submissive wives. Neither of these inferences seem plausible. There is no evidence that judicial opinion has altered significantly, and the few available scraps of empirical information [1] concerning marital behaviour indicate a growth of husbandly consideration rather than cruelty. Further, it is unlikely that judicial opinion and personal relationships within the family could change radically in so short a period as ten years. The third possibility is that the extension of womens', especially married womens', occupations in the environment of full employment since 1939 has emancipated some women from cruel husbands upon whom they were previously financially dependent. Perhaps the new independence has also been accompanied by the spread of knowledge. Many wives in the lower social classes may only recently have learnt that the Herbert Act established cruelty as a ground of divorce. These factors could reasonably be held to account for the rise in cruelty petitions. A fourth hypothesis must, however, be considered. A high proportion of all divorce cases are undefended.[2] Many of these result, it is frequently

[1] e.g. Geoffrey Gorer, *Exploring English Character* (1955), esp. chs. IX and X.

[2] Over 90 per cent. No figures showing the ratio of undefended to defended petitions brought under the Legal Aid Scheme are published. The author believes the proportion to be in the region of 84 per cent.

alleged, from prior agreement between the spouses and are "faked."[1] If this is true, the grounds for such petitions will be chosen to suit the personal convenience of the parties. If they merely wish to divorce without immediate expectation of marriage to other partners, desertion provides a comfortable ground which is still, if the couple are sensitive to such considerations, socially more respectable than adultery and personally less distasteful than cruelty. If, on the other hand, speed and certainty of timing are important, the choice must lie between adultery and cruelty. Although adultery is easy to "fake," it presupposes a degree of social sophistication usually limited to the upper social classes. The conventional routines of early morning tea in a hotel bedroom with the chambermaid as witness, or the few days spent in a hired flat, are expedients outside the customary range of working-class behaviour. Cruelty has the disadvantage of being restricted, in practice, to wives' petitions, but it remains for working-class people the easiest and cheapest matrimonial offence to "fake." Thus, it could be argued that if it has become an upper-class convention, when a couple agree to part speedily, for the husband to commit, or pretend to commit, adultery, a similar working-class convention is being established whereby the husband pretends to behave with cruelty. On this view, the proportionate increase in cruelty petitions, which have continued their steady rise since the introduction of Legal Aid in 1950, provides statistical evidence in support of the assertion that many people treat the law with contempt by committing matrimonial offences in order to secure divorces.

One serious criticism can be urged against this view. Many petitions filed by working-class people are now

[1] A "faked" divorce may be defined as one in which the parties, having decided to dissolve their marriage, deliberately conduct themselves so that one commits a statutory matrimonial offence on the basis of which the other agrees to petition for divorce. Such conduct is likely to be, but is not necessarily, technically collusive or connivent.

pursued with financial help under the Legal Aid scheme.[1] The statistical information published annually in the Reports of the Law Society on the working of Part I of the Legal Aid and Advice Act is difficult to interpret. First, it is not based on the calendar year, but on a period running from April to March. Secondly, it does not distinguish, under the heading "Divorce,"[2] between civil aid certificates issued for "pure" divorce (i.e. to petitioners and respondents) and those for such other related matters as enforced maintenance and the representation of co-respondents. Third, it does not show

[1] Very little information about the occupations or incomes of persons assisted by the Legal Aid scheme is available. It is a cardinal feature of the administrative arrangements that neither the Law Society nor practitioners are called upon to assess the financial resources of applicants or to fix their contributions, This responsibility is carried out by the National Assistance Board in accordance with the provisions of the Legal Aid (Assessment of Resources) Regulations, 1950. These regulations are complicated : their object is to derive a figure of an applicant's disposable income and disposable capital, i.e. the income remaining after meeting necessary commitments and the free capital that can readily be realised. If an applicant has a disposable income of less than £156, or a disposable capital of less than £75, he obtains the legal services of the scheme free of charge. Above these minima, contributions are levied according to a sliding scale of charges. The variations in applicants' personal circumstances and commitments make any generalisation about their incomes impossible, but rather more than a third of legal aid certificates are granted to people whose incomes and capitals are so small that they are excused any contribution. In 1954, 41 per cent. made either no contribution (36 per cent.) or one of less than £10. (*The Fifth Report of the Law Society on the Operation and Finance of Part I of the Legal Aid and Advice Act, 1949* (1956), Appendix II, Part II, p. 38.) The sliding scale operates in such a way that it would not be worth the while of a person whose disposable income was £300 a year or more to use the scheme for an undefended divorce costing £75. The administration and financial arrangements of the scheme are described in the *First Report of the Law Society . . .* (1951).

[2] *The Fifth Report of the Law Society* . . . (1956), Appendix II, Part I. This table allocates successful applications according to the court for which they were granted. The distinction between col. (10) "Divorce Department" and col. (11) "Private Practitioner" arises because certificates granted for the divorce court to applicants who either contribute nothing or an amount of £10 or less are handled directly by the Law Society's Divorce Department—the successor to the old Services Divorce Department. Persons who contribute more than £10, petition the divorce court through a private solicitor. In 1954, 26 per cent. of all legal aid applications granted for the divorce court were on behalf of those required to contribute £10 or less.

the distribution of legal aid petitions by ground. It is thus impossible to estimate even the proportion of civil aid certificates granted in respect of divorce petitions. It is a reasonable assumption that two-thirds of the "Divorce" certificates are granted to actual petitioners.[1] On this basis, in 1954, although 79 per cent. of all legal aid cases related to matrimonial matters,[2] only 52 per cent. were petitions for divorce.[3] It follows, therefore, that approximately 45 per cent. of the total number of divorce petitions in 1954 were filed by assisted persons.[4] Misunderstanding of the tables published in the Law Society's annual Reports has led to the frequent assertion that two-thirds of all divorce petitions are brought by persons assisted under the Legal Aid scheme. A representative of the Law Society even gave evidence to this effect to the Morton Commission.[5] The widely quoted calculation by which the National Marriage Guidance Council sought to show the disproportion between government expenditure on assisted divorce on the one hand, and grants for reconciliation work on the other, similarly exaggerated the number of Legal Aid petitions.[6]

In 1954, 16 per cent. of all petitions alleged cruelty.[7] It is probable that the proportion under legal aid is higher and, taking 20 per cent. as a guess, the actual number would be in the region of 2,600. On present information, the trend of cruelty petitions filed by assisted persons since 1951 cannot be estimated. However,

[1] This estimate has been made on the basis of private information which the author believes to be reliable.

[2] In the year ending the 31st March 1955, 24,019 civil aid certificates were issued, and 19,477 applications were granted for "Divorce." *The Fifth Report of the Law Society* . . . (1956), *op. cit.*, Appendix I, Part III and Appendix II, Part 1.

[3] i.e., two-thirds of 19,477 as a proportion of 29,036.

[4] It should be noted that the figure for all divorce petitions in 1954 is based on the calendar year and that for petitions filed by assisted persons on the period 1st April 1954, to 31st March 1955. It is impossible to relate the legal aid petitions to the calendar year.

[5] Evidence, 29th Day, p. 754, Q. 7165.

[6] *ibid.*, 5th Day, pp. 107–108.

[7] Table X above.

if the figure suggested for 1954 is near the mark, two comments can be made on the assertion that the rise in cruelty petitions is an indication of the growth of "faked" divorces. Middle-class people are unlikely to choose cruelty as a "faked" ground, and, though working-class petitions certainly account for more than half the total filed on this ground, they probably do not amount to more than one in ten of all petitions. Further, whilst some legal aid divorces are undoubtedly "faked," common sense suggests that it is very much more difficult to work a "faked" petition through the Law Society's elaborate procedures than through a private solicitor. The explanation of the rising trend of cruelty petitions remains obscure. It is, clearly, an index of the growing financial independence of working-class wives, of the penetration of knowledge about divorce and the facilities of the Legal Aid scheme amongst working-class women, and also, perhaps, of an increasing habit of "faking" divorce petitions. This latter suggestion, though seemingly plausible, should be regarded with caution. There is no measure at present of the extent to which any one of these factors contributes to the final result.

Tables XI and XII give information about two important social aspects of divorce. Table XI shows the incidence of divorce by duration of marriage ; Table XII the incidence of divorce by the number of children of the marriage.

These tables, though highly suggestive, permit only three firmly based and important conclusions. In the first place, they demonstrate an astonishing similarity and stability over a relatively long period of time. It is remarkable that the distribution of dissolved marriages by duration and number of children should have changed so little in a half century during which the law of divorce, the access to the court, the size and standard of living of the family, the position of women, and familial, parental and sexual relations have changed so much. Secondly,

TABLE XI. DISTRIBUTION OF MATRIMONIAL PETITIONS, 1898 TO 1945, AND DISSOLUTIONS AND ANNULMENTS OF MARRIAGE MADE ABSOLUTE, 1951 TO 1954, BY DURATION OF MARRIAGE; ENGLAND AND WALES [1]

Duration of marriage Years	Annual Averages [2]			
	1899 to 1903	1926 to 1930	1941 to 1945	1951 to 1954
	(percentages)			
1–5	14·7	14·6	15·2	9·9
5–10	30·4	34·0	31·8	31·3
10–20	42·5	38·2	37·7	38·1
Over 20	12·4	13·2	15·3	20·7
	100·0	100·0	100·0	100·0

TABLE XII. DISTRIBUTION OF MATRIMONIAL PETITIONS, 1898 TO 1945, AND DISSOLUTIONS AND ANNULMENTS OF MARRIAGE MADE ABSOLUTE, 1951 TO 1954, BY NUMBER OF CHILDREN OF MARRIAGES; ENGLAND AND WALES [3]

Number of Children	Annual Averages [2]			
	1899 to 1903	1926 to 1930	1941 to 1945	1951 to 1954
	(percentages)			
None	39·9	40·8	41·0	33·4
1	23·8	30·9	31·3	32·7
2	15·6	16·7	16·7	19·1
3–6	18·4	11·2	10·7	14·1
7 or more	2·3	0·4	0·3	0·7
	100·0	100·0	100·0	100·0

[1] Figures for 1899–1903 adapted from Appendix III, Table XIII, Appendices to the Minutes of Evidence and Report . . . (Cd. 6482), 1912, *op. cit.*, p. 34; those for 1926–1930 and 1941–1945 from Table XXXV. The Registrar-General's *Statistical Review of England and Wales for 1946–1950, Text, Civil*, p. 63; those for 1951–1954 adapted from Table P3, The Registrar-General, *op. cit.*, *Tables, Part II Civil*, 1951 *passim*.

[2] Figures for 1899–1903 include all matrimonial petitions (i.e. for dissolution, nullity, judicial separation and restitution of conjugal rights) filed in England and Wales. Figures for 1926–1930 and 1941–1945 relate only to petitions for dissolution and nullity filed at the Principal Divorce Registry in London and cover more than half the petitions filed during the two periods in England and Wales. Figures for 1951–1954 include all petitions for dissolution and nullity in England and Wales. Thus, the figures for the different periods are not strictly comparable but none other is available, and there is no reason to think that the trends indicated are distorted by the different bases of compilation.

[3] Figures derived from the same sources as those in Table XI, but those for 1899–1903 from Table XV, p. 35, and those for 1951–1954 from Table P4.

recent experience is that 59 per cent. of all divorces occur amongst marriages which have lasted more than ten years. This proportion has remained surprisingly stable since the end of the nineteenth century, though it has shown a slight tendency to rise. Thus the persistent assertion that easier facilities for divorce have led to widespread divorce-mindedness with the result that many more young people now rush into and out of unthinkingly contracted marriages, is not in accord with the facts. It appears, also, when the rising proportion of divorces amongst marriages of more than twenty years' duration is read against the background of increasing expectation of life, that the divorce court is now taking over functions which, in the past, were the undertaker's prerogative. Third, the reiterated conviction that divorce exacts an alarming toll of unstable and emotionally deprived children must be qualified by the knowledge that, for the last fifty years, a third of all dissolved marriages have been childless. It is impossible to determine from the published statistics the number of divorces amongst marriages the children of which had grown up when the petition was filed. As, however, 20 per cent. of all divorces now take place after the marriage has lasted more than twenty years, the proportion of divorces which do not involve defenceless children must be considerably higher than a third.[1]

The number of broken marriages cannot be measured by divorce statistics alone. The existence, at least until the Legal Aid scheme was brought into operation in the autumn of 1950, of two systems of matrimonial jurisprudence has already been emphasised in Chapter I. The divorce division of the High Court catered for the better off by dissolving their marriages. The magistrates' courts served

[1] It appears that 20,000 of the 36,000 children whose parents were divorced in 1954 were under sixteen years of age. This point is discussed on p. 162, fn. 2. It is important to remember that, in the context of divorce statistics, " children " are defined as any issue of the marriage whatever their age when the petition is filed.

the wives[1] of the poor by making maintenance orders which preserved intact the bond of matrimony but enabled them to live apart from their husbands. Table XIII shows the number of maintenance orders made and the number of divorce petitions filed since the beginning of the century.

TABLE XIII. NUMBER OF PETITIONS FOR DISSOLUTION AND NULLITY FILED AND MAINTENANCE ORDERS (MARRIED WOMEN) MADE 1901 TO 1954; ENGLAND AND WALES[2]

Period	Petitions dissolution and nullity	Maintenance orders[3] (married women)
	(annual averages)	
1901–1905	812	7,595
1906–1910	809	7,309
1911–1913[4]	965	7,637
1919–1920	4,874	11,087
1921–1925	2,848	9,101
1926–1930	4,052	10,813
1931–1935	4,784	9,617
1936–1940	7,535	10,401
1941–1945	16,075	13,418
1946–1950	38,901	19,208
1951–1954	33,132	14,489

[1] A husband may apply for a separation order, but cannot obtain a maintenance order against his wife. Husbands' applications are rare.

[2] The Maintenance Orders statistics, 1900–1950, have been usefully extracted from the many official sources and are published in a table by J. E. S. Simon in Minutes of Evidence Royal Commission on Marriage and Divorce, 7th and 8th Days (1952), p. 207. The figures for 1951–1954 have been added from the *Criminal Statistics, England and Wales* (1955), Table XII.

[3] These orders include only those made on the application of wives. A substantial number of orders for maintenance were made against husbands and other family heads on the application of the Poor Law authorities before 1948. Between 1901 and 1913 they averaged around 4,000 a year, between 1920 and 1929 around 3,000 and then climbed sharply from some 3,000 in 1931 to some 5,000 in 1938. Unfortunately, the statistics do not distinguish between maintenance of wives, children and other relatives. But it is clear that the numbers of maintenance orders shown in Table XIII underestimate, by an unknown amount, the actual total in the period before 1939.

[4] Maintenance order figures are not available for the years 1914–1918.

The statistics concerning the matrimonial jurisdiction of magistrates' courts, published by the Home Office, are deplorably scanty and uninformative. They do not show, at least in useful detail, the different grounds on which orders are made. No information is given as to the duration of marriage or number of children of women on whose applications maintenance orders are made. Further, it is not known how many maintenance orders have been rescinded *de facto* by the return of a wife to her husband or *de jure* by application to the court. Table XIII must therefore be interpreted with caution, and allowance made for the unknown proportion of " dead " orders. A full estimate of the total number of " live " orders cannot be made. The annual Report of the National Assistance Board shows, however, some 70,000 clients in 1955 [1] who described themselves as married but living apart from their husbands. This description includes " not only ' deserted ' wives, i.e. wives who have been abandoned by their husbands, but also wives who, for good or bad reasons, have themselves left their husbands, and wives who have separated from their husbands by mutual consent." [2]

Divorce petitions have increased fortyfold during the last fifty years whereas maintenance orders have only doubled. From 1926 to 1935 there were roughly twice as many orders as divorces but, after 1946, the relative positions of the two series have been reversed. It seems reasonable to assume that many of the pre-1939 maintenance orders represented the applicants' desire for divorce frustrated because they could not afford to pursue an action in the High Court. In this period, therefore, the number of marriage breakdowns which left a public record included those dissolved by divorce and those disrupted by " live " maintenance orders. Such orders created, in Professor Wootton's phrase, " a class, as it were, of homeless spirits, neither married nor unmarried,

[1] p. 13. [2] Cd. 9210, 1954, p. 18.

but suspended between the chance of heaven in a happy marriage with a new partner and the certainty of hell in life with the old one."[1] The Legal Aid scheme has altered this situation. As poverty no longer bars the way to the High Court, and the facts which must be proved to obtain a maintenance order, are, in some cases, the same as those necessary to secure a divorce,[2] many maintenance orders are now no more than the preliminary step which wives take to secure or supplement their incomes before filing a divorce petition.[3] On this view, the maintenance order of 1955 is likely to become the decree absolute of 1956.[4] Of how many current

[1] Barbara Wootton, *Holiness or Happiness* (The Twentieth Century, Nov. 1955), p. 415.

[2] "Adultery is a sufficient reason for both kinds of order, but desertion for however short a time justifies a maintenance order while it must have lasted three years to be a ground for divorce. Wilful neglect to provide reasonable maintenance is a ground for a maintenance order in a court of summary jurisdiction (as in the High Court), but not in itself a ground for divorce. Cruelty which is a ground for divorce is not necessarily a ground for a maintenance order. To claim such an order by reason of the husband's cruelty, the wife must show that it was "persistent," but, on the other hand, she will get the order on proof that he was persistently cruel to her children, and also in certain cases, by reason of a conviction for assault, and in some other cases of acts akin to cruelty. Unsoundness of mind which may be a ground for divorce is not a ground for a maintenance order, while such an order can be made by reason of the husband being a habitual drinker or a drug addict. . . . As against the wife's claim to maintenance the husband may raise defences arising from her own matrimonial conduct, and it is especially provided that proof of her adultery is such a defence." (O. Kahn-Freund, in W. Friedmann, ed., *Matrimonial Property Law* (1955), pp. 307–308).

[3] A divorce does not rescind a maintenance order. A petitioner has the option of keeping what she has already been granted in the magistrates' court, or applying to the High Court for maintenance. The great advantage of retaining the magistrates' order lies in the relative ease of enforcement. The enforcement procedures of the High Court are cumbersome and unsatisfactory.

[4] The Matrimonial Causes Act, 1950, facilitates the conversion of a maintenance order into a divorce. Sec. 7 provides:

(i) A person shall not be prevented from presenting a petition for divorce . . . by reason only that the petitioner has at any time been granted . . . an order under the Summary Jurisdiction (Separation and Maintenance) Acts, 1895–1949, upon the same or substantially the same facts as those proved in support of the petition for divorce.

(ii) On any such petition for divorce, the court may treat the . . . said order as sufficient proof of the adultery, desertion, or other ground on which it was granted. . . .

maintenance orders this is true it is impossible even to guess, as the number of wives with " live " maintenance orders who petition for divorce is unknown. It appears reasonable to assume that the proportion is substantial and likely to rise.[1] Thus the common controversial habit of using divorce figures as a measure of broken marriages, or of the alleged, progressive disintegration of the family in the twentieth century, is invalid.[2] An index of marriage breakdowns would have to combine both divorces and maintenance orders ; on present information such a calculation is impossible though, before 1939, the numbers of divorces seriously underestimated the total of publicly recorded, broken marriages. Moreover, the formalities of marriage are nowadays more commonly observed than fifty years ago. The unrecorded, broken cohabitation of 1900 will today be counted as a broken marriage. The gloomy picture of marital instability frequently drawn from the rapid increase in divorce since 1900 is greatly exaggerated.

This summary of the available statistical information concerning divorce establishes or suggests six main conclusions.

[1] A wife may apply for a maintenance order with or without a non-cohabitation clause (i.e. a separation order). If such a clause is inserted, it is a bar to divorce on the ground of desertion during the order's existence. The standard, printed form of order used contains a non-cohabitation clause, and, in the past, many courts did not strike it out when a maintenance order only was applied for and granted. Some wives subsequently discovered that their divorce petitions were barred for this reason. In recent years great care has been taken by solicitors to ensure that the unwanted clause is struck out.

[2] Two witnesses before the Morton Commission, Canon Hugh Warner (Evidence, 6th Day, p. 151, Q. 1191) and Mr. J. E. S. Simon, Q.C., M.P. (7th–8th Day, p. 200) thought there was " statistical evidence that wider facilities for divorce do lead to a grave unsettling of home life " (Warner). " It is frequently claimed by those who advocate easy divorce that the denial of facilities would merely result in the parties living separated, and possibly in an illicit union. If this were correct each extension of the grounds for divorce should cause a fall in the number of spouses living separate. . . . On the contrary, each extension of the facilities for divorce has weakened the marriage tie generally, and this has been reflected in an increase in separated as well as in divorced spouses " (Simon). This argument ignores reality. It could be valid only on the assumption that, since 1923, all spouses had equal means of access to the divorce court.

(1) The increase in divorce since 1900 has resulted from many complex changes. There have been extensions of the grounds for divorce and, of greater significance, a widening access to the High Court for the lower social classes. Today, full employment and legal aid ensure that poverty is no bar to divorce. Social and demographic changes have affected the expectation of life, the proportion of the population who marry, and the age at marriage. The structure and functions of the family, the position of women, and prevailing conceptions of desirable familial, parental, and sexual relationships have all changed. These—and other—interdependent variables have been operating within a society conditioned by continuously expanding industrialism and intermittent war. The present situation is the result of the coincidence in point of time of a multiplicity of social changes. Any attempt to select a *primum mobile*, or to arrange factors in order of importance, is necessarily an essay in futility.

(2) The distribution of divorce by duration of marriage and by the number of children of the marriage has been remarkably stable since 1900. The high proportion of divorces amongst marriages which have lasted for more than ten years does not support the popular assertion that easier facilities for divorce have created a divorce-minded population which rushes carelessly and unthinkingly into and out of easily dissolved marriages at the first sign of marital disharmony. Similarly, the high proportion of divorces amongst childless couples or amongst those whose children have grown up, must qualify the frequently expressed anxiety that every divorce represents an addition to the unhappy nursery of emotionally disturbed or deprived children.

(3) Whilst the increasing number of divorces clearly demonstrates a decline in public respect for the supernatural sanctions invoked by religious marriage ceremonies, there is no evidence that respect for the institution

of marriage has weakened. Indeed the high proportions both of divorced persons who marry new partners and of married couples in the whole population suggest a steadily increasing enthusiasm for marriage.

(4) Wives are now as likely as husbands to petition for divorce. The only statistically significant grounds are adultery, desertion, and cruelty. A high and roughly equal proportion of petitions allege adultery or desertion, but cruelty has been increasing rapidly during the last ten years.

(5) Statistical evidence derived from the operation of the Legal Aid scheme since 1950 permits the inference that knowledge and practice of divorce have spread extensively amongst the lower social classes.

(6) Available information is inadequate to provide any index of changes in the numbers of broken marriages since 1900. The statistics and changes in social function of magistrates' courts' maintenance orders, suggest, when viewed alongside divorce statistics and against the background of changing social habit and recent demographic history, that the rise (if, indeed, there has been a rise) in the rate of marriage breakdown during this century has been greatly exaggerated in recent discussions.

Such limited conclusions are the most that can safely be derived from the unsatisfactory statistical data. They serve to define the extent of our ignorance rather than the range of our knowledge about divorce. Of the many gaps in the information necessary to an informed judgment, two are especially distressing. Apart from slight and hazardous gleanings from Legal Aid statistics, there are no means, short of expensive investigations impossible for private persons, of discovering the distribution of divorce in rural and urban areas, or by occupation and income, or by social class. It is astonishing that the only published facts illuminating this most important aspect of divorce relate to the years 1907 and 1908 and to the period 1896–1921.[1] Without such information, no serious study of the causes and significance of divorce in England can be attempted. Secondly, the paucity of data about the familial circumstances and subsequent history of wives who are granted maintenance orders in the magistrates courts is deplorable. Once again the only useful published information about such orders relates to the years 1907 to 1909.[2] Until such material is regularly collected, the incidence, causes, and consequences of broken marriages must remain the dominion of the many moralists who are unable to distinguish between knowledge and their own dogmatic presuppositions.

[1] Sir John Macdonnell provided the Gorell Commission with a table showing, for 1907 and 1908, " the number of petitions presented by persons apparently belonging to the working classes " (Appendices to the Minutes of Evidence of the Royal Commission on Divorce and Matrimonial Causes (Cd. 6482, 1912), Table XVa, p. 35). He defined working-class by the husband's occupation at the date of marriage, and concluded that the proportions of working-class petitions were 29 per cent. in 1907 and 26 per cent. in 1908. Statistics of divorce by occupation were published annually in the Civil Judicial Statistics in the period 1896–1921.

[2] Sir John Macdonnell also provided the Gorell Commission with a table showing the number of separation (maintenance) orders county by county, thus indicating their distribution between rural and urban areas. (*ibid*, Table XIIa, p. 33). The Gorell Commission circulated a detailed questionnaire to all Clerks to Justices throughout England and Wales. Their answers provided information that is not available today (*ibid.*, pp. 46–59). The Morton Commission received some scraps of information in evidence. The Justices' Clerks Society provided a table showing some useful details of the matrimonial work of police courts in seven industrial towns in 1951. However, the explanatory notes that accompany the table are too slight to permit any useful conclusions to be drawn (12th–13th Day, p. 354). Mr. A. J. Chislett, Clerk to the Justices, Wallington Petty Sessional Division, sampled 100 consecutive maintenance orders made by his court, in which 29 per cent. were in respect of women whose marriages had lasted less than five years, 22 per cent. between five and ten years, 30 per cent. between ten and twenty years, and 19 per cent. more than twenty years (35th Day, p. 873). The Marriage Law Reform Society gave some details about magistrates' orders made by the court in Acton, Middlesex (9th Day, p. 237). The only government publication which contains useful details is the *Report of the Departmental Committee on Imprisonment by Courts of Summary Jurisdiction in Default of Payment of Fines and Other Sums of Money* (Cd. 4649, 1934), p. 37 *et. seq.*

CHAPTER III

THE VICTORIAN FAMILY: ILLUSION AND REALITY

THE scanty statistics outlined in the last chapter contribute little towards an understanding of the social significance of divorce. They exhibit the falsity of some dogmatic assertions, but permit few constructive affirmations. The ability to count does not necessarily confer a capacity to explain, and even the most comprehensive statistics of divorce would be meaningless unless the trends they indicated were interpreted as part of the changing history of the family.

Many moralists today bewail the disintegration of the family, the growth of irresponsibility, and the resulting corruption of morality in our society. Indeed, their threnodies on the family are the small change of current journalism, the recurring theme of ecclesiastical pronouncements, and the reiterated platitudes of schoolmasters, magistrates and social workers—the self-appointed clergy of our irreligious age. The High Master of St. Paul's School reports that:

> When the late Archbishop of York declared that the home is the greatest casualty of our time, this warning was endorsed by the experience of priests and probation officers, of teachers and magistrates, and even of those politicians whose economic policies have stimulated this gradual dissolution of home life.[1]

Miss Hall explains that:

> the most urgent problems which confront sociologists, social administrators and workers today are such

[1] A. N. Gilkes, art. "Faith in the Family," the *Sunday Times*, 21st October 1956.

symptoms of a sick society as the increasing numbers of marriage breakdowns . . .[1]

The Assistant Bishop to the Archbishop of Canterbury asserts in a pamphlet, *The Breakdown of the Family*, that " the life of the family is seriously threatened " because, *inter alia*, " people make greater demands on one another in married life," " easy divorce has changed the attitude of people to marriage," and " the conditions of modern industrial life threaten the family." [2] Professor James finds many causes for the present " widespread moral collapse and domestic disintegration." Amongst them he emphasises that :

> The husband-wife relationship as a complementary partnership in a joint personality has been resolved into a dualism of male and female rights, status and freedoms, so that the fundamental nature and purpose of marriage have been lost in a struggle for equality and social justice in isolation from the biological and domestic context in which, in its natural setting, the institution of marriage occurs.
>
> The bureaucratic Welfare State is too large and too impersonal to inculcate that instinctive loyalty which binds together members of a family or group in a sense of common duty to each other and to the society of which they are an integral part. . . . Never was it more apparent that a sound social life must be based on a system of values grounded in a moral and spiritual order, yet it is this crucial ethical factor that is largely inoperative in modern society. Thus, in the regulation of marriage and family relationships confusion of thought and practice prevail through divided counsels and the absence of a universally recognised standard with sufficient moral compulsion to serve both as a rule of life for the individual and a rule of criticism upon society.[3]

These formidable indictments of the present-day family all assume a falling off from the higher standards and

[1] M. P. Hall, *The Social Services of Modern England* (1952), p. 8.
[2] Stephen Neill, *The Breakdown of the Family* (1949), pp. 1–7.
[3] E. O. James, *Marriage and Society* (1952), pp. 187–188.

nobler aspirations of the past. Indeed, present anxieties about divorce are only one aspect of these general and gloomy assessments of the corrupting consequences of recent social change. Current criticisms of the family rest upon a comparison, sometimes explicit but usually concealed, of the stability and moral certainties of Victorian family life with today's shortcomings and laxity. Knowledge of the Victorian family and an examination of the causes and course of subsequent change are thus essential to any discussion of the present significance of divorce.

The Victorians were more family conscious than any generations in our history. The sanctity and dignity of the family is an ever recurring theme in their literature ; the health and vitality of the family was their constant preoccupation. Early- and mid-Victorian attitudes can be illustrated and clarified in many ways. A generation which held the integrity of the family to be the foundation of stable social life and frequently applauded the fruitful consequences of unaccustomed royal virtue, could not for long maintain its parents' faith in the Malthusian account of the consequences of Christian marriage. The *Introduction* to the Census of 1851 reflected a new outlook.[1] Written by William Farr, a great Victorian to whose pioneering statistical work the Registrar General's office owes much of its usefulness, it rejected Malthus's popularisation of the view that the " perpetual tendency in the race of man to increase beyond the means of subsistence is one of the general laws of animated nature " on grounds which underlay the ebullient mood of the 'fifties and 'sixties. Population and prosperity, Farr argued, grew together as cause and effect. " Numbers may either be diminished by celibacy and licentiousness or be multiplied by marriage," and the history of marriage in England disclosed the secret of growing prosperity. Lord Hardwicke's Marriage Act in the middle of the eighteenth

[1] *Occupations*, vol. I, p. liii *et seq.*

century led to " the social reform of the family," " the increase of marriage and of population," and " the increase in the industry of Great Britain." All this, Farr assured his readers, " was accomplished without any miraculous agency, by the progress of society, by the diffusion of knowledge and morals—by improvements—and improvements chiefly in the institution of marriage." Reviving faith in Lord Bacon's maxim that " true greatness consisteth essentially in population and breed of men " was accompanied by extreme hostility to any interference with the privacy of family life. W. Cooke Taylor, an authority on the factory system, thus stated his fear that factory legislation which limited childrens' hours of work would disrupt the family.

> The family is the unit upon which a constitutional government has been raised which is the admiration and envy of mankind. Hitherto, whatever else the laws have touched, they have not dared to invade this sacred precinct ; and the husband and wife, however poor, returning home from whatever occupations or harassing engagements, have there found *their* dominion, *their* repose, *their* compensation. . . . There has been a sanctity about this . . . home life which even the vilest law acknowledged and the rashest law respected. . . . But let the State step in between the mother and her child . . . domestic confidence is dissolved, family privacy invaded and maternal responsibility assailed. For the tenderness of the mother is substituted the tender mercies of the State ; for the security of natural affection, the securities of an unnatural law. Better by far that many another infant should perish in its innocence and unconsciousness than to be the victim of such a state of things.[1]

For all the Victorian generations the family was an omnipresent reality. Characteristically, Walter Bagehot

[1] Quoted H. L. Beales, *The Victorian Family* in H. Grisewood (ed.), *Ideas and Beliefs of the Victorians* (1949). This broadcast talk is the only general account of the Victorian family in print. My debt in this chapter to Mr. Beales's learned and suggestive article will be obvious to all readers.

appealed to the sentiment of family when, in his brilliant *The English Constitution* of 1865, he traced "how the actions of a retired widow and an unemployed youth become of such importance."

> A *family* on the throne is an interesting idea. . . . It brings down the pride of sovereignty to the level of petty life. No feeling could seem more childish than the enthusiasm of the English at the marriage of the Prince of Wales. They treated as a great political event, what, looked at as a matter of pure business, was very small indeed. But no feeling could be more like common human nature as it is, and as it is likely to be. The women—one half the human race at least—care fifty times more for a marriage than a ministry. . . . A princely marriage is the brilliant edition of a universal fact, and, as such, it rivets mankind. We smile at the *Court Circular* ; but remember how many people read the *Court Circular* ! Its use is not in what it says, but in those to whom it speaks . . . a royal family sweetens politics by the seasonable addition of nice and pretty events. It introduces irrelevant facts into the business of government, but they are facts which speak to "men's bosoms" and employ their thoughts. . . . Accordingly, so long as the human heart is strong and the human reason weak, royalty will be strong because it appeals to diffused feeling, and republics weak because they appeal to the understanding.[1]

Farr, Cooke Taylor, and Bagehot were imposing on their different material a representative conception of the family as a little sovereign commonwealth. The importance and maintenance of such a family was the main theme of the endless moralising literature of the period. Manuals of conduct [2] describing and extolling it had, by the 'eighties, joined Samuel Smiles's *Thrift* and *Self Help*

[1] W. Bagehot, *The English Constitution*, 3rd ed. (1891), pp. 38–39.

[2] The books of Rev. J. B. Brown, *The Home* : *In its Relation to Man and to Society* (1883) and Rev. J. R. Miller, *Home Making of the Ideal Family Life* (n.d.) are examples.

as the inevitable choice for School and Sunday School prize-givings. But in Victorian days, as at other times, the moralist's ideal was imperfectly realised.

The character of the Victorian family cannot be described apart from its changing occupational and class setting. Different people's families functioned differently. There was no "representative family" whose life and experience were shared by all social strata. In this respect, the acceleration of industrial development, with its accompanying growth of towns which sucked in, decade by decade, an increasing proportion of the growing population, had a strikingly paradoxical effect. It weakened the family of the wage earning class as it strengthened that of the middle class. But it was the middle-class family which became the exemplar of moralists in the decades after the Great Exhibition, compelling conformity from above and attracting aspirants from below. The main outlines of its assertive history are clear and well documented. The autobiographies, diaries, letters and novels, of admirers and dissidents alike, provide a running commentary on this greatest of Victorian success stories.

I

As industrialism floated its rapidly expanding executive class to affluence or modest competence, it also transformed the home environment of the middle-class family. Gas gave new light to the family parlour or drawing-room as well as new subscribers to the circulating libraries and, later, new cooking stoves to the kitchen. The increasing use of water closets helped to found a new occupation, and to condition English plumbers in ways of thought from which they have not yet fully emancipated themselves or their victims. Railways, the agents of suburban colonisation, carried boys to the new public schools and their families to the seaside for the annual family holiday. The growth of manufacturing industry and the parallel reorganisation of the distributive trades established a new reliance on the shopkeeper. These—and many other—transforming additions to the physical environment and equipment of the middle-class family between the mid-eighteenth and mid-nineteenth centuries are nowhere better illustrated than in the pages of Mrs. Isabella Beeton's, *Book of Household Management.*[1] Unlike those of her predecessors,[2] Mrs. Beeton's *magnum opus* was not merely a cookery book ; it was a manual for the middle-class domestic manager, comprising, according to its sub-title,

> information for the mistress, housekeeper, cook, kitchen-maid, butler, footman, coachman, valet, upper and under house-maids, lady's maid, maid-of-all-work, laundry maid, nurse and nurse-maid, monthly, wet, and sick nurses, etc., etc., also sanitary, medical and legal memoranda : with a history of the origin, properties, and uses, of all things connected with home life and comfort.

The usefulness and appeal of this astonishing book to the middle-class housewife can be measured by its sales. First issued in parts in 1859, it came out as an 1172-page book, price 7s. 6d., in 1861 ; by 1870 it had sold over two million copies.

[1] There are two lively and interesting accounts of Mrs. Beeton and her husband. Nancy Spain, *Mrs. Beeton and her Husband* (1948) and H. Montgomery Hyde, *Mr. and Mrs. Beeton* (1951).

[2] The exception is the fascinating book of Alexis Soyer, *The Modern Housewife or Ménagère* (1849), which guided Mr. and Mrs. Baker of Bifrons Villa, St. John's Wood, through the domestic perils of ascending social mobility from small shopkeeper to wealthy merchant. By 1853 it had sold 30,000 copies. In that year Soyer added a touch of cruel realism and spoilt his sales. " The too bold speculation of your unfortunate but devoted husband " reduced the Bakers to the poverty from whence they sprang and sent Mrs. Baker back to the kitchen and Soyer's recipes for boiled ox feet. Soyer's career is described in the delightful and elegant biography of Helen Morris, *Portrait of a Chef* (1938).

The character of the mid-Victorian families whose physical comfort was secured by Mrs. Beeton's prescriptions, had been moulded by many social and economic influences. The middle ranks of society were growing in numbers and in wealth or, if not wealth, at least the hope of aspiring to it. Stable or expanding incomes gave most of them a settled and optimistic outlook on their economic future and the ability to command cheap domestic service on a scale roughly indicated below.

Income (£ per annum)	Number of servants	Total Servants' Wages Bill (£ per annum)
100	1	5
250	2	18 15s.
500	3	62 10s.
1,000	5–7	125
5,000	14 (includes 8 males)	465
20,000	43 (includes 25 males)	1,475 [1]

In 1851 there were more than a million domestic servants, more than double the women and girls then employed in all the textile trades. On the eve of the Kaiser's war they still formed the largest single occupational group. The household duties of the middle-class wife were limited to supervising, and complaining about, her servants. The change in her situation since the eighteenth century was admirably described in an extract, dated 1853, from Margaretta Grey's diary.

It appears to me that, with an increase of wealth unequally distributed, and a pressure of population,

[1] The figures for incomes of £100–£1,000 are the estimates of J. H. Walsh, *A Manual of Domestic Economy* (1857), p. 606. They are quoted by J. A. Banks, *Prosperity and Parenthood* (1954), p. 74, which contains an excellent and detailed account of domestic service in this period. I have added the estimates for income of £5,000 and £20,000. They are taken from Alfred Cox, *The Landlord's and Tenant's Guide* (n.d., *c.* 1853), pp. 109–111.

there has sprung up among us a spurious refinement, that cramps the energy and circumscribes the usefulness of women in the upper classes of society. A lady, to be such, must be a mere lady, and nothing else. She must not work for profit, or engage in any occupation that can command money. . . . Men in want of employment have pressed their way into nearly all the shopping and retail businesses that in my early days were managed, in whole or in part, by women. The conventional barrier that pronounces it ungenteel to be behind a counter, or serving the public in any mercantile capacity, is greatly extended. The same in household economy. Servants must be up to their several offices, which is very well; but ladies, dismissed from the dairy, the confectionary, the store-room, the still-room, the poultry yard, the kitchen-garden, and the orchard, have hardly yet found themselves a sphere equally useful and important in the pursuits of trade and art to which to apply their too abundant leisure. . . . We must submit to the changes which the progress of art . . . forces upon us. What is done with abridged labour and greater effect on a large scale in the factory, need not be done with time and many pains by many hands in the family. But what I remonstrate against is the negative forms of employment: . . . the crippling of talent under false notions of station, propriety, and refinement, that seems to shut up a large portion of the women of our generation from proper spheres of occupation and adequate exercise of power.[1]

Victorian middle-class women lost much when industrialism and urbanisation took many of the old household jobs out of the home. The leisure they gained became the mark of respectability and refinement so long as it was filled only with futile domesticities. Marriage was the only socially approved occupation open to women, and their earlier lives were organised within the family to that end. "Women don't consider themselves as

[1] Josephine E. Butler, *Memoir of John Grey of Dilston* (1869), p. 326, fn. 1.

human beings at all," wrote Florence Nightingale in a private note in 1851, "there is absolutely no God, no country, no duty to them at all, except family."[1] Outside the family married women had the same legal status as children and lunatics ; within it they were their husbands' inferiors. By marriage they moved from dependence on fathers or male relatives to dependence on husbands. To the Pauline conclusion that they two shall be one flesh, the Victorian husband added the explanation : "and I am he." The common law asserted this unity by regarding husband and wife as one person.[2] The married woman had practically no right to hold property ; her personal estate passed to her husband on marriage ; she could sue in the courts only in her husband's name ; and had no right to the custody of her legitimate children above the age of seven. A husband was entitled to enforce his right to his wife's *consortium* by attachment of person, and could force her to return to him. Women could exercise political rights only as the Sovereign or, if rate-payers, as voters for the Boards of Poor Law Guardians. Even the Sovereign had her moments of doubt. ". . . I am every day more convinced," she confided to her uncle Leopold in 1852, "that *we women*, *if* we *are* to be *good* women, *feminine* and *amiable* and *domestic*, are *not fitted to reign*. . . ."[3] Lord Tennyson truly phrased the maxim of the age when he wrote

> Man with the head and woman with the heart
> Man to command and woman to obey ;
> All else confusion.

The legal powers of husbands over their wives reflected the personal status of women in the family. But their

[1] Quoted C. Woodham Smith, *Florence Nightingale* (1950), p. 93.

[2] The best account of the legal position of women in this period is that of Erna Reiss, *The Rights and Duties of Englishwomen* (1934).

[3] A. C. Benson and Viscount Esher, (ed.), *The Letters of Queen Victoria*, vol. II, 1844–1853, p. 444.

subjection, as John Stuart Mill called it, was sexual as well as social. It is significant that submissiveness is always the quality most stressed by the manuals of conduct. Men thought of women, and women thought of themselves, as passive, submissive instruments of male gratification who must dutifully and joylessly endure the lawful embraces of their husbands. Their only legitimate satisfactions from sexual intercourse were those of motherhood, and these issued from pain and suffering. The conspiracy of silence [1] about sex was in part the creation of urban ignorance—countryfolk have no opportunities for such refinements. In part, also, it was a middle-class evangelical reaction from those free and easy habits of the sceptical Whig aristocracy which led Lord Carlisle to remark, " I was afraid I was going to have the gout the other day, I believe I live too chaste : it is not a common fault with me." Nor was it, comments Lord David Cecil, " a common fault with any of them. . . . Even unmarried girls were suspected of having lovers ; among married women the practice was too common to stir comment." [2] Sexual adventurousness was possible for a wealthy, primogenitary class that stuck to the rule of securing a male heir of known parentage ; and its members were not often put to the inconvenience and expense of obtaining a divorce by Private Act of Parliament. There is an element of naïvety in Mr. Haw's observation that the rarity of such Private Acts in the eighteenth century did not present " the Church with a challenge to her teaching which demanded a decisive answer in any way comparable to the statutory legislation which was to follow." [3] The middle-class system of inheritance

[1] It was occasionally broken in curious ways. In 1841 the Rev. G. D. Haughton published his account of the future under the title *On Sex in the World to Come*. He thought that " Religion has been deeply injured by the uninteresting representations which are usually given of the Life to Come," and promised his readers " a foundation for more cheering hopes, and brighter anticipations " (pp. v–vi).

[2] David Cecil, *The Young Melbourne* (1939), pp. 10–11.

[3] Reginald Haw, *The State of Matrimony* (1952), p. 138.

required the austerer morality which Dr. Arnold's example diffused throughout the public schools, where boys' sexual instincts were disciplined by cold water and sublimated in muscular Christianity. (Girls, being thought to have no sexual instincts, were spared the cold water.)

Few aspects of the period are more astonishing than the successful imposition of middle-class standards on the overt sexual behaviour of the aristocracy. " That d.....d morality," which disconcerted Lord Melbourne, covered early-Victorian England like a fog. The occasional flickering light, Lord Palmerston,[1] perhaps, not troubling to conceal his preference for the old ways, served only to emphasise the gloom. The unmentionableness of sex and the necessary chastity of women were important contributions of the nonconformist and evangelical revivals to Victorian morality. The new attitudes were well established [2] when Thomas Bowdler's *The Family Shakespeare. In which nothing is added to the Text ; but those Words and Expressions are ommitted which cannot with Propriety be read aloud in a Family* was first published in 1818. Mr. Bowdler succeeded, to the satisfaction of the Edinburgh reviewer, in removing from " three plays of a rather ticklist description—Othello, Troilus and Cressida, and Measure for Measure . . . many passages . . . which a father could not read aloud to his children—a brother

[1] Under the aristocracy's control over appointments to the Queen's Household, the Royal Palaces sheltered easy going habits of which their mistress never learnt. The Lord Chamberlain, Lord Conyngham, provided for his mistress by installing her as housekeeper in Buckingham Palace, and the Lord Steward, Lord Uxbridge, followed his thrifty example. Lord Palmerston, when Foreign Secretary and the Queen's guest at Windsor Castle, was in the habit of relaxing from cares of state in the bedroom of one of the Queen's Ladies of the Bedchamber. On one occasion he disturbed the wrong lady and her protests roused the Castle. This abuse of royal hospitality was the origin of Victoria's detestation of Palmerston. (These details are taken from the book of Roger Fulford, *The Prince Consort* (1949), pp. 60–61.)

[2] The best account of the factors in this transition is still the most scholarly book of Maurice J. Quinlan, *Victorian Prelude* (Columbia University Press, 1941).

to his sister—or a gentleman to a lady."[1] By the 'sixties they had permeated, and been reinforced by, the literature[2] acceptable on the bookstalls of that keen censor, Mr. W. H. Smith. Hippolyte Taine, the French critic, writing in 1864, discerned the instructions which their readers gave to English novelists.

> Be moral. All your novels must be such as may be read by young girls. We are practical minds, and we would not have literature corrupt practical life. We believe in family life, and we would not have literature paint the passions which attack family life. We are protestants, and we have preserved something of the severity of our fathers against enjoyment and passions. Amongst these, love is the worst. Beware against resembling in this respect the most illustrious of our neighbours. Love is the hero of all George Sand's novels. Married or not, she thinks it beautiful, holy, sublime in itself; and she says so. Don't believe this; and if you do believe it, don't say it. It is a bad example. Love thus represented makes marriage a secondary matter. It ends in marriage, or destroys it, or does without it, according to circumstances; but whatever it does, it treats it as inferior; it does not recognise any holiness in it, beyond that which love gives it, and holds it impious if it is excluded. . . . George Sand paints impassioned women; paint you for us good women. George Sand makes us desire to be in love; do you make us desire to be married.[3]

[1] *Edinburgh Review* (1821), pp. 52–53.

[2] The one, and in many ways surprising, exception is Surtees. *Sponge's Sporting Tour* was first published in book form in 1853; *Handley Cross; or, Mr. Jorrocks's Hunt* in 1854. But they were the product of, and largely read by rural society. They caused anxiety when they became popular with the urban public. ". . . cheap editions have been called for by the reading public within the last few years. I have heard it gravely stated that hunting books lack refinement. . . . Yet the people who complain of Mr. Jorrocks will devour the sexual novels of the modern female novelists." Thus an admirer of Surtees, writing in 1900 (G. F. Underhill, *A Century of Fox-Hunting* (1900), pp. 235–236).

[3] H. A. Taine, *History of English Literature* (trans. V. Van Laun, 1878), vol. II, pp. 354–355.

Perhaps Taine's judgment was too harsh. The early- and mid-Victorians were sensitive to the claims of love and affection as the basis of happy married life, but alive also to the miseries of imprudence. The anxious discussion in the 'fifties and 'sixties of the "proper time to marry," which Mr. Banks describes,[1] pointed to a cautious avoidance of hasty marriage. The desire to maintain both a wife and middle-class social station could only be reconciled by the postponement of marriage until such time as male earnings sufficed for both. The increasing age of marriage and the inviolable rule of female chastity together created the most repugnant aspect of Victorian middle-class social life. When Victorians spoke and wrote of the "*Great Social Evil*" they referred, not to working class housing, or the sanitary condition of manufacturing towns, or the working lives of agricultural labourers, but to prostitution. The character of the middle-class family and the relations between men and women within it cannot be understood without a brief reference to this dark beastliness which lay behind the conspiracy of silence.

The historical as distinct from the moral or psychological [2] definition of prostitution in this period must recognise the existence of those economic and social forces which led to the organic manufacture of prostitutes.

[1] *op cit.*, ch. III.

[2] The historian has not yet received much help from psychologists in the investigation of these problems. Dr. Edward Glover, for example (H. Grisewood (ed.), *op. cit.*, *Victorian Ideas of Sex*) is unwilling to admit that the Victorian situation was in any way distinctive. His view appears to rest on three grounds. First, that many Victorians "were themselves violently anti-Victorian." Secondly, "modern investigations have shown that a surprisingly large number of prostitutes are mentally backward to the point often of borderline deficiency." Third that, historically, sexuality is a constant. Any emphasis on environmental factors Dr. Glover regards as absurd, naïve and adolescent. In terms of Dr. Glover's explanation of Victorian prostitution, the decline in numbers and social importance of prostitutes since 1850 can be explained only in terms of a theory of the chronologically fluctuating incidence of mental deficiency amongst women.

Overcrowding, the Poor Law, unemployment, and intermittent employment all contributed to maintain the supply. A persistent demand came from middle-class men frustrated of normal outlets. William Acton, a surgeon, whose *Prostitution, Considered in its Moral, Social and Sanitary Aspects*, first appeared in 1858, made a clear diagnosis.

> The laws which society imposes in the present day in respect of marriage upon young men belonging to the middle class are, in the highest degree, unnatural, and are the real cause of most of our social corruptions. The father of a family has, in many instances, risen from a comparatively humble origin to a position of easy competence. His wife has her carriage; he associates with men of wealth greater than his own. His sons reach the age when, in the natural course of things, they ought to marry and have a home for themselves. It would seem no great hardship that a young couple should begin on the same level as their parents began, and be content for the first few years with the mere necessaries of life; and there are thousands who, were it not for society, would gladly marry on such terms. But here the tyrant world interposes; the son must not marry until he can maintain an establishment on much the same footing as his father's. If he dare to set the law at defiance, his family lose *caste*, and he and his wife are quietly dropt out of the circle in which they have hitherto moved. All that society will allow is an engagement, and then we have the sad but familiar sight of two young lovers wearing out their best years with hearts sickened and with hope long deferred. . . . I know there are thousands who are living in sin, chiefly in consequence of the impossibility (as the world says) of their marrying. Some go quietly with the stream, and do as others do around them . . . many, perhaps most of them, are wretched under the convictions of their conscience . . . yet they dare not offend their family, alienate their friends, and lose their social position by making what the world calls an imprudent marriage. . . . It is difficult to suggest any remedy for

this evil. But the mischief is on the increase with our increasing worship of money.[1]

Prostitution operated through the double standard of morality to accommodate both the recognised waywardness of men and the purity of the middle-class wife and home. Many Victorians were hypocritical, but to indict whole generations on that ground is unbalanced. Hypocrisy and complacency were not the only attitudes. An ever present undercurrent of anxiety was expressed in many ways. Sometimes, as with Mr. Gladstone's honourable, but often misconstrued, personal efforts at rescue work, the response was individual;[2] often, as with J. B. Talbot's London Society for the Protection of Young Females or the many Moonlight Missions, it was organised. The system of prostitution was the squalid basis of much Victorian rectitude and respectability. It must be understood and interpreted as an essential element in Victorian sexual morality.

The middle-class family drew its strength from growing numbers and rising incomes. Within it, women had an inferior personal and sexual status; outside it, men pursued irregular relationships. In the family hierarchy, stations were known and fixed under paternal, but authoritarian, rule. Women's usefulness was restricted to such domestic trivialities as reflected their husband's

[1] pp. 168–170. In the nature of the case, it is impossible to make a reasonable estimate of the numbers of prostitutes. In London, Acton observes, they have been "variously estimated according to the opportunities, credulity, or religious fervour of observers, and the width of interpretation they have put upon the word." Estimates for London in the 1850's ranged from 80,000 to 8,600. The latter figure was a Metropolitan Police estimate for 1857. Estimates of numbers in other towns varied in like proportion. An indication of the range of Victorian writing about prostitution is given in the bibliography of O. R. McGregor, "The Social Position of Women in England, 1850–1914" (*The British Journal of Sociology*, vol. VI, No. 1), pp. 55, fn. 47.

[2] Gladstone's lifelong efforts for the redemption of prostitutes occasioned much malicious gossip and some embarrassing incidents. They are fully described in the biography of Philip Magnus, *Gladstone* (1954), esp. pp. 105–110.

station, and to continuous childbearing. Within the established social scheme, its dependent members enjoyed neither personal freedom nor individual independence. This family code owed much to, and was sanctified by, evangelical religion which reinstated the Pauline conception of marriage and reinforced the sexual degradation of women. It could not escape the notice of the practical man, Mr. G. M. Young remarks, that

> the virtues of a Christian after the Evangelical model were easily exchangeable with the virtues of a successful merchant or a rising manufacturer, and that a more than causal analogy could be established between Grace and Corruption and the Respectable and the Low. To be serious, to redeem the time, to abstain from gambling, to remember the Sabbath day to keep it holy, to limit the gratification of the senses to the pleasures of a table lawfully earned and the embraces of a wive lawfully wedded, are virtues for which the reward is not laid up in heaven only. The world is very evil. An unguarded look, a word, a gesture, a picture, or a novel, might plant a seed of corruption in the most innocent heart, and the same word or gesture might betray a lingering affinity with the class below.[1]

" We have no data," remarks Mr. H. L. Beales, " upon which the statistician can work to establish levels or trends of happiness and unhappiness, harmony and frustration. Even Bentham had failed to devise a felicific calculus." [2] The historian cannot measure the quality of life within this family system. He can only conclude that the final judgment must allow for the diseased tyranny of *The Way of All Flesh* as well as for Trollope's domestic felicities.

[1] G. M. Young, *Victorian England : Portrait of an Age* (1936), p. 2. This is the most brilliant and erudite study of the Victorians yet written. The passing of the years serves only to enhance its quality.

[2] H. L. Beales, *op. cit.*, p. 357.

II

If the consequences of industrialism for the middle class are clear, its impact on working people is indistinct, and has been much disputed. In the two decades before 1850, a school of moralists and social reformers created a picture of the working-class home under early industrialism which historians long accepted, and which is still the stock-in-trade of much current thinking. This account begins with the peasant or domestic worker's family of pre-industrialist days when it was largely a self-sustaining economic unit. There was a division of labour between members of the family ; men reaped and women and children bound the sheaves. Women and children spun the yarn, men specialised in weaving. The family home was the workshop, parental discipline served also as industrial discipline, and education and technical training were the home responsibility of parents. When, according to this view, agriculture was commercialised and the textile trades went into the factory, the family disintegrated. The familial division of labour was destroyed ; men, women and children went out to work, and the working-class home became no more than a dormitory annexe to the factory. As the economic unity of the home was destroyed, so also the moral values it sustained and implanted in children were corroded. The factory system destroyed parental affection and incited sexual licence amongst working-class people. Peter Gaskell, a Manchester surgeon, surveying conditions in 1833, thought

> The chastity of marriage is but little known or exercised ; husband and wife sin equally, and an habitual indifference to sexual rights is generated, which adds one other item to assist in the destruction of domestic habits.[1]

[1] *The Manufacturing Population of England* (1833).

His conclusion was the same as the young Disraeli's, writing in his "Young England" phase, twelve years later.

> There are great bodies of the working classes of this country nearer the condition of brutes than they have been at any time since the Conquest. Indeed I see nothing to distinguish them from brutes, except that their morals are inferior. Incest and infanticide are as common among them as among the lower animals. The domestic principle wanes weaker and weaker every year in England ; nor can we wonder at it, when there is no comfort to cheer and no sentiment to hallow the Home.[1]

Disraeli's two nation diagnosis was echoed in similar terms by Friedrich Engels who thought that "next to intemperance in the enjoyment of intoxicating liquors, one of the principal faults of English working men is sexual licence . . . the social order makes family life almost impossible for the worker."[2] Such views passed from the moralists to the novelists. They appear, in a suitably bowdlerised form, in Mrs. Gaskell's *Mary Barton* (1848) and in *North and South* (1855). All mix gross exaggeration, especially with regard to the extent of children's and married women's employment in factories, with some element of truth. They shed more light on their middle-class authors' presuppositions than upon working-class behaviour.

The effect of industrialism on the working-class family in this transitional period has never been fully studied. Such a study is possible, but must overcome many difficulties. Unlike the middle class, working people were inarticulate and, in any case, had no leisure in which to record intimacies in private diaries. Most of the available

[1] B. Disraeli, *Sybil* (1845). The quotation is from the "Young England" ed. (1904), p. 228.

[2] *Condition of the Working Class in 1844* (trans. 1936), pp. 128–129. Engels at any rate shared one proletarian fault. He maintained as a mistress, first Mary, and later, Lizzie Burns ; much, we are told, to the Marx's embarrassment. (M. Beer, *Fifty Years of International Socialism* (1935), pp. 77–78.)

information about their lives derives from middle-class observers whose writing is often prejudiced and distorted. One further difficulty is the slow, uneven spread of industrialism which affected different occupational groups at different times in different areas of the country. No generalisation about the working-class family in the middle years of the century is possible. All that can be attempted here is a brief indication of the main problems and the lines upon which solutions emerged.

The physical environment of the working-class home both gained and lost from industrialism. The transference of domestic work from insanitary, overcrowded cottages created possibilities of homemaking, and destroyed little of value. The trades that were still in the home in 1850, lace-making, straw-plaiting, glove making, framework knitting, nail making—and more besides, produced the worst conditions. It was of the homes of people such as these that Henry Mayhew wrote a moving essay in 1850 under the title of *Home is Home, be it never so Homely*. He describes places " so very *homely* as to allow neither ease, peace, comfort, and hardly affection to be enjoyed in them." [1] In the long run mechanisation offered an emancipation permanently denied to the domestic worker. But it was a long run advantage. If industrialism gave workers, especially skilled workers, rising wages and improving standards of life, it brought with it also new insecurities and a new environment. The rapid growth of towns posed problems of health and housing, government and police, on a scale that no community had ever faced before. Industrialism did not, as Gaskell, Disraeli and Engels thought, impoverish and demoralise [2] workers

[1] In Viscount Ingestre (ed.), *Meliora : Or Better Times to Come*, 2nd. ed. (1852), p. 263.

[2] All these matters, including family life under the domestic system, are discussed in great detail, and with abundant documentation, in the important book of Ivy Pinchbeck, *Women Workers and the Industrial Revolution, 1750–1850* (1930). Indeed, much that today passes as a new interpretation of the period is implied or stated by Dr. Pinchbeck.

whose lives and families had been secure and carefree in an earlier age. In 1850 it was keeping alive three times as many people as in 1750 at a standard of living certainly no lower than that endured by their progenitors. The real disaster was that too many of the old ways of life and working survived to be carried forward, together with those that had been revolutionised by machinery, into the age of great cities.

To say that industrialism promised relief from the miseries and grinding poverties inseparable from most human lives in ages past, to hold up the Irish, who starved in 1846 when their potatoes rotted, as a warning to carping critics, does not erase or mitigate the recorded sufferings of the generations who endured that posterity might live in decency and comfort. The physical environment of most urban working-class families was squalid, beastly and brutalising. In 1854 John Simon, Medical Officer to the City of London, urged the establishment of a Ministry of Health.

> I would beg any educated person to consider what are the conditions in which alone animal life can thrive ; to learn, by personal inspection, how far these conditions are realised for the masses of our population ; and to form for himself a conscientious judgment as to the need for great, if even almost revolutionary, reforms. Let any such person devote an hour to visiting some very poor neighbourhood in the metropolis, or in almost any of our large towns. Let him breathe its air, taste its water, eat its bread. Let him think of human life struggling there for years. Let him fancy what it would be to himself to live there, in that beastly degradation of stink, fed with such bread, drinking such water. Let him enter some house there at hazard, and—heeding where he treads, follow the guidance of his outraged nose to the yard (if there be one) or the cellar. Let him talk to the inmates : let him hear what is thought of the bone-boiler next door, or the slaughter-house behind ; what of the sewer-grating before the door ; what of the Irish basket-makers

> upstairs—twelve in a room, who came in after the hopping, and got fever; what of the artisan's dead body, stretched on his widow's one bed, beside her living children. Let him, if he have a heart for the duties of manhood and patriotism, gravely reflect whether such sickening evils, as an hour's inquiry will have shown him, ought to be habit of our labouring population. . . .[1]

But, despite the work of Simon and his colleagues, these were, and for long remained, the habit of the labouring population. With horrifying overcrowding, the inadequate provisions of a private enterprise educational system, and the omnipresent poverty of a class who mostly lived from hand to mouth, the family could not be a stable, going concern. Children were brutally socialised, and sexual relations imperfectly regulated. In this respect, habits changed little in themselves, though the age of marriage, or its irregular substitute, fell; and, in the town, the old sanctions of a small rural community ceased to operate. What middle-class people regarded as a new and dangerous decline in working-class moral standards was no more than the persistence, in a new world, of old habits which urban life and investigating civil servants exposed to open view.

The essential changes in working-class family life were its setting of urban poverty, and the altered code by which middle-class people judged its quality. The latter point comes out clearly in the stream of comment about those human derelicts—if they were human—of an industrialising society, the agricultural labourers. The Rev. Lord Sidney Godolphin Osborne, whose authoritative letters to *The Times* on the social condition of rural society, under the initials S.G.O. fill two volumes in incomplete reproduction, thus wrote of his native Dorset.

[1] Edward Seaton, (ed.) John Simon, *Public Health Reports* (1887), vol. I, p. 144.

> Is it not notorious that, very generally, the cottages in which the poor dwell are so constructed that anything like a separation of the sexes at night is next to impossible? Is it not the fact that in ten thousand cases, father, mother, brothers, and sisters are forced to undress and lie down to rest in one and the same room? So common is this state of things, that I am satisfied it has affected the whole tone of feeling of the upper towards the lower classes; we have got into a way of thinking depravity, like rags and broken windows, to be the regular, if not the natural accompaniment of poverty.[1]

Depravity was inseparable from leisureless lives passed in brutality and squalor, from which only drink gave momentary release. The record of prostitution, juvenile delinquency,[2] infanticide, baby farming, and child murder[3] is nauseating testimony. But the final judgment on the horrors of the middle years of the century lies not with Gaskell or Engels, but with the Rev. Dr. Robert Vaughan whose optimistic assessment of the urban tendencies of his day was published, in 1843, under the title *The Age of Great Cities; or, Modern Society Viewed in its Relation to Intelligence, Morals and Religion.* He deplored the prevalent evils of the "new form of social existence," but insisted "the wonder, all things considered, is not that it is so great, but rather that it is not greater."

This brief account has said nothing of the aristocratic family. It has been concerned only with the dynamic elements of mid-nineteenth-century society, with the quick and not the dying. The character of the middle- and working-class family units a hundred years ago has

[1] Arnold White (ed.), *The Letters of S.G.O.* (n.d. 189?), vol. I, p. 75.

[2] See e.g. Mary Carpenter, *Reformatory Schools for the Children of the Perishing and Dangerous Classes* (1851) and *Juvenile Delinquents, their Condition and Treatment* (1853).

[3] There is a massive literature of which the following are examples. The Report of Dr. Hunter in *Sixth Report of the Medical Officer of the Privy Council* (Cd. 3416, 1863), p. 454 *passim*, and *Report of the Select Committee on the Protection of Infant Life* (P.P. 1871, vol. VII), James Greenwood, *The Seven Curses of London* (1868), sec. I.

been sketched to provide a point of reference for, and a measure of, those changes which have shaped our mid-twentieth-century experience.

III

The middle-class mid-Victorian family which nowadays attracts the melancholy nostalgia of moralists was annihilated by external pressures and internal tensions. The sense of economic security and expansiveness which had cradled it in the good years after 1850, dissolved in the years of falling prices and imperial adventure after the 'seventies. Real incomes did not fall, but the cost of maintaining increasingly elaborate middle-class appearances absorbed a larger proportion of their resources.[1] The range of material wants widened. People travelled more, entertained more, and employed more domestics at higher wages. And always in the nursery were the survivals of regular and inevitable pregnancies, watched over by cheap mother substitutes. Then, as now, parents' duty to their offspring was not fulfilled unless they secured for them an adult station in the social hierarchy no lower, or, if possible, higher than that in which they were reared. As industrial technology diversified and professional work became more skilled, the maintenance of social status increasingly required a longer and more expensive education.[2] Thus, by the 'seventies, well-stocked nurseries conflicted with established social habits and parental obligations.

These were the circumstances in which, if Cupid proposed, the advocates of mechanical methods of birth control disposed. Readers of the *Forsyte Saga* will recall

[1] There is detailed discussion in the essential book of J. A. Banks, *op. cit.*

[2] Much interesting information about the rising cost of education is assembled in the book of G. G. Leybourne and Kenneth White, *Education and the Birth Rate* (1940).

how young Euphemia Forsyte justified the break in family tradition when Aunt Susan was cremated in 1895: "Well I think people have a right to their own bodies, even when they're dead." This remark leads Galsworthy to reflect on Forsyte breeding habits. Their birth rate had "varied in accordance with the rate of interest." Ten per cent. had sired ten children, but when the rate fell to 3 per cent. they adopted the practice of "mild reproduction." "A distrust of their earning powers, natural where a sufficiency is guaranteed, together with the knowledge that their fathers did not die, kept them cautious. If one had children and not much income, the standard of taste and comfort must of necessity go down . . ." Thus the Forsytes conformed to the tendencies of the age.

The trial, in 1877, of Annie Besant and Charles Bradlaugh for reprinting and circulating a forty-year-old birth control pamphlet, initiated widespread public discussion, and resulted in the immediate formation of the Malthusian League to which Professor Glass [1] traces the promotion of the modern birth control movement with its system of clinics. The League's main object was the reduction of working-class poverty through family limitation. At that time, however, its economic arguments had greater influence on the better off than on the poor to whom its arguments were directed. Family limitation began first amongst the higher social classes and spread downwards progressively, decade by decade. Amongst those who married between 1851 and 1861, the differences in family size at the top and bottom of the social pyramid were small; for those marrying between 1881 and 1886, such difference had become significantly clearer. The table on the next page shows the changing situation.

[1] D. V. Glass, *Population Policies and Movements in Europe* (1940), p. 35. Ch. I is the authoritative account of the whole birth control movement in England.

AVERAGE FAMILY SIZE IN EACH SOCIAL CLASS AS A PROPORTION OF THE AVERAGE FOR ALL SOCIAL CLASSES TOGETHER [1]

Social class	Percentage of average of all classes — Women marrying 1851–1861	Percentage of average of all classes — Women marrying 1881–1886
1. Professional and higher administrative in finance & commerce	86	72
2. Employers in industry and retail trade	98	86
3. Skilled workers	101	102
4. Intermediate between 3 and 4	100	102
5. Unskilled labourers	105	112
6. Textile workers	99	93
7. Miners	110	132
8. Agricultural labourers	106	113

The percentage gap between the classes with the smallest and largest families, the professional group and miners, had risen, by the 'eighties, from 24 to 60 per cent.

The extension of the birth control habit to most social groups during the last seventy years has almost eliminated the large family. Women married between 1870 and 1879 averaged 5·8 children each, those who married in 1925 (ending their reproductive lives in 1950) contrived only 2·21.[2] The elimination of the large Victorian family is strikingly illustrated by the table at top of page 84.

Eighty years ago three-fifths of all families had five or more children, by 1925 two-thirds had two or less. The trend has not been reversed. "Large families," Professor Titmuss recently remarked, "are becoming reproductive deviants. As such, they may soon become anthropological curiosities." [3] There are still differences between the family size of the various social strata, though

[1] *Report of the Royal Commission on Population* (Cd. 7695), 1949, p. 28. The unsatisfactory categories of "social classes" are those of the Registrar-General.

[2] D. V. Glass and E. Grebenik, "The Trend and Pattern of Fertility in Great Britain," *Papers of the Royal Commission on Population* (1954), vol. VI, Pt. I, p. 3.

[3] 'British National Conference on Social Work,' *The Family* (1954), p. 12.

GREAT BRITAIN: DISTRIBUTION OF WOMEN (PER 1000) WITH VARIOUS NUMBERS OF LIVE BIRTHS FOR SELECTED MARRIAGE GROUPS [1]

Number of women (per 1000) with specified numbers of live births	Date of first marriage						
	1870 to 1879	1890 to 1899	1900 to 1909	1910	1915	1920	1925
0	83	99	113	122	150	138	161
1 or 2	125	231	335	373	447	456	506
3 or 4	181	258	277	282	254	258	221
5 to 9	434	340	246	200	139	136	106
10 or more	177	72	29	23	10	12	6
All	1,000	1,000	1,000	1,000	1,000	1,000	1,000

less marked than at the end of the nineteenth century. The table below indicates the experience of the last fifty years by dividing women into two groups according to their husbands' manual or black-coated occupations.

GREAT BRITAIN: FAMILY SIZE AND SOCIAL STATUS [2]

Date of first marriage	Number of live births per woman in:	
	Non-manual group	Manual group
1900–1909	2·81	3·96
1910–1914	2·36	3·36
1915–1919	2·07	2·94
1920–1924	1·90	2·72

The rapid fall in the number of children born to married couples has not been accompanied by any unwillingness to get married. The proportion of each generation which has married has remained remarkably stable, at around 86–88 per cent., over the last century.

The lifting of the crushing, debilitating burden of too frequent pregnancies was the most important, single

[1] D. V. Glass and E. Grebenik, "The Trend and Pattern of Fertility in Great Britain," *Papers of the Royal Commission on Population* (1954), vol. VI, Pt. I, p. 3.

[2] *Ibid.*, p. 4.

factor affecting the social position of married middle-class women. Their declining birth rate banished the horse-hair sofa, that uncomfortable symbol of Victorian fecundity, from the drawing-room to the attic, and enabled married women to contribute to, and benefit from, the emancipatory activities of the "women's rights" movement. After 1850, sharpening conflict between the family code and demographic reality forced a few pioneering women into an organised attack on the prevailing conception of their "proper sphere." The Census of 1851 showed that, in the age group 40–45, one-quarter of the women and one-fifth of the men were unmarried.[1] A disparity between the numbers of girl and boy babies born and surviving to maturity, emigration, and some men's preference for bachelorhood, deprived twenty-five out of every hundred women (the proportion amongst the middle class was certainly higher than the national average) of the chance to marry. A social organisation built on the assumption that marriage was women's proper sphere, made no provision for single, propertyless gentlewomen.[2] The pitiful lives and increasing numbers of these social outcasts—the old maids to be, the superfluous or, in W. R. Greg's finally contemptuous phrase, the "redundant women"[3]—disturbed educated opinion in the 'fifties. At that time the only respectable alternatives to marriage were

[1] Noel A. Humphreys (ed.), *Vital Statistics: A Memorial Volume of the . . . Reports and Writings of William Farr* (1885), p. 46.

[2] The article of Harriet Martineau, "Female Industry" (printed anon.) in the *Edinburgh Review* (1850), vol. CCXXII, which drew out the consequences of the excess of women, made a deep impression at the time. The literature on this topic is voluminous; the most intelligent and best informed contemporary discussion is that of Anon (John Duguid Milne), *Industrial and Social Position of Women in the Middle and Lower Ranks*, 1st. ed. (1857).

[3] The original article, "Why are Women Redundant?" was reprinted in the book of W. R. Greg, *Literary and Social Judgments* (1868). It expresses the conventional point of view. Greg was answered by, amongst others, Frances Power Cobbe in *Fraser's* (1862) with "What Shall we do with our Old Maids?" reprinted in her *Essays on the Pursuits of Women* (1863).

authorship and governessing, and both had become overcrowded, sweated trades. The first issue of *The Englishwoman's Journal* in 1858 thus described the reality which inspired so many romantic novelists.

> . . . [governessing] is the only profession open to an educated woman of average ability. Few are aware of the extent to which women of the lower classes [work] ; —but while *all* our lady readers have received instruction from some class of governess, there is probably not one who has not also some relative or cherished friend either actually engaged in teaching, or having formerly been so engaged. We find families who have no link with the army, the navy, or the church, who in all their wide-spread connection have kept aloof from trade ; —but from the highest to the lowest rank in which a liberal education is bestowed, we shall find some cousin or friend who is a governess. Indeed, it is not a question of rank at all, for the unmarried female members of the small merchant's family enter the profession from natural necessity, and the fortuneless daughters of the highly connected clergyman have often no other resource. It is a platform on which the lower and upper classes meet, the one struggling up, the other drifting down . . . here is the one means of breadwinning to which access alone seems open—to which alone untrained capacity is equal or pride admits appeal.[1]

Something had to be done to break down the male monopoly over respectable occupations. Something had to be done, too, for the reform of girls' education. Their early training, customarily complete when all the polite futilities essential for decorous entry to the marriage market had been acquired, was an embarrassment in the labour market.

This was the effective origin of the "women's movement,"[2] and these the problems tackled by able, selfless pioneers during the following decades. The initiatives

[1] *The Englishwoman's Journal* (1858), vol. I, p. 1.

[2] The standard history is that of Ray Strachey, *The Cause* (1928). The most useful book is still that of E. A. Pratt, *Pioneer Women of Victoria's Reign* (1897).

of Frances Buss and Emily Davies and many others resulted in provision for girls' schooling and higher education. The example of Miss Nightingale, and the early persistence of Emily Faithfull, Jessie Boucherett and Sophia Jex-Blake helped to create new occupational opportunities for unmarriageable women. By the early twentieth century the hard, and sometimes brutal, struggle for entry into the higher professions had achieved some successes. There were only a handful of women doctors, senior civil servants and the like, but enough to establish precedents for the future. Most Edwardian workers in white blouse occupations clustered round the schoolroom, the hospital ward, the shop counter, and the typewriter. They came mainly from the suburbs, from a class that hardly existed when the Society for Promoting the Employment of Women was founded in 1859, to help those " who have been born and bred ladies (to) preserve the habits, the dress, and the countless moral and material associations of the rank to which they were born." [1] Their lower middle-class jobs stemmed from the technological and social diversification of industrialism, and owed more to the joint stock company than to pioneering feminists.

The conditions under which working women lived and laboured were beyond the knowledge and sympathies of most mid-Victorian advocates of women's rights. Only prostitutes received their sustained attention. The ravages of venereal disease had become in the 'sixties a source of great anxiety to the naval and military authorities. The Admiralty prepared a Contagious Diseases Bill which became law without parliamentary debate in 1864. This Act imposed the principles, common to many continental countries, of compulsory or voluntary medical examination and treatment of prostitutes in eleven garrison towns in England and Ireland. In 1866

[1] The formation and objects of the Society are described by Jessie Boucherett in *The Englishwoman's Journal* (1864), vol. XIII, pp. 17–21.

and 1869 the system was extended to eighteen towns, including Canterbury and Winchester. The discipline for the women was stiffened by introducing a register of prostitutes and periodical compulsory medical examinations. Specially drafted plain clothes medical police administered the Acts, though their harshness was somewhat mitigated by provision, under the 1866 Act, of religious instruction for prostitutes detained in hospital.[1]

The silent introduction of this system of government supervised prostitution unexpectedly produced the most violent and acrid agitation of mid-Victorian years. Josephine Butler, then President of the North of England Council for Promoting the Higher Education of Women, and wife of Canon Butler, became leader of a movement for repeal.[2] The twenty-year campaign for the repeal of the Contagious Diseases Acts which Mrs. Butler and James Stansfeld carried to success in 1886, is of great historical importance. It has been unduly neglected, in part, perhaps, as a result of the repugnant character of its work. The repealers suffered for, and safeguarded the principle of personal liberty. It is characteristic of the mid-Victorians that, with all their myopic limitations, their finest qualities are clarified, not in the great issues that now fill chapters in the history books, but in the squalid pages of evidence to the Royal Commission upon the Administration and Operation of the Contagious Diseases Acts. There [3] John Stuart Mill, facing practical ethical issues of the personal rights of prostitutes, gave vitality and nobility to the formal propositions of *On Liberty*. The repealers also forced a disconcerted and resentful public to examine the underlying presuppositions of sexual morality. After Mrs. Butler's stormy career women could no longer be excluded from such discussions,

[1] The history of the imposition and repeal of the Acts is described in the book by J. L. and Barbara Hammond, *James Stansfield* (1932).

[2] Josephine Butler's own moving account of her experiences was published as *Personal Reminiscences of a Great Crusade* (1896).

[3] Evidence, vol. II, 1871, ch. 408–411.

public or private ; the double standard of morality took on the appearance of seedy casuistry ; and the conspiracy of silence about sex, natural reticence to the previous generation, was seen to be a conspiracy.

From the 'eighties onwards the implications of Mrs. Butler's crusade and the widening use of contraceptives, emphasised the irrelevance of old pruderies. The changing sexual outlook of middle-class people was matched by new physiological and psychological investigations.[1] These redefined differences in sexual function in terms which, for many thoughtful people, destroyed the conception of women as an inferior and subordinate sex. The meaning of this knowledge was interpreted for a wide public by the writings of Havelock Ellis [2] which, more than any others, mark the watershed between the Victorians and ourselves. The acid of science began to eat into old ignorance and established faiths, as it pushed forward to new masteries. Eleven years before the *Origin of Species* shattered evangelical self-confidence, the Rev. Dr. Cumming had assured an Exeter Hall audience that " religious men have ceased to be afraid as they used to be, of the discoveries of science. Religious men, on the contrary, hail them. They used to be in fear lest light from the stars should put out the Sun of Righteousness ; they used to be apprehensive lest the hammer of the geologist should break the Rock of Ages. . . ." [3] Cumming's optimistic predictions were sadly falsified. After thirty years' experience of Darwin's bulldog, Huxley, snapping

[1] A clear indication of their content and social meaning can be quickly obtained from the books of Havelock Ellis, *The Task of Social Hygiene* (1912), and Patrick Geddes and J. Arthur Thomson, *Sex* (1914).

[2] The biography of Houston Peterson, *Havelock Ellis* (n.d.) contains a useful bibliography of Ellis's writings.

[3] Cumming's lecture is reprinted in the symposium *Lectures Delivered before the Young Men's Christian Association* (1886), vol. III. He was a fashionable, evangelical preacher in his day and a favourite of Queen Victoria's. He built his reputation on predictions of the imminent end of the world. His popularity declined when, immediately after one such prophecy, it became known that he had negotiated and signed a long lease for a new house. He was the subject of a savage essay by George Eliot.

at their heels, religious men hailed the discoveries of science no longer. Some, impervious to science, fell to the Higher Criticism ; and agnosticism spread amongst intellectuals whilst indifference and weakening social compulsions reduced congregations in town and country alike. The power of religious faiths to command intellectual loyalties and regular public observance had weakened. Family pews were emptying, family prayers were going out of fashion and the family Bible, in its opulent binding and gilt clasps, joined the family photograph albums at the bottom of a dusty cupboard. The evangelical faith which had once sustained the family code was perishing in an atmosphere of scepticism and indifference.

IV

Such were the influences which destroyed the middle-class mid-Victorian family. They permeated Edwardian society and have conditioned our own mid-twentieth-century experience. Their most obvious result has been the extension of civil, legal and political rights to women. The inferior half of the Victorian community have now become, formally at least, equal citizens. This social revolution was not limited to women. Their experience as part of recent democratic movements was skilfully delineated by Beatrice Webb's suggested paraphrase of a passage in Sir Almroth Wright's attack on the " votes for women " campaign. (Mrs. Webb's paraphrases are inserted in brackets.)

> The failure to recognise that man [*the capitalist*, *the white man*] is the master, and why he is the master, lies at the root of the suffrage [*the trade union*, *the colonial nationalist*] movement. By disregarding man's [*the capitalist's*, *the white man's*] superior physical force, the power of compulsion upon which all government is based is disregarded. By leaving out of account those

> powers of the mind in which man [*the capitalist*, *the white man*] is the superior, woman [*the worker*, *the black man*] falls into the error of thinking that she [*they*] can really compete with him, and that she [*they*] belong[*s*] to the self-same intellectual caste. Finally, by putting out of sight man's [*the capitalist's*, *the white man's*] superior money-earning capacity, the power of the purse is ignored.[1]

The pathological posturings of Mrs. Pankhurst and her supporters, and the tactics of some present-day nationalist movements, have much in common. The agents of change do not always reveal the meanings of change.

Women's approach to full citizenship was the outward reflection of a deeper transformation in personal relationships, in the attitudes of women to themselves and society and of society to them. Half a century ago there was a ferment of adjustment to exciting ideas, and a fervent exploration of new possibilities. For some, the acquisition of new freedoms distorted the nature of old tyrannies and produced eccentricities of thought and behaviour that help to clarify the nature and problems of the social changes in which they participated. Many influential women, for example, embarked on an " anti-man " crusade [2] to establish their conception of female superiority and degraded male inferiority. This common view underlined the comfort which Mrs. Butler offered to a friend about to be confined in 1893.

> I know it must be very horrid to go, as it were, a beast to the shambles. . . . But your ever faithful God is near you, dear. You remember how sweet and lovely Jesus always was to *women*, and how he helped their *woman* diseases, and how respectful he was to

[1] Almroth Wright, *The Unexpurgated Case against Woman Suffrage* (1913), pp. 71–72. Mrs. Webb's comment appeared in " The Awakening of Women," Special Supplement, *The New Statesman*, 1st November 1913.

[2] There was shrewd prediction in the amusing novel by Walter Besant, *The Revolt of Man*, 8th ed. (1886). He pictures the triumph of the " women's movement," the ensuing subjection of men, and their mid-twentieth-century revolt.

> them, and loved them, and forgave the sins of the most sinful. And he was born of a woman—a woman *only*. No man had a hand in *that*.[1]

Such attitudes conditioned the thinking of many suffragettes. In a widely circulated pamphlet of 1913 Christabel Pankhurst warned women against marriage.

> For severely practical, common-sensible, sanitary reasons women are chary of marriage. When the best-informed and most experienced medical men say that the vast majority of men expose themselves before marriage to sexual disease, and that only an "insignificant minority," as one authority puts it—25 per cent. at most—escape infection; when these medical authorities further say that sexual disease is difficult, if not impossible, to cure, healthy women naturally hesitate to marry. Mr. Punch's "advice to those about to marry—Don't!" has a true and terrible application to the facts of the case. "Sacrifice yourself, sacrifice yourself," is a cry that has lost its power over women. . . . Now that women have learnt to think for themselves, they discover that woman, in sacrificing herself, sacrifices the race.[2]

The fantastic idiocy of Miss Pankhurst's belief that three-quarters of the male population suffered from venereal disease is significant not for the light it throws on her sense of proportion, but because it illustrates an aspect of the revolt against the mid-Victorian family code.[3]

[1] Quoted A. S. G. Butler, *Portrait of Josephine Butler* (1954), pp. 58–59. (Italics in original.)

[2] Christabel Pankhurst, *The Great Scourge and How to End it* (1913), pp. 99–100. How to end it was simple. "The only cure is Votes for Women." We have since discovered the antibiotics to be more effective.

[3] Of course, there was a grain of truth amongst the wild exaggeration. The social problem was posed in the novel by Hubert Wales (pseud. William Pigott), *The Yoke*, 1st ed. (1907); 2nd ed. (1908), then suppressed. A young, widowed lady of almost unbelievable piety and purity is obsessed with fears for the health of her twenty-year-old stepson. She is so convinced of the prevailing corruption that, after much anxious prayer and meditation, she decides it is her repugnant but moral duty to sacrifice her own body to her stepson's needs. Those with depraved tastes will find the scene in which she explains and justifies her action to the stepson's fiancée less tragic than the author intended.

Many thought, medical considerations apart, that marriage was a tyranny corrupting to all free women. They admired the heroine of Grant Allen's story (her name, inevitably, was Herminia) who rejected a proposal of marriage because

> I know what marriage is—from what vile slavery it has sprung ; on what unseen horrors for my sister women it is reared and buttressed ; by what unholy sacrifices it is sustained and made possible. I know it has a history. I know its past : I know its present. . . . I must keep my proper place, the freedom which I have gained for myself by such arduous efforts. I have said to you already, " So far as my will goes, I am yours ; take me. . . . But more than that—no. It would be treason to my sex. Not my life, not my future, not my individuality, not my freedom." [1]

Some joined organisations to promote " bachelor motherhood "—a revealing phrase—and answered advertisements in their journals offering vacancies in shorthand-writers' offices to " the girls who do." [2] The aspects of personal relationships between men and women which novelists explored, troubled many who had to face the practical difficulties of reconciling beliefs and behaviour. The Rev. the Hon. Edward Lyttelton, who became Headmaster of Eton, was conscious of an " urgency of need which has perhaps not existed before " to help parents to an understanding of the sexual difficulties of the young. He prefaced his sensible *Training of the Young in the Laws of Sex* (1901) with a biting comment on the " stupidity and cruelty typical " of the moral code which corrupted his boys.

> A thoroughly conventional man in good society would sooner that his son should resort with prostitutes than that he should marry a respectable girl of a distinctly lower station than his own : indeed, it is

[1] *The Woman who Did* (1895), pp. 39–40.
[2] Appearing in, e.g., *The Adult*, vol. II, No. 5 (1898).

> not going too far to say that he probably would rather that his son should seduce such a girl, provided there were no scandal, than marry her.[1]

These and similar attitudes, he added, gave upper-class boys a " view of womanhood " that was " nothing but barbarous."

These are examples of the ways in which middle-class men and women groped towards new standards and new relationships when the middle-class family code began to crumble. They do not illustrate the representative attitudes and behaviour of their day, but they explain the sources and chart the course of change. Their influence appears in the insistence of the Royal Commission on Divorce of 1909 that there is " no satisfactory solution of the problem which is raised as to the personal relations between husband and wife . . . except by placing them on an equal footing. . . ." [2]

For most people, awareness of the delicate problems of personal relationships, and the willingness to seek harmonious solutions develops only in circumstances of material security. In the middle years of the nineteenth century, the conditions in which working people lived did not permit such sophisticated speculation. Only in their breeding habits were they able to emulate their financial betters. Working-class women did not seek freedom in the right to work and had no need of societies to promote their employment. There were no conspiracies of silence about sex in their overcrowded homes, or frustrations bred by aimless domesticities. We have no evidence upon which to base sound judgments of changes in the internal relationships and tensions in working-class families, and such changes are less important than those which have transformed urban life and mitigated economic insecurity.

The character of the modern working-class family has

[1] p. 43.
[2] *Report* (Cd. 6478, 1912), p. 89.

been determined by the growth of social policy through which it has acquired, in our own generation, some capacity to take a middle-class view of life. Mr. Beales has defined social policy as " a collective term for the public provisions through which we attack insecurity and the debilitating tendencies of our 'capitalist' inheritance."[1] This attack developed from many quarters. The universality of social policy is meaningless unless interpreted as an integral part of the productive equipment of industrialism. After 1850, the expanding productivities of the new economic system were increasingly seen to rest on a rational exploitation of human as well as material resources. The preventible human wastage of unregulated industrialism carried with it social and economic costs that could not, in the long run, be equated with technological efficiency. Long hours of work, the employment of young children, and a diseased, illiterate labour force, inadequately housed, contributed both to competitive inefficiency and social instability. By the 'eighties such relationships, probed and demonstrated by investigating civil servants, doctors and the like, began to be defined and measured in the inescapable certainties of statisticians' tables. Two illustrations will suffice. In a period when German and American industrial competition caused anxiety and falling profit margins, the education of working people could no longer be safely or profitably left to the private enterprise of quarrelsome religious organisations. The labour market required new technical skills, and education, therefore, had to become a public service. Nor could urban poverty be left to look after itself at a time when universal male suffrage, fears of war, and socialism seemed to threaten established institutions. When Charles Booth in 1887 initiated a series of statistical investigations which established beyond argument that

[1] H. L. Beales, *The Making of Social Policy* (Hobhouse Memorial Lecture, 1946), p. 7.

30 per cent. of the population of London and other towns lived in grinding poverty, politicians had new terms of reference forced upon them. Political loyalties to country or party could no longer be assumed, they had to be canvassed by rational appeals to an electorate which contained many who had ceased to accept filth and squalor as part of the natural order. Hence were derived school meals and school doctors, labour exchanges and national insurance, the public provision of working-class housing, and public responsibility for town planning. These and the many other similar twentieth-century responses to the social consequences of industrialism, are now embodied in what today we describe, inelegantly and inaccurately, as the " welfare state." Their significance is misinterpreted if, in origin, they are attributed to philanthropic zeal or humanitarian sentiment. They are now, as Mr. Beales insists, social imperatives that condition all our lives.

> The various branches of our social policy are not mere sweeteners of the hard rigours of a system of individualist compulsions. They represent social provision against waste of life and resources and against social inefficiency—not concessions. They are positive elements in a world of public as well as private enterprise. They supercede rights of property hitherto accepted, systems of discipline now obsolescent or dead. They represent . . . the new principles of social obligation inherent in a society based upon the unmeasured productivities of machines.[1]

These new principles of social obligation were the framework within which a working-class family unit appropriate to the conditions of industrialism became established. Working-class people could not themselves perform the familial duties prescribed by the middle-class family code. The very bases of this conception—a clean and decent home and the leisure to pursue family life

[1] H. L. Beales, *op. cit.*, pp. 9–10.

within it, the health and education of children, the protection of dependents—were only secured by collective action and public provision. Herein lies the essential and distinctive difference between the middle- and working-class family's experience in the industrialising society of the last hundred years. The economically secure middle-class family could easily be a self-helpful, independent unit ; the working-class family became a going concern only within the protective shelter of expanding social services.

A century ago middle- and working-class families shared little in common save their high fertilities. They have travelled by very different routes into the twentieth century towards similarities of function and behaviour. If poverty and squalor are still unhappily the experience of a declining number of citizens, the mass of the population is no longer drilled in iron ranks of inescapable misery. The high productivities of modern industry, the partial reduction of morally indefensible economic and social inequalities, and the diffusion of political power and responsibility are today increasingly standardising the lives and amenities of all social strata. The small family of consciously conceived children has become the common aim of most parents. At a time when middle-class people can no longer push their homemaking and domestic responsibilities on to cheap domestic servants, the fashionable psychiatry has announced the compensatory discovery that mothers are important for young children. Two world wars have demonstrated the impossibility of running modern economic systems without the large-scale employment of women.[1] Women still face a conflict between motherhood and employment outside the home, though its setting and meaning have changed since the time when it was evidenced by infanticide, baby farming,

[1] The book of Gertrude Williams, *Women and Work* (1945) is the best account of the extension of women's employments during the last half-century.

and high infant and maternal mortalities. The typical working-class mother of 1900 could expect to live for twelve years after her family had been reared. Today, Professor Titmuss reminds us, with increasing expectation of life and declining family size women enter their "reproductive grazing ground"[1] with more than half their adult lives to run. Differences in biological function between men and women, on which the Victorians erected and enforced conceptions of social superiority and inferiority, are now commonly regarded as the complementary foundations of equal participation in social and family life. The authoritarian, paternally dominated family has gone the way of some other dictatorships, taking with it the double standard of sexual morality. This element in the Victorian family code has disappeared from most people's thinking nowadays, though some moralists seem anxious to return to it. Sir Basil Henriques, for example, thus distilled his magisterial experience at a conference held to discuss the problem of the unmarried father.

> If girls in schools . . . can be made to be proud of their vocation, and if boys can be taught from the day they go to school to show courtesy towards the girls, then as they grow older I am inclined to think that they will treat other girls as they would their own sisters and if they must indulge in sexual intercourse then they will do so with prostitutes and not with girls who have not chosen that profession, but who have chosen the glorious profession of motherhood.[2]

Sir Basil concluded his address by affirming his belief that "the sanctity of women cannot be impressed upon men unless it is mixed up with the knowledge that the girl is built in the image of God." It is difficult to

[1] R. M. Titmuss in *op. cit.*, p. 12. This essay is a striking commentary on present-day trends.

[2] *Verbatim Account of Extraordinary Meeting of National Council for the Unmarried Mother and her Child*, 29th November 1955, p. 9.

feel that morality has been damaged by the widespread rejection of such notions and the behaviour they imply. It is a positive gain that knowledge and enjoyment have replaced furtiveness and shame as the attitudes which many men and women now bring to their sexual relationships.

These are the directions in which the break-up of the mid-Victorian family code have led. Some[1] welcome these changes as elements in the establishment of a democratic family in which the loyalties of compulsion and obedience have been replaced by those of affection and choice, though moralists now deplore them as leading to the disintegration of family life. Victorian beliefs and practice have been stressed both because our own situation is the product of their dissolution and also because they still provide contemporary moralists with a stereotype of the desirable family code and approved behaviour. Indeed, the Victorian family now survives only in the minds of middle-class moralists, the successors in our generation of Gaskell, Engels and Disraeli. Historical forgetfulness and middle-class myopia are always characteristic of such thinking. Bishop Neill, for example, remarks with charming naïvety

> I have often wondered why it is that, apparently, the Victorian family, so much more severe and restricted than that of our own day, produced so much less neurosis in the children that grew up in it. I mean, of course, the *real* Victorian family, as you will find it brilliantly portrayed in the novels of, for example, Trollope, and not the nightmare of Butler's *Way of all Flesh*. I am inclined to think, though of course I cannot

[1] e.g., Barbara Wootton, "Holiness or Happiness," *Twentieth Century*, Nov. 1955, and R. M. Titmuss, *op. cit.* It is instructive to compare the picture of the family drawn in moralising literature with that which emerges from Professor Titmuss's definitive study of war-time social policy, *Problems of Social Policy* (1950). He considers that the solidarity of the family, with its local roots, provided the social cohesion by which the civilian population successfully resisted bombing.

> prove, that it was because in that world you knew exactly where you were. There were rules, very strict rules, based on intelligible principles. If you broke the rules you knew just where you were. That is very different from the capricious world in which most of our children have to grow up today.[1]

In the perspective of a century's change such comparisons are socially irrelevant and wildly unhistorical. They ignore the working-class family whose experience of industrialism cannot truthfully be described in terms of breakdown and disintegration. The middle-class, mid-Victorian family code has disintegrated. But free men and women in the mid-twentieth century need not mourn the passing of a system of " faith unfaithful," of " honour rooted in dishonour." There is today a growing capacity and willingness to ground familial relationships in the practice of social and personal equality, and to substitute knowledge for ignorance as the basis of conduct. Current discussions of divorce have been distorted by a misunderstanding of the character and origins of the new democratic family unit. Such misunderstandings feed the hypochondria of moralists who diagnose a diseased present because they worship a past they do not understand.

[1] *op. cit.*, p. 16. Bishop Neill does not disclose the historical and clinical techniques by which he has been able to compare the incidence of neurosis amongst Victorian and mid-twentieth-century children.

CHAPTER IV

CHRISTIAN MARRIAGE

UNTIL recent years Christian teaching has dominated all discussion of marriage and divorce and has determined the standard of accepted behaviour. Any examination of present-day conflicts about marriage and divorce must therefore begin with an understanding of the Christian position. The account that follows avoids, as far as possible, the hortatory and polemical literature. It is largely derived from the elaborate and considered evidence presented by the Christian churches to the Royal Commissions on Marriage and Divorce appointed in 1909 and 1951.

The main branches of the Christian church agree that marriage is a divine institution ordained by God as an inviolable contract between one man and one woman terminable only by death. This doctrine is held by all the great Christian communions which, like the Church of England, derive from the teaching of Jesus Christ their

> understanding of what marriage rightly is according to the will and purpose of God. His teaching requires that " a man leave his father and mother and cleave to his wife ; and they twain shall be one flesh ; so then they are no more twain, but one flesh " (St. Mark, 10, vv. 7 and 8). His teaching requires that marriage shall be lifelong : " Whosoever shall put away his wife and marry another commiteth adultery against her, and if a woman shall put away her husband and be married to another, she commiteth adultery " (St. Mark, 10, vv. 11 and 12). Accordingly the Church affirms " that marriage is a union permanent in its nature and lifelong." [1]

[1] Royal Commission on Marriage and Divorce, Evidence (1953), 6th Day, p. 145.

The Christian churches agree about God's law but differ widely about His intention for its practical application. For conduct and legislation the important question is whether God intended lifelong, monogamous marriage to be an ideal standard to which earthly marriages should approximate, or an invariable rule to be observed in all cases. At this point the Roman and protestant churches divide. For the Church of England, as for all protestant churches, marriage is not a sacrament.[1] According to Article XXV of the Thirty-nine Articles, only Baptism and the Supper of the Lord are sacraments. Matrimony is " not to be counted for (a Sacrament) of the Gospel (because it has) not any visible sign or ceremony ordained of God." For the Roman Church marriage is a sacrament, and " a consummated marriage between two baptised persons cannot be broken by any human power." [2] The clearest statement of the Roman position was made by Monseigneur Moyes, Canon of the Archdiocese of Westminster and a Prelate of the Roman Court, in evidence to the Gorell Commission.

> (1) Marriage between Christians is not only a contract, but a sacrament of the New Law, in which the union of the parties is wrought and ratified by God. In this sacrament, the parties themselves—not any officiating clergyman—are the ministers, each giving consent to the other, and God accepting and sealing the consent of both.
>
> (2) When such marriage is validly celebrated between competent persons, and is consummated, so that there is fulfilled in their union the words of Our Lord, " and they two shall be in one flesh " (Mark. vv. 8) there

[1] There are, of course, many members of the Church of England who hold that marriage is a sacrament.

[2] Rev. G. P. Dwyer, *The Catholic Faith* (n.d., *c.* 1954). This is a bound volume of the leaflets issued by the Catholic Enquiry Centre. The quotation is taken from Leaflet 15, p. 1. Christians sometimes, and papists frequently, confuse their readers by phrasing matters of belief as if they are matters of fact. In the present instance, it is notorious that many marriages have been and are, in fact, broken by " human powers."

exists between them a God-made bond of matrimony, or *vinculum matrimonii* in its completeness. The knot is of God's own knitting, and Christ teaches that it is God Himself who is the "Joiner."

(3) Because the union is thus of God's making and a Divine work, it has the paramount and immutable character of Divine law, and is absolutely indissoluble except by death of either party. It cannot be unmade by any act of the parties themselves, seeing that it is a covenant which they themselves have not made, but is one into which God Himself has entered as the Joiner. As a matter of Divine law, or God's own ordinance, it is intangible by any created power and no human authority whether ecclesiastical or civil, can have any authority to dissolve it. As neither the Pope nor the Church can claim to override or alter anything which is of Divine law, neither can exercise any dispensing power to loose the complete and consummated bond of matrimony. "What God has joined together, no man may put asunder." The Catholic Church teaches that this principle laid down by Christ is absolute. . . .[1]

For the Roman Church the ordinance of Christ concerning marriage has the paramount and immutable character of divine law. The Church of Scotland, on the other hand, asserts that "this law is no arbitrary imposition"[2] and agrees with the Church of England[3] that Christ intended its interpretation to be left to the Church.

As is well known, the Church of Scotland at the time of the Reformation, in common with other churches of the reformed family, rejected the Roman doctrine of marriage as one of the seven sacraments. The ground of this rejection was the different reformed conception

[1] Royal Commission on Divorce and Matrimonial Causes, Evidence, vol. II (Cd. 6480), 1912, p. 427.

[2] Royal Commission on Marriage and Divorce, Evidence, 22nd Day, p. 566.

[3] "But in this as in all things our Lord left the Church liberty to deal as best it can with sinful conditions" (Archbishop of Canterbury, *Problems of Marriage and Divorce* (1955), p. 20).

> of the nature of the sacrament and the fact that marriage as an ordinance of creation was not instituted by Christ in the days of His flesh . . . in common with other reformed Churches the Church of Scotland took the view that Scripture permits divorce on two grounds—adultery and desertion . . . (the Church of Scotland recognises) that the Church has, ever since the Reformation, held it to be in accordance with the mind of Christ that the civil authority should be empowered to dissolve the marriage tie, the grounds on which such a course may be based having from 1573 been not only infidelity but desertion—facts which import that the union between the parties has already been dissolved.[1]

Similarly the Methodist Church believes

> that there are courses of conduct which so violate the pledges and obligations of marriage that, of themselves, and in fact, they destroy it as a union of heart and soul. In such cases the marriage ceases to be what it is divinely intended to be, a oneness in body and spirit, resting on mutual understanding, fidelity and love.[2]

Neither the evidence given to the recent Royal Commission nor the Archbishop of Canterbury's pamphlet *Problems of Marriage and Divorce*, published in 1955, contain a clear statement of the grounds on which the Church of England permits divorce to its members. But in answer to a question by one of the recent Royal Commissioners, Sheriff Walker, the Archbishop stated the principle behind his acceptance of divorce.

> I think one would say that the moral principle is that in each ground for divorce there is a frustration of one or more of the purposes of marriage. The purposes

[1] Royal Commission on Marriage and Divorce, Evidence, 22nd Day, p. 566. It should be noted that, according to the evidence, p. 571, " there is a body of lay and ministerial opinion which believes that the Church should not recognise divorce at all or at most recognise it only on grounds of infidelity."

[2] *ibid.*, 3rd and 4th Days, p. 64.

> of marriage are the procreation of children, natural relations, and the comfort that one ought to have of the other. Adultery breaks the union of man and wife, desertion deprives him of the partner, one of the purposes of marriage, cruelty frustrates one of them, also insanity and sodomy and bestiality. I think you could say, could you not, that they all frustrate one or more of the purposes of marriage.[1]

The Archbishop's view on this point is shared by sections of Church of England opinion which do not accept his doctrinal position on other matters relating to divorce. The Modern Churchmen's Union, founded in 1898 for the advancement of liberal religious thought, said in evidence

> We are as anxious as anyone else to uphold the Christian ideal of marriage . . . an ideal which is sometimes expressed in the ambiguous phrase "the indissolubility of marriage." But we believe that this ideal is best maintained not by the rigorist view that marriage is incapable of dissolution but by the recognition that in certain cases divorce is necessary and permissible as being the lesser of two evils.[2]

This preliminary examination of the Christian outlook discloses a fundamental difference between the Roman and protestant churches. Both derive their doctrine of marriage from the law of God, both interpret the law of God differently.

The Roman Church's doctrine of indissoluble marriage does not mean, however, that no marriage can ever be dissolved. It maintains extensive grounds of nullity under which a supposed marriage is declared to have been null from the beginning.[3] Some fifteen direment

[1] Royal Commission on Marriage and Divorce, Evidence, 6th Day, p. 155, Q. 1260.

[2] *ibid.* Evidence, 19th Day, p. 507.

[3] I have based the following account on the evidence of Monseigneur Moyes to the Royal Commission on Divorce and Matrimonial Causes, Evidence, vol. II (Cd. 6480), 1912, p. 427 *et seq.*

impediments, which preclude God's acceptance of the marriage, include disparity of religion ; a solemn vow of chastity or entering a religious order made before the consummation of a marriage ; duress or violence ; madness ; impotency ; consanguinity (even the marriage of first cousins is prohibited without prior dispensation) ; and the solemn and public betrothal before the marriage of one of the parties to another person. Such nullities must arise from causes antecedent to the marriage and not from causes supervening after the marriage. To this rule there is one exception. The passage in St. Paul's First Epistle to the Corinthians : [1]

> If any brother hath an unbelieving wife, and she is content to dwell with him, let him not leave her. And the woman which hath an unbelieving husband, and he is content to dwell with her, let her not leave her husband. For the unbelieving husband is sanctified in the wife, and the unbelieving wife is sanctified in the brother : else were your children unclean ; but now are they holy. Yet if the unbelieving departeth, let him depart : the brother or the sister is not under bondage in such cases. . . .

is held to establish the so-called Pauline Privilege according to which if one of the unbelieving parties becomes a Christian, and the other refuses to live peaceably with the convert, the marriage can be annulled. Under the procedure of the Church such nullity suits go before the Diocesan Court from which there is an appeal to Rome. The law of this Church has no civil validity in England and a faithful papist, blamelessly obeying his Church, may be treated by English law as a criminal. This circumstance was explored by Sir Lewis Dibdin [2] and Monseigneur Moyes during the latter's evidence

[1] I. vii., 12–15.

[2] One of the Commissioners, he was Judge of the Arches Court of Canterbury and of the Chancery Court of York and one of the foremost English Canon Lawyers of his day.

to the Royal Commission on Divorce which reported in 1912.[1]

DIBDIN: Supposing the party—say the man—who had that decree (i.e. of nullity) from the Church remarried in fact in England, how would that be regarded in the Church?

MOYES: He would be regarded as perfectly free to marry.

DIBDIN: Although according to the law of the State he would be a bigamist?

MOYES: Yes, quite so; he would be a bigamist, I suppose.

DIBDIN: But the Church would not put him under censure?

MOYES: Oh no, not with regard to the law of the State; the Church would leave him to reckon as best he might with the civil penal effects.

DIBDIN: They could not help that?

MOYES: They could not help that. But with regard to the matter of conscience, he is married to the second person and not the first.

DIBDIN: It would not be considered an offence, independent of the marriage law, to have broken the law of the State?

MOYES: No; the Church would hold that the enactment on the part of the State was entrammelling the law of Christ.

DIBDIN: The law of the Church comes before the law of the State?

MOYES: In matters of conscience like this.

DIBDIN: And though he had committed bigamy, the Church would think he had not only committed no wrong, but would not officially discourage him from doing so.

MOYES: Would not officially discourage him from doing so.

DIBDIN: And his children who were considered legitimate by the law of the land they would regard as——?

[1] Evidence, vol. II (Cd. 6480), 1912, p. 430. Q. 23,013–23,021.

MOYES: As illegitimate by the law of the Church, but as legitimate if either party were in good faith as to the validity of the first marriage.

DIBDIN: That would be a remarkable position? [1]

Since 1936 the doctrine of nullity, stripped of the more extravagant features practised by the Church of Rome,[2] has increasingly attracted powerful sections of Church of England opinion. Their acceptance of civil divorce implies not an approval of the principle, but only a recognition of the sinfulness of men and women. The duty of the Church, they hold, is to bear constant witness to the Christian ideal of indissoluble marriage. But the increase in the number of divorces during recent years has been so large that many ecclesiastics are alarmed lest the Church of England should appear to compromise this ideal by being too tolerant of its laity's sinfulness or ambivalence. Accordingly, the Church of England is now engaged in stiffening its marriage discipline. This process has not so far resulted in an outright attack on the provisions of the Herbert Act. It has taken the alternative course first, of anathematizing as adulterous the marriages of divorced persons and, secondly, imposing ecclesiastical penalties on such of its members as have been divorced. The first course involves only linguistic action which seeks to alter the generally accepted meaning of adultery. In common speech (and in law) adultery has always meant voluntary sexual intercourse between a married person and someone of the opposite sex. Its

[1] The argument runs both ways. Just as papists may use the law of their Church to regularise their consciences even though such action may bring them into conflict with the law of the land, so also they may use the civil law of divorce to regularise a situation approved by canon law. "Catholics may also usefully avail themselves of civil proceedings for dissolution in order to regularise their civil status in a case where a matrimonial union into which they have entered has been found to be invalid and null according to the law of the Church" (Royal Commission on Marriage and Divorce, Evidence, of Catholic Union of Great Britain, 16th–17th Day, p. 427).

[2] "Some of the reasons for which they grant nullities we also hold; but others we think are very difficult to establish" (Archbishop of Canterbury, *op. cit.*, p. 13).

meaning as now interpreted on behalf of the new school of thought by the Archbishop of Canterbury has moved into the realms of metaphysics.

> We must . . . analyse the word " adultery " and examine its moral content before considering how Church discipline shall deal with it. Our Lord himself used the word in two different senses. He applied it to a man who, after divorcing his wife, marries another. He also said that " whosoever looketh on a woman to lust after her hath committed adultery with her already in his heart " (Matt. 5, 28). Here are two kinds of adultery ; and how many who would never be guilty of the former must plead guilty to the latter ! There is another form of adultery, morally more detestable than either of these, when a man (or woman) coveting his (or her) neighbour's wife (or husband) invades the marriage and violates by adultery. There is another form, less open perhaps to moral objection than the other three, the adultery incurred in a second marriage after divorce which is totally unconnected with the breakdown of the first marriage, where, so to speak, the first marriage is dead, and buried beyond apparent recall and the second marriage often comes as a real blessing to both parties and to the children. And it is evident that even though every one of these conditions is (as breaking in fact or in thought the marriage bond) adultery, yet they differ greatly in the degree of moral reprobation for which they call.[1]

Widespread acceptance of this new terminology outside Church circles seems unlikely. Its common use would require a knowledge of one's neighbour's intimate thoughts and behaviour too detailed to be acquired in the course of normally polite neighbourly intercourse, though such suggestions are made. The writer of a pamphlet,[2] recently published by the Mothers' Union, suggests that the continued use of the word " marriage " to describe second marriages after divorce is " an illogical abuse of language. If the second union could be called

[1] Archbishop of Canterbury, *op. cit.*, pp. 12–13.

[2] J. L. C. Dart, *God's Law of Marriage* (n.d. *c.* 1954), pp. 13–14.

by some such term as "legal concubinage" much of the difficulty would disappear. . . ." The unpleasant possibilities of such a proposal are exemplified in the remark of a Rural Dean about Sir Anthony Eden, published in his Parish Magazine in 1952.

> The news that the *hitherto* respected Foreign Secretary has entered into a *so-called* "marriage" with the Prime Minister's niece during the lifetime of his own wife has come as an outrageous shock to Christian sentiment throughout the land. It is a grievous thing for a country when it is shown that its rulers have no respect for the laws of God.[1]

Relations between the Archbishop of Canterbury and an adulterous (to the fourth degree of moral reprobation) Prime Minister[2] must require on both sides the exercise of considerable Christian charity. Though the Church of England now regards marriages of divorced persons as adulterous and impossible of celebration in church, it does not forbid them to its members. The Archbishop makes the point forcibly.

> Let me say quite frankly that in some cases where a first marriage has ended in tragedy, a second marriage has, by every test of the presence of the Holy Spirit that we are able to recognise, been abundantly blessed. For this very reason I do not find myself able to *forbid* good people who come to me for advice to embark on a second marriage. . . . I tell them that it is their duty as conscientiously as they can to decide before God what they should do. If they remarry, they will never again be able to bear a full and clear witness to our Lord's declaration of what marriage is: but . . . they must decide whether this lasting spiritual loss is in their judgement outweighed by a call of God to seek spiritual gain in a second marriage.[3]

[1] Quoted by A. P. Herbert, *The Right to Marry* (1954), p. 4. This carefully documented book is invaluable. It is written with Sir Alan's characteristic wit, clarity and pungency.

[2] It is distasteful to cite personal instances, but they have been forced into, and have thus become part of, public discussion. Fairness requires the further comment that many politicians merit the same ecclesiastical censure.

[3] *op. cit.*, pp. 23–24. (Italics in original.)

Such spiritual guidance seems to assume a laity equally skilled in casuistry.

The Church of England's new insistence on using rude words to describe people respectably married according to law and social usage is accompanied by the disciplining of divorced members of the Church. The only effective penalty now remaining is the refusal of re-marriage in church. In 1936 the four Houses of Convocation, the "Parliament" of Church of England clergy, passed a Resolution

> That in order to maintain the principle of life-long obligation which is inherent in every legally contracted marriage and is expressed in the plainest terms in the Marriage Service the Church should not allow the use of that Service in the case of anyone who has a former partner living.[1]

Despite clerical opposition,[2] bishops now dissuade their clergy from marrying divorced persons in church although

[1] Quoted by A. P. Herbert, *op. cit.*, p. 5.

[2] The main body of organised opposition within the Church of England is represented by the Modern Churchmen's Union. Their opinion in evidence to the Royal Commission was "... the Church has no justification for denouncing all second marriages as being null and void. A second marriage can in many cases be a true Christian marriage" (Evidence, 19th Day, p. 508). The Union also gave evidence, p. 509, of support for its views amongst clergy in the diocese of London and Chelmsford. Of 885 clergymen in these dioces, 479 approved and 406 disapproved the refusal of their Church to remarry divorced persons. If the almost equally divided opinions of the clergy of London and Chelmsford are representative of the whole country (there are no means of knowing that they are not) then the Union was entitled to tell the Royal Commission (p. 510) that "we stand for the point of view in the Church which has not been adequately, represented by the Archbishop. . . ." It added further that its views had the support of the majority of the laity of the Church of England. This makes the reply of the Archbishop of Canterbury to the Chairman of the Royal Commission, who asked if a memorandum presented by the Archbishop stated the attitude of the Church of England, very puzzling. "I do not say that all our proposals would have universal assent but the general approach and the main principle which we maintain, that it is a matter of tightening up and not relaxing the laws, will have the support of, I think, practically the whole Church. I may add that the Modern Churchmen's Union has submitted evidence *roughly in line* with ours" (Evidence, 6th Day, p. 147, my italics). The only valid conclusion that can be drawn by an outside observer is that, at the moment, the mind of the Church of England is unsettled, and does not appear to be adequately interpreted by the archbishops and bishops.

this right has been secured to the laity by a succession of Acts of Parliament since 1857, and is still the law of England. Until 1937, a clergyman of the Church of England was bound to marry the innocent party in a divorce suit in church. The Herbert Act altered the law to meet the conscientious scruples of some clergymen by freeing all clergy from the obligation to marry persons whose marriages had been dissolved on any grounds. By this Act the clergy may do as they please. The Archbishop of Canterbury may refuse to solemnise a marriage at which the Dean of St. Paul's, a leading member of the Modern Churchmen's Union, would be happy to officiate. The bishops cannot directly forbid clergy to exercise a discretion granted to them by Act of Parliament, but, acting as a body, they can achieve the same result. The Modern Churchmen's Union told the recent Royal Commission that

> it is virtually impossible to find a clergyman willing to risk the disapproval of his Bishop by conducting the remarriage even of the innocent party to a divorce suit in his Church.[1]

Bishops have no legal power to compel their clergy to frustrate the intention of Parliament, though they possess other methods of persuasion. Sir Alan Herbert quotes [2] a clergyman who points out.

> They can refuse to visit a Parish for Confirmations or other occasions ; they can cut off diocesan grants ; they can deny all preferment (and this would weigh heavily with younger men). Unless therefore a clergyman is independent financially as well as morally he would find himself very awkwardly placed in face of his Bishop's disapproval.

Archdeacon Grantley is a vanished type nowadays, and rigorist bishops freely enforce practices which they cannot forbid, by working, as Sir Alan tartly remarks, " on the poverty of their subordinates." The laity are in no better position than the clergy. The Church forbids the

[1] Royal Commission on Divorce, Evidence, 19th Day, p. 508.
[2] A. P. Herbert, *op. cit.*, p. 38.

spiritual benefits of a church wedding to a faithful, previously unmarried member who wishes to marry a divorced man whose first wife is still alive. It insists that the merits of such a marriage depend, not on the character of the couple, but on the continued physical existence of the previous wife. Should she commit suicide, the bishop can straightway marry the couple in the Cathedral.

The extension of this practice during the last fifteen years has proved embarrassing, so the Church of England is attempting now to escape some of the awkwardness by reviving the ecclesiastically more convenient rules of nullity. A decree of nullity [1] carries none of the religious

[1] In law there may be petitions for a decree of nullity in the cases of marriages void or voidable. These were defined by the Master of the Rolls in 1947 (*De Reneville* v. *De Reneville* (1947), 64 T.L.R., p. 85) : "A void marriage is one which can be regarded by every court in any case in which the existence of the marriage is in issue, as never having taken place, and one that can be so treated by both parties to it without the necessity of any decree annulling it ; a voidable marriage is one that will be regarded by every court as a valid subsisting marriage until a decree annulling it has been pronounced by a court of competent jurisdiction." In England, marriages are (I) void if (*a*) one or both of the parties was under sixteen years of age at the date of the ceremony, or (*b*) there is a pre-existing marriage, or (*c*) after disappearance, one spouse has been presumed dead, or (*d*) the parties are related by the prohibited degrees of consanguinity or affinity, or (*e*) at the date of the ceremony one of the parties was a lunatic, or (*f*) there was no real consent ; and (II) voidable if (*a*) common law grounds of incapacity (i.e. inability to consummate the marriage), or (*b*) statutory grounds of nullity exist. (The statutory grounds are laid down in the Matrimonial Causes Act, 1950, sec. 8.) A decree of nullity is retroactive. It says that a marriage never existed and, if the parties behaved as though one did, they were acting under a delusion. This is the legal theory, the practical application has been qualified. In *Eaves* v. *Eaves* (1940), ch. 109, Lord Goddard, L.C.J., said : ". . . the marriage is valid until it is annulled by a decree of the court and those actions which have taken place during the marriage on the footing that it is subsisting or in direct contemplation of a marriage which afterwards takes place cannot be affected by a subsequent decree of annulment." The Herbert Act provided that children born to a marriage subsequently annulled under certain of its provisions are to be deemed legitimate. The Law Reform (Miscellaneous Provisions) Act, 1949 (sec. 4), gives the status of legitimacy to the children of all voidable marriages. Thus non-existent marriages can produce legitimate children. The distinction between a decree of nullity in the case of a voidable marriage and a decree of divorce is, to a layman at any rate, elusive. The above account of the law, the cases, and quotations from judgments has been taken from the book of J. C. Arnold, *The Marriage Law of England* (1951), esp. chs. II and III.

disadvantages of a decree of divorce. Like the Roman Church, the Church of England (or a section of it) holds that divorce, though legally dissolving a marriage, does not break the spiritual bond. Nullity, on the other hand, declares that a marriage has never existed despite outward appearances and, no spiritual bond having been created, the parties are free to marry again in church. The "official" evidence presented to the recent Royal Commission on behalf of the Church of England stresses that solicitors should always, where grounds exist, advise clients to petition for nullity rather than for divorce.

> On certain occasions when we are approached about marriage in church, a divorce decree is produced. We then say we cannot perform the marriage, but sometimes additional evidence is provided, which shows that from the point of view of the Church there never was an original marriage at all, the marriage was null and void. . . . On enquiry we find that very often the parties concerned did not even know that they could have applied for a decree of nullity; in other cases, the solicitors had advised them that a decree of divorce was more easily obtainable and cheaper. . . . What we are suggesting . . . is that lawyers . . . should enquire whether it would be possible for the parties to claim a decree of nullity. That would relieve us a great deal.[1]

The implications of this attitude can best be understood in terms of concrete instances. If Mary divorces John on the grounds of his sodomy,[2] she cannot remarry during John's lifetime with the Church's blessing because she took him for better for worse. If Jane obtains a decree of nullity on the ground that, unknown to her, James suffered from syphilis[3] when they were married, she is relieved by the Church of her obligation to keep him in sickness and in health and may be remarried with full

[1] Royal Commission on Divorce, Evidence of the Bishop of London, 6th Day, p. 148, Q. 1171.

[2] Matrimonial Causes Act, 1950, sec. 1 (1).

[3] *ibid.*, sec. 8 (1) (*c*).

Anglican rites and a white wedding. The explanation of the Church's refusal to remarry Mary in church whilst extending its blessing to Jane, lies in a theologically significant distinction between sodomy and syphilis. Sodomy is a ground for divorce, syphilis a ground for nullity. " Every divorce," the Archbishop of Canterbury explains, " is created by sin somewhere, and every marriage after divorce is involved in that sin." [1] John's sodomy necessarily involved Mary's second marriage in sin whereas James's syphilis left Jane and her second husband morally untainted. These two situations present relatively uncomplicated ethical problems compared with those which arise when a spouse can petition either for nullity or for divorce. Three months after marrying Mary, John discovers that she is subject to recurrent fits of epilepsy. He is told that he may petition for a decree of nullity provided he does so within one year of the celebration of the marriage.[2] Impressed, however, with the words of the marriage service, he conceives it to be his duty to hold her in sickness. Two years after they have been married, Mary deserts him and John ultimately petitions for divorce on that ground.[3] In this case the Church will penalise John for attempting to live up to his marriage vows. Had he petitioned for nullity within a year of his marriage, the Church would hold that his marriage to Mary had never existed and would have solemnised his next attempt. Because he tried to make the best of it and failed, through no fault of his own, he and his second wife are excluded from the blessings of a marriage in church because " every marriage after divorce is involved in . . . sin." The grounds of nullity cited in these examples were considered by a Commission appointed by the Archbishops of York and Canterbury in 1949. The Commission thought that,

[1] *op. cit.*, p. 20.
[2] Matrimonial Causes Act, 1950, sec. 8 (1).
[3] *ibid.*, sec. 1 (1) (*b*).

> with the exception of wilful refusal to consummate, the additional grounds for nullity introduced by Parliament in 1937 . . . may be accepted, and recommends that consideration be given to incorporating its findings in the Canon Law of the Church of England.[1]

The old Ecclesiastical Courts, and hence the Church of England today, accepted as grounds of nullity only disabilities arising *ex causa precedenti*; wilful refusal to consummate the marriage is regarded as anomalous because it arises *in causa subsequenti*. The Church therefore proposed that wilful refusal should become a ground of divorce.[2]

The distinction between nullity and divorce puzzled Lord Keith, one of the recent Royal Commissioners.

> LORD KEITH: I gather you do not think that there is any element of, shall I say, ecclesiastical refinement in the view that is taken by the Church as between divorced persons and those whose marriages are annulled?
>
> ARCHBISHOP OF CANTERBURY: I am bound to say it seems to me, if I may dare to put it so, as plain as a pikestaff.[3]

Other protestant churches have not joined the rigorists of the Church of England in their return to medieval doctrines, and still retain a historical recollection of the Reformation. The Church of Scotland is certain "that Scripture does not debar the re-marriage by a minister of any class of divorced persons."[4] The Regulations of the Methodist Church

[1] *The Church and the Law of Nullity of Marriage* (1955), pp. 47–48.

[2] Royal Commission on Marriage and Divorce, Evidence, 6th Day, p. 140.

[3] *ibid.*, 6th Day, p. 153, Q. 1222.

[4] *ibid.*, 22nd Day, p. 567. In 1949 a Special Committee of the General Assembly reported that "the present position whereby re-marriage by a minister is forbidden to one who has been divorced as defender on the ground of adultery, but permitted to all other divorced persons, is quite untenable and requires amendment"

. . . deny the right of re-marriage to none where it could be shown there was a genuine amendment of life and a true desire to establish a new union on a basis of faith in God and dependence on Him; that is, only where it was clear that there was a real evangelical awakening.[1]

The number of divorced persons whose second or subsequent marriages were solemnised in church is shown by the table below. Comparable statistics for Scotland are not available; and those for England for 1952 only.

MARRIAGES OF DIVORCED PERSONS BY MANNER OF SOLEMNISATION, ENGLAND AND WALES, 1952[2]

	Total number of marriages	Marriages of divorced persons
TOTAL	349,308	40,205
Civil marriages	106,777	35,349
Marriages with religious ceremony:		
Total	242,531	4,856
Church of England and Church of Wales	173,282	58
Roman Catholics	33,050	241
Methodists	16,640	2,004
Other Nonconformists	15,528	2,222
Jews	1,876	122
Others	2,155	209

Only fifty-eight couples found Church of England clergymen willing to marry them in church, but the Roman Church married 241 and the other protestant churches, over 4,000.

Protestant opinion on matters relating to marriage and divorce during recent years, shows some confusion. The Methodist Church,[3] the Church of Scotland,[4] and that

[1] Royal Commission on Marriage and Divorce, Evidence, 3rd–4th Day, p. 65.

[2] The Registrar-General's *Statistical Review of the Year 1952, Text*, p. 252.

[3] "The Methodist Church . . . accepted the recent changes in English divorce law (Matrimonial Causes Act, 1937) as a reform long due. . . ." Royal Commission on Marriage and Divorce, Evidence, 3rd–4th Day, p. 64.

[4] "With reference to the Bill before Parliament (the Herbert Act) the General Assembly approve generally of the proposal to extend the grounds of divorce. . . ." *ibid.*, 22nd Day, p. 578, Q. 5044.

section of the Church of England represented by the Modern Churchmen's Union [1] have all accepted the main principles of the Herbert Act. The "official" Church of England has not overtly declared itself opposed to the principles of the Act though it now actively and mischievously [2] penalises Church of England members who exercise their rights under it. Against protestant differences of doctrine and emphasis must be set the consistency with which the Roman Church maintains that, under God's law, divorce is always forbidden, though nullities, which have the same practical consequences as divorce, may be obtained on many grounds. Christians agree, however, that separation is always preferable to divorce. The Roman Church holds that

> judicial separation is particularly appropriate for persons who believe in the indissolubility of marriage and feel that they would give pain and scandal to their relatives and friends if they became involved in divorce proceedings.[3]

The Rev. E. C. Urwin, representing the Methodist and associated Churches, told the Morton Commission that separation "is a lesser evil than divorce." [4] The Church of England stressed the several theological and, it alleged, moral benefits of separation as the alternative to divorce.

> A separation, while witnessing to the fact that a marriage has broken down, at the same time bears a telling witness to the true conception of marriage as a life-long obligation. It demonstrates that even when living together has become impossible, the obligation remains so firm as to prevent the parties making a fresh

[1] "I think on the whole we (the Modern Churchmen's Union) should agree that it (the Herbert Act of 1937) was a beneficial step." Royal Commission on Marriage and Divorce, Evidence, 19th Day, p. 510, Q. 4307.

[2] "If people conspire to defeat the intention of an Act of Parliament that is a public mischief" (Lord Goddard, L.C.J., 1953). Quoted A. P. Herbert, *op. cit.*, p. 11.

[3] Evidence, 16th–17th Day, p. 429. [4] *ibid.*, 3rd–4th Day, p. 72, Q. 629.

union. And, of course, it does keep the door open to a reconciliation.

Of course separation inflicts frustration and hardship upon many people who see no reason why they should not be free to marry again. But whoever succeeded in raising the moral tone of any society without causing the frustration of some natural desires and the hardship of having to forego them ? The choice is simple : either for the well-being of the nation public understanding of what marriage requires is to be raised, or for the convenience of individuals it is to be left to find its own level; if it is to be raised, the necessary price must be paid.

In fact, to prefer divorce to separation and thus replace some illicit unions by fresh legal unions is only to paper over the cracks. Though the illicit union can now become a legal marriage, the moral situation is completely unchanged. . . . It is of real moral importance that things should be called by their right names. Separation does at least secure that illicit unions cannot borrow the title of marriage or the status of legitimacy. And a person who chooses a separation in preference to a divorce is helping to keep reality in this realm.

Further, it is not all frustration and hardship to the separated person. If by divorce he may marry again, and claim thereby to have become a good citizen, he will become satisfied with himself and his own moral sense will be blurred. If he endures the hardship of a separation, his conscience may at any time reassert itself and he may be driven to repentance and reconciliation : in which case the way back is still open.[1]

There seems to be an element of inconsistency between the above quoted view of the Memorandum submitted by the Church of England to the Morton Commission and the advice given by the Archbishop of Canterbury to members of the church seeking guidance.

Let me say quite frankly that in some cases where a first marriage has ended in tragedy, a second marriage has, by every test of the presence of the Holy Spirit that we are able to recognise, been abundantly blessed.

[1] Evidence, 6th Day, p. 144.

> For this very reason I do not find myself able to *forbid* good people who come to me for advice to embark on a second marriage . . .[1]

Confusion amongst Christians concerning the nature of marriage or the permissibility and consequences of divorce, becomes worse confounded in relation to the types of behaviour within marriage which are approved or disapproved by different churches. All that is here possible is to give a brief indication of one or two of the main difficulties.

Christians agree that one of the main purposes of marriage is the regulation of sexual relations. The most recent pronouncement of the Church of England's Moral Welfare Council declares, and all denominations would freely assent, that

> Only the Christian religion can put sex in its proper and God-given place, and only the Christian religion can provide the grace to live out in practice what this implies. . . . In the end, therefore, it is the Church, which claims to have the revelation of the true nature of God and of Man, *which should say what sex is really for and how it should be used.*[2]

On one further aspect of the use of sex all Churches agree. They hold that sexual activity must be restricted to married couples, and condemn pre-marital and extra-marital intercourse. Nevertheless, common experience and the Registrar General's statistics show the limited influence which this prohibition at present exerts on actual behaviour.[3]

[1] *op. cit.*, p. 23. (Italics in original.)

[2] Rev. W. P. Wylie, *The Church Cares* (1955), pp. 4 and 12. (Italics in original.)

[3] " If we add together for 1953 the number of illegitimate births in England and Wales and the number of babies born within the first eight months of marriage, the total of children who must have been, so to speak, illegitimately conceived, amounts of some 82,800—a figure equivalent to nearly one in every three legitimate births occurring in that year " (Barbara Wootton, " Holiness or Happiness," *Twentieth Century*, November 1955, p. 411).

For the last half century or so science has enabled people, in Professor Titmuss's striking phrase, " to control their own fertility." Contraceptives today give many the capacity to determine, albeit sometimes unsuccessfully, the results of their sexual behaviour—a capacity generally possible to earlier generations only through abstinence or criminal abortion.[1] The fall in the birth rate since late Victorian times has great social, biological, and, because its immediate cause has altered sexual habits, theological significance. All Churches have been forced to provide guidance for members who wish to know if the use of contraceptives is unchristian. The guidance they offer differs widely.

The Roman Church insists that birth control is a grievous sin against the law of God.

> The conjugal act is destined primarily by nature for the begetting of children, those who, in exercising it, deliberately frustrate its natural power and purpose sin against nature and commit a deed which is shameful and intrinsically vicious.[2]

Papists who practise birth control reject God's partnership in their marriage and say, in effect, to God

> We shall have the pleasure, You shall not have the soul. We shall make it impossible for this creature to be born. There shall not be a child because we do not trust You to do Your share if a child is born.[3]

Any attempt to frustrate the natural consequences of copulation is condemned without qualification. This does not imply a prohibition of marital intercourse in circumstances in which, through the sterility or age of husband or wife, conception is impossible. In such instances the decision not to complete the act by creating

[1] It is commonly estimated that there are still 100,000 abortions every year. The history and early methods of contraception are described by N. E. Himes, *Medical History of Contraception* (Baltimore, 1936).

[2] " Christian Marriage," *Encyclical Letter Casti Conubii* (1930), p. 26.

[3] Rev. G. P. Dwyer, *Birth Control* (n.d., *c.* 1953), p. 10.

a soul is God's. Fecund papists are, however, permitted to use the alleged "safe period," provided there is serious cause and both partners agree. This is justified because

> . . . this form of self-control is very different from what is popularly called birth control. Here no positive action on the part of the couple thwarts the act. The act is complete as far as they can make it. Nature, God's design, is here complete when the two have accomplished their part. Doubtless, here is a natural check designed by God Himself.[1]

This exception to the general rule of the Roman Church has caused protestant theologians some difficulty. "To many minds untrained in the subtleties of casuistry," Professor James remarks, "the ethical distinction between this and other forms of birth control may not be very obvious."[2] The Roman clergy's pronouncements about sex are like those of lifelong teetotallers about drink, dogmatic but necessarily inexperienced. Perhaps this accounts for the undertone of hysteria present in much of their writing about sexual matters; and also for the evident repugnance with which it is regarded by many protestants.[3]

With the exception of a small minority of High Anglicans, most protestants regard the practice of birth control as now[4] no more unnatural than the habit of

[1] Rev. G. P. Dwyer, *Birth Control* (n.d., *c.* 1953), p. 14.

[2] E. O. James, *Marriage and Society* (1952), p. 160.

[3] There is some evidence that the Roman Church's prohibition of birth control influences the actual behaviour of its members to much the same extent as the general Christian prohibition of pre-marital and extra-marital intercourse influences the community as a whole. See, e.g., E. Slater and M. Woodside, *Patterns of Marriage* (1951), p. 208 *et seq.* There is discussion of the experience of Eire in D. V. Glass (ed.), *Introduction to Malthus* (1953), p. 27 *et seq.*

[4] Opinion in the Church of England has changed radically during the last fifty years. The Lambeth Conference of 1908 passed the following resolution: "The Conference regards with alarm the growing practice of the artificial restriction of the family, and earnestly calls upon all Christian people to discountenance the use of all artificial means of restriction as demoralising to character and hostile to national welfare" (R. T. Davidson (ed.), *The Five Lambeth Conferences* (1920), p. 327.

sleeping on interior sprung mattresses. They judge the use of contraceptives by their effect on the happiness and healthiness[1] of parents and children.[2] They hold it wrong altogether to evade the responsibilities of parenthood. The Methodist Church says

> For Christian people the determining issues are moral and spiritual. They can only be decided by the individual conscience in the sight of God. The use of a contraceptive method can only be justified if the marriage bond and married love are thereby truly honoured and not debased, if the obligation to parenthood is the better fulfilled and not evaded, if family life is enriched and not impoverished, and if increase and not diminution of good comes to society.[3]

The Church of England also, according to the view of the majority of bishops at the Lambeth Conference of 1930, leaves the decision as to the use of scientific methods of contraception to the individual conscience of the laity who must always bear in mind the duty of child-bearing. Some guidance concerning the amount of child-bearing necessary to fulfil the Christian duty was given by the Archbishop of Canterbury to the Mothers' Union in 1952.

[1] The Roman clergy are in the habit of asserting in public discussion and in writing that contraception is damaging to health. "There are good medical grounds," asserts the Superior of the Catholic Missionary Society, "for holding that the practice of birth prevention can cause sterility, neurosis and other evils" (Rev. G. P. Dwyer, *op. cit.*, p. 8). Of the assertion that birth control causes sterility, Dr. Lewis-Faning, who carried out an investigation of "Family Limitation and its Influence on Human Fertility during the Past Fifty Years," *Papers of the Royal Commission on Population* (1949), vol. I remarks (p. 15): "(there is) clear indication that the use of birth control does not appreciably reduce the power to reproduce." The assertion that birth control causes neurosis must be set against Father Dwyer's view that abstinence from sexual relations is "a high way of the cross." Father Dwyer does not state the nature of the "other evils" caused by birth control. It is only fair to add that Father Dwyer prefaces his assertions with the statement: "This is not a medical pamphlet."

[2] See, e.g., Rev. F. F. Rigby, *Discussion on Marriage* (1954, p. 62, or Rev. A. H. Gray, *Men, Women and God. A Discussion of Sex Questions from the Christian Point of View*, 19th ed. (1951), p. 109 *et seq.*

[3] *Methodist Declaration on the Christian View of Marriage and the Family*, pp. 27–28, quoted Rev. E. C. Urwin, *Can the Family Survive?* (1944), p. 71.

> I have got into trouble for saying this before, but I am going to repeat it! One child deliberately willed as the limit is no family at all but something of a misfortune, for child and parents. Two children accepted and willed as the ideal limit do not make a real family—a family only truly begins with three children.[1]

According to this view, the planned Church of England family should not consist of less than three children.

The practical consequences of Christian beliefs for some of the main problems of marriage and divorce today may now be summarised and compared with those established by the Royal Commission on Divorce and Matrimonial Causes which reported in 1912. That Report observed that opinions were maintained by "persons equally learned, equally able, equally pious and honest, equally disinterested and humane, and equally public spirited" in favour of each of the following principles:

That all marriages are indissoluble.
That Christian marriages are indissoluble.
That marriage is dissoluble on the ground of adultery only.
That marriage is dissoluble on the grounds of (1) adultery, or (2) desertion.
That marriage is dissoluble on other serious grounds based upon the necessities of human life.[2]

Different branches of the main Christian Churches still maintain each of these principles. In recent discussion and in evidence to the Royal Commission which has just reported each of the following additional principles has been asserted by one or some of the Christian Churches:

No divorced person may be re-married in Church.
The innocent party to a divorce suit may be re-married in Church.
Any repentant divorced person may be re-married in Church.

[1] *An Address to Official Workers of the Mothers' Union* (1952), p. 6.
[2] (Cd. 6478), 1912, p. 30.

Only the Christian religion can say what sex is really for and how it should be used.
The use of scientific methods of birth control are contrary to the Law of God.
The use of scientific methods of birth control are a matter for the individual Christian conscience.

The Law of God is thus held to justify an extensive range of irreconcilable propositions concerning the possibility of divorce, the rights of divorced persons, and sexual behaviour within marriage. There is a general consistency of view within each church, with the exception of the Church of England which contains amongst its membership supporters of each principle advanced by all the other denominations. It may well be that, as the Church of Scotland told the present Royal Commission, "... it is sometimes forgotten that the area of agreement between them (the branches of the Christian Church) is far wider than the area of disagreement."[1] Unhappily the area of disagreement extends over these very issues which are most important for personal conduct and governmental legislation. In Britain today, the concept of "Christian marriage" has a content so variable as between different Christians that it can provide neither a standard for personal conduct nor criteria for the legislator. This difficulty is aggravated by the insistence of each body of Christian opinion that its divinely derived conclusions about marriage, divorce, and sex are not only true as such but also embody, independently of their divine origin, what is good for society. The legislator has therefore to reckon with competing doctrines claiming both divine sanction and the social good as their justification. He must also, in a democratic society, give weight to considerations urged by those who reject Christianity and derive their conception of the social good from secular sources.

[1] Evidence, 22nd Day, p. 566.

CHAPTER V

THE MORTON COMMISSION I

THE EVIDENCE

EARLIER chapters have traced the community's attitude towards divorce and experience of its consequences. Similarly the results of the break-up of the mid-Victorian family code have been indicated. Some welcome these changes as elements in the transition to a democratic family unit in which the rights of individuals are emphasised even at the expense of institutional claims. On this view, the family is strengthened as the servitudes which used to be enforced by law and custom are replaced by new loyalties grounded in personal choice. Others deplore change as leading to the destruction of family life and therefore to the corruption of morality; and they are in the habit of interpreting the rapid increase of divorce in the aftermath of Hitler's war as an index of domestic decay. This cleavage of opinion concerning the health of the contemporary family is the background of all evidence about divorce submitted to the Morton Commission. It has been admirably summarised by Professor Wootton.

> On the one side stand those who hold that the family and marriage, as institutions, have a value in their own right, over and above their effect on the welfare of any individuals affected by them. In the extreme case, this value may be held to outweigh everything else and to preclude divorce altogether. Whom God hath joined together let no man put asunder—no matter how wretched their lives may be. In a more moderate version, the inherent sanctity of marriage as such is reckoned as only one amongst many factors

involved ; and a balance is struck between this value on the one hand and the happiness of the parties and of their children on the other. Whom God hath joined together man may put asunder provided that the situation is sufficiently desperate ; but the *presumption* is that they ought to stay joined. On the other side stand those who appraise the virtue both of marriage in general and of any particular marriage in terms only of the earthly, though not necessarily the material, welfare of the persons concerned. To them, divorce is inherently neither good nor bad, but should be judged in much the same way as one judges the decision to resign from a job. In principle it is a private matter ; though even on this view it will be recognised that legal protection is necessary for those whose interests are involved, but who, owing to youth or possibly to economic dependence, are unable adequately to look after themselves. Whom man hath joined together, man may put asunder—but only with due consideration for the interests of the helpless.[1]

The practical difficulties caused by this division of attitudes (which, without prejudice, Professor Wootton called the "religious" and the "utilitarian") were sharpened in 1951 when Mrs. Eirene White moved [2] the second reading of her private member's Bill to enable either a husband or a wife who had lived apart for seven years without prospect of reconciliation, to obtain a divorce. Her proposal was well received by the House of Commons which gave the Bill its second reading. The Bill would have introduced new principles, repugnant to the "religious" attitudes, by enabling a "guilty" partner to dissolve a marriage against the will of the "innocent" spouse, and have destroyed the ecclesiastically derived doctrine of the matrimonial offence. Accordingly, Mrs. White accepted the government's offer of a Royal Commission as a *quid pro quo* for its withdrawal.

[1] Barbara Wootton, "Holiness or Happiness," *Twentieth Century*, November 1955, p. 407.

[2] Hansard, vol. 485, col. 926 *et seq.*

A Commission of nineteen members, under the chairmanship of Lord Morton of Henryton, was appointed in September 1951

> to inquire into the law of England and the law of Scotland concerning divorce and other matrimonial causes and into the powers of courts of inferior jurisdiction in matters affecting relations between husband and wife, and to consider whether any changes should be made in the law or its administration, including the law relating to the property rights of husband and wife, both during marriage and after its termination (except by death), having in mind the need to promote and maintain healthy and happy married life and to safeguard the interests and well-being of children ; and to consider whether any alteration should be made in the law prohibiting marriage with certain relations by kindred or affinity.

These wide terms of reference created the opportunity for an investigation as thorough and far reaching as that undertaken by the Gorell Commission. This chapter will examine the evidence obtained by, and submitted to, the Morton Commission on the main issues, as they affect England and Wales,[1] between the " religious " and the " utilitarian " attitudes to divorce.

The views of the Christian churches have already been set out in detail and discussed in Chapter IV. It is here necessary to emphasise only one general aspect of their evidence to the Morton Commission. The churches stated their distinctive theological presuppositions, and all insisted on the divinely revealed truth of their differing beliefs. But all agreed that the practical policies stemming from their theological convictions coincided with those dictated by the secular good of society. In the extreme case, the Roman church justified its opposition

[1] This chapter does not attempt any discussion of the situation in Scotland. The general problems there are the same as those in England, although a different historical experience and legal system have resulted in detailed variations.

to all divorce because " we believe, not simply on religious grounds, but also on social and patriotic grounds, that the extension of facilities for divorce will make our society not better but worse." [1] The Church of England noted that " there are very many, perhaps a majority, who do not hold " the Christian standard of marriage. " That being so, the Royal Commission could not base its recommendations solely on the grounds of Christian doctrine," but

> it must be the desire of all responsible people that by the will of its citizens and by the operation of the nation's laws, the national standards and habits should approximate as far as possible to the Christian standard. Thus, whether explicitly on Christian grounds or simply on grounds of national well-being, the principle should be to adhere as far as possible to the Christian standard and to allow departures from it only regretfully and owing to " the hardness of men's hearts " and with as little detriment as possible to the stability of the family as the indispensable unit of a sound national life.[2]

Humanists similarly desire to protect society by preserving the stability of the family. The memorandum submitted to the Commission by the Ethical Union explained that

> the essential of morality is reliable behaviour founded on mutuality of interests. . . . If there must be a normal pattern of sexual relations, and if among western nations that pattern has historically and ideally been determined as life-long monogamous union, the law must confirm this and protect the institution of the family as the assumed and approved foundation of society . . . this is the first function of the marriage law in our society.[3]

[1] Minutes of Evidence, Royal Commission on Marriage and Divorce, 16th–17th Day, p. 428.

[2] *ibid.*, 6th Day, pp. 137–138.

[3] *ibid.*, 29th Day, p. 765.

All the evidence before the Commission, whether Christian or not, advocated policies directed to securing the stability of the family and hence the general social good. Discussion of the supernatural or secular sources from which such policies are derived is, therefore, unnecessary. The most important practical question which the Commission faced was the effect of divorce on the stability of the family.

All who wed in Registry Offices are reminded that "marriage, according to the law of this country, is the union of one man with one woman voluntarily entered into for life, to the exclusion of all others." Some couples may reflect, perhaps sardonically, that the Superintendent Registrar is quoting a phrase from the judgment of Lord Penzance in *Hyde* v. *Hyde and Woodmansee* (1866), a case which fittingly resulted from the polygamous enthusiasms of Brigham Young.[1] The constant reiteration of this definition by lawyers and ecclesiastics serves only to

[1] Mr. and Mrs. Hyde had contracted a Mormon marriage according to the law of Utah by a ceremony at which Brigham Young himself officiated. Later, Hyde came to live in England and, when he learnt of Mrs. Hyde's subsequent marriage in Utah to Joseph Woodmansee, he petitioned for divorce in the country of his new domicil. The court will only proceed with a divorce petition if it is first satisfied that the marriage sought to be dissolved actually exists. Indeed, as Mr. C. P. Harvey remarks (*op. cit.*, p. 130), a valid marriage "is the only condition precedent to divorce which cannot be circumvented somehow." Lord Penzance refused to accept Hyde's polygamous union as a marriage in the following famous paragraph: "Marriage has been well said to be something more than a contract—to be an institution. It creates mutual rights and obligations, as all contracts do, but beyond that it confers a status. The position or status of husband and wife is a recognised one throughout Christendom: the laws of all Christian nations throw about that status a variety of legal incidents during the lives of the parties and induce definite rights upon the offspring. What then is the nature of the institution as understood in Christendom? Its incidents vary in different countries but what are its essential elements and invariable features? If it be of common acceptance and existence it must needs (however varied in different countries its minor incidents) have some pervading identity and universal basis. I conceive that marriage understood in Christendom may for this purpose be defined as the voluntary union for life of one man and one woman, to the exclusion of all others" (35 L.J. (P. and M.), p. 58, quoted J. C. Arnold, *The Marriage Law of England* (1951), pp. 3–4).

emphasise its inaccuracy. Although for most people marriage remains, in fact and intention, a lifelong union, it has become in law " simply a union for three years certain, terminable thereafter at the option of the parties." [1] The principle underlying English divorce jurisdiction is that the respondent must have committed a statutory matrimonial offence [2] against the petitioner. Moreover, not only must the respondent be guilty but the petitioner must either be innocent of, or able to persuade the court to exercise its discretion to condone, any such offence. Only such a spouse can petition. Divorce is, therefore, a legal remedy optionally available for the innocent and a penalty to be suffered by the guilty. If the guilty spouse is the husband he is under penalty to maintain his former wife and to support the children of the marriage.[3] If the wife is the guilty party, then, subject to an exceptional award of a small " compassionate allowance," she will be punished by losing any right to income from her former husband. If both spouses are equally guilty, then, subject to the court's excercise of discretion,[4] neither can petition for divorce. Collusion, connivance, and condonation are absolute

[1] C. P. Harvey, " On the State of the Divorce Market," *Modern Law Review* (April 1953), vol. XVI, no. 2, p. 129.

[2] As set out under sec. 1, Matrimonial Causes Act, 1950. The one exception to the principle is, s.s.(d), when the respondent " is incurably of unsound mind." This exception is usually justified on the ground that incurable insanity is a direct visitation from God.

[3] As a rough rule, the court awards a sum sufficient to bring the wife's income (if any) up to one-third of the joint income.

[4] This brief summary of the law is necessarily crude. The Court of Appeal laid it down in the leading case on the exercise of discretion in favour of the petitioner's adultery, *Blunt* v. *Blunt* [1943] A.C. 517, that the court should have regard to " the interest of the community at large by maintaining a true balance between respect for the binding sanctity of marriage and the social considerations which make it contrary to public policy to insist on the maintenance of a union which has utterly broken down." Thus the court has now come to exercise its discretion in accordance with social realities, and a decree may even be awarded to both parties where both seek the exercise of the court's discretion and injustice would be done if it were exercised in favour of one party only. This is very odd because the Court of Appeal's conception of " public policy " cannot be reconciled with the doctrine of the matrimonial offence.

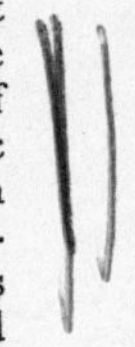

bars to relief. Collusion partly consists of presenting a petition, or withholding a just defence, by agreement between the parties. What may constitute collusion is a highly technical matter about which lawyers disagree, but the following examples bring out the important, practical considerations :

(*a*) John and Mary have amicably reached a parting of their ways. John says : " We both are certain that our marriage has broken down, and both of us want a divorce. I have never committed any matrimonial offence, but I shall now commit, or pretend to commit, adultery so that you can petition for divorce."

(*b*) John and Mary have reached a quarrelsome parting of their ways. John says : " I find our marriage intolerable and I am leaving you. You may as well know that I have been committing adultery for months past. I shall send you evidence and you can, if you want, use it to get a divorce." Mary replies : " Send the evidence, I'm delighted to get the chance to be free."

In circumstances (*a*) Mary's petition would be barred as collusive if the court learnt of the agreement ; in (*b*), Mary's petition would be honourably and successfully filed. The distinction between these two cases rests on the principle that in (*a*) there is no real injury because the parties had agreed, whereas, in (*b*), Mary is injured even though she is pleased that an opportunity for divorce has occurred.[1] Connivance implies an anticipatory consent, active or passive, to adultery committed by the other spouse.[2] Condonation is the reinstatement to the former

[1] " The fact that both spouses desire a divorce *a vinculo* does not make them guilty of collusion, provided they have not entered into any agreement obnoxious to the court ; and an agreement between the parties not involving an imposition on the court or a suppression of facts, but merely facilitating proof and smoothing the asperities of litigation is not collusive or otherwise objectionable, though it is liable to be looked into by the court " (Rayden's *Practice and Law in the Divorce Division*, 5th ed. (1949), p. 138). It is thus permissible to smooth " the asperities of litigation " provided that they have resulted from rough, domestic asperities. Any attempt to smooth domestic asperities before litigation necessarily runs a serious risk of becoming collusive.

[2] *ibid.*, pp. 132–133.

marital position of a spouse who has committed matrimonial offences of which the other spouse is fully aware. The decision to condone, or not to condone, is at the discretion of the innocent spouse. A guilty spouse cannot refuse to consent to the condonation.[1] In some respects the principles of divorce law are contrary to the general theory of English law. Dr. R. M. Jackson explains that the divorce court

> . . . contrary to the general theory of our law . . . regards everyone as a suspicious character. Every petitioner has to swear, usually twice over (once in writing and once orally), that he or she is innocent of any matrimonial offence. Not content with this, a period which was six months until 1946 and is now six weeks must elapse between the decree nisi and the decree absolute so that anonymous letter writers may suggest to the Queen's Proctor that some petitioner has committed adultery; the honesty of litigants must then be checked by a detective service run on public money.[2]

In certain circumstances an appeal within six weeks from a decree absolute is allowed. Apart from this, a decree absolute cannot be challenged even if it is subsequently discovered to have been obtained by a fraud upon the court.

A central issue confronting the Morton Commission was the retention or abolition of the matrimonial offence as the basis of divorce law at a time when all citizens

[1] Rayden's *Practice and Law in the Divorce Division*, 5th ed. (1949), p. 139.

[2] *op. cit.*, p. 53. A *canard* concerning the evidence of the Earl of Desart to the Gorell Commission has been widely circulated. (The Earl was Treasury Solicitor, and hence Queen's and King's Proctor, from 1895 to 1909. His evidence appears in the second volume of the Gorell Commission's Minutes of Evidence (Cd. 6480), 1912, pp. 135–146.) He has been recently credited, e.g., by Sir Hartley Shawcross (Hansard, vol. 485, col. 1001), by several speakers in a House of Lords debate (Hansard, 24th October 1956), and also by the Marriage Law Reform Society (in their evidence to the Morton Commission, 9th Day, p. 224) with the statement that, during his term of office, 75 per cent. of all divorces were, in fact, divorces by consent. The Earl of Desart made no such statement; indeed, the tenor of his evidence like that of his successor, Sir Thomas Barnes, to the Morton Commission, was emphatically to the contrary.

have access to the High Court, and few regulate their marital behaviour in accordance with the theological and social presuppositions underlying the doctrine. Much of the evidence submitted may be classified according to attitude on this main point. On the one hand, there were "abolitionists" who wished to make away with the matrimonial offence; on the other, were "institutionalists" who insisted on its retention.[1]

The "abolitionist" case was urged on two main grounds. First, that divorce has become, in many cases, a degrading farce which has brought law and the administration of justice into public disrepute. In practice, it was alleged, spouses commit matrimonial offences in order to get divorced, and there is a strong probability that many of the undefended cases, which make up about 90 per cent. of the total, result from collusive agreements. This view was put forcibly to the Commission by Professor L. C. B. Gower.

> The only point on which opinions may differ is as to the proportion of divorces which may be regarded as collusive or based on bogus grounds. Among the upper income groups I would say that it is well over half the total of undefended cases, although among the poorer classes, whose cases are handled under the Legal Aid Scheme, it seems to be considerably lower. . . . But whatever the proportion, there is no doubt that many divorces are now granted where there are no true grounds, and that provided the parties are in agreement there is never the slightest difficulty in obtaining a dissolution.
>
> This state of affairs has two consequences:
>
> (1) It enables the party who is the less anxious for a divorce to hold up to ransom the other who is eager to obtain one, and thus to extort unduly favourable financial arrangements from him.

[1] My distinction between "abolitionists" and "institutionalists" approximately corresponds to Professor Wootton's distinction between the "utilitarian" and "religious" attitudes to divorce. I think the former preferable because emotively neutral.

(2) It involves the parties often in the degrading business of actual or pretended adultery and always in deceiving the court, it forces the lawyers to be unwilling participants in a travesty of justice and it brings the whole administration of the law into disrepute.[1]

Professor Gower did not suggest that solicitors or their managing clerks act in concert with petitioners to present false cases to the court. He had in mind the type of situation described to the Commission by another solicitor, Mr. W. J. C. Heyting.

> I feel that there is a considerable amount of collusion in one form or another, but . . . solicitors are not parties to it and the reason for that is this ; the more intelligent people are, the more they know perfectly well what the law is on this subject and they just don't tell their solicitors the whole truth in the matter. The solicitor may have very strong suspicions and it is his duty to ask his clients specifically about collusion and draw the client's attention to the law on this matter. I am sure in the vast majority of cases he does this. But if a client denies it, there is very little more the solicitor can do whatever his suspicions may be.[2]

Professor Gower doubted whether there is any remedy other than abolishing divorce altogether or introducing divorce by consent and divorce based on a period of separation in the absence of consent. The former solution is politically impracticable. The latter " would not, in fact, make divorce much easier than it is at present ; in the main it would merely allow the parties to do openly what they now do clandestinely." [3] Professor

[1] Evidence, 1st Day, p. 15. [2] *ibid.*, 10th Day, p. 304, Q. 2338.

[3] A similar comment was made by a witness, Mr. Arthur Macmillan, a barrister whose attitude to divorce is that " of a believing member of the Church of England " and very different from that of Professor Gower. In his Memorandum, Mr. Macmillan wrote : " It must . . . be remembered that, in practice, though not by law, divorce by consent exists, and is constantly obtained." He added further : " It is quite wrong to think, as many people seem to think, that this statement reflects in any way on either the Judiciary or on the legal profession. The discussions of man and wife in the privacy of their home are necessarily unknown by outsiders," *ibid.*, 5th Day, p. 127.

Gower's proposals were inspired by his anxiety to free the administration of justice from what another distinguished lawyer, Professor Glanville Williams, described as "the squalor now found in the divorce court and the collusion and perjury that are now found there." [1]

"Institutionalists" who wish to retain the matrimonial offence as the basis of divorce law rebutted Professor Gower's conclusions by denying the truth of his and similar assertions as to the extent of collusion. The evidence on this point of the General Council of the Bar of England and Wales [2] is representative of the "institutionalist" attitude. Mr. R. J. A. Temple, Q.C., replying to Lord Morton, made two comments on Professor Gower's evidence. First,

> Collusion in the sense in which I understand the witness (i.e. Professor Gower) defined it, or suggested that it was taking place, amounted not only to the presentation of a false case, but had much graver implications. The solicitor is, of course, much more closely identified with the lay client than the barrister, and it is quite impossible for anything like the suggested

[1] Evidence, 16th–17th Day, p. 449.

[2] The General Council of the Bar gave evidence twice. On the first occasion (1st Day) their representatives told the Commission, "What the General Council puts forward can be said to represent the views of practising and non-practising barristers. As far as this memorandum is concerned . . . though it does not, of course, by any means represent the view of every member of the Bar, it does probably represent the greatest measure of agreement between us" (p. 44). On the second occasion (16th–17th Day) their representatives prefaced their evidence by saying : ". . . some members of the Bar have gained the impression . . . that such evidence has been put forward as representing not only the views of the general Council of the Bar but also of the Bar as a whole. We would like to re-emphasise [*sic*] that this is not the case. Our written evidence was prepared by a special committee composed mainly of practitioners of the Probate and Divorce Bar, and it was subsequently approved by the majority, but not all, of the members of the General Council of the Bar. There was no question of the Bar as whole being consulted . . . and . . . the memorandum cannot and is not claimed to, represent the views of members of the Bar as a whole." (p. 441.) In view of these conflicting statements, it is difficult to discover whose views are represented by the General Council's evidence. It is clear, however, that it would be unsafe to take it as representing the views of barristers generally.

> number of cases to be collusive, bogus or false, without, in my view, the solicitor becoming aware of it. Now, the implication that I draw from that, and I may be wrong, is that the suggestion is that the solicitor or his managing clerk is acting in concert with the petitioner to present to the court a false case. That is a very grave statement to make, and I, for one, am utterly unable to accept it.[1]

Mr. Temple effectively answered a criticism of the present system that was never made to the Commission by any witness. Professor Gower's point was not that solicitors deceive the court, but that they are deceived by their clients in circumstances in which, though they may suspect deception, they have neither the means nor the inducement to discover the truth. When Lord Keith asked Mr. Temple to consider this possibility as supporting the assertion that there are, in fact, many divorces by consent, he replied,

> . . . such a conclusion would be entirely unwarranted. The lay client, in my experience, is not a person who goes to a solicitor with a prepared and fraudulent case in his or her pocket, knowing that if he or she tells the solicitor the true facts the solicitor will say, " You cannot go on with this." I do not think people do that sort of thing. I think . . . that the lay client is a fairly naïve sort of person . . .[2]

The lay client underwent some puzzling changes of character during the Bar Council's evidence. This " fairly naïve " person began his marital career in their Memorandum by exhibiting a high degree of sophisticated vigour. His attitude to marriage and divorce, though casual, was enterprising ; and was thus described to the Commission :

> We are attracted to each other. We will go round the corner to the registrar's office and then sleep together legally. If it doesn't work out, we can go round the

[1] Evidence, 2nd Day, p. 46. [2] *ibid.*, 2nd Day, p. 59, Q. 541.

> other corner and get a decree nisi at no particular cost in a month or so, and in a further six weeks we shall be free to do the same thing all over again with a different partner.[1]

Such inconsistency is as surprising as the contempt shown for the lay client is unattractive.

The Bar Council's second comment on Professor Gower's evidence was to deny that 50 per cent. of divorces are collusive or bogus.[2] It would have been more helpful to the fairly naïve lay reader if their witnesses had dealt with what Professor Gower actually asserted: that " well over half the total of undefended cases " from the upper, and a " considerably lower " proportion from the lower, income groups may be regarded as collusive or based on bogus grounds. Neither Mr. Temple nor Mr. Latey discussed the possibility that the incidence of collusion may vary with petitioners' incomes, although they quoted with approval the Lord Chancellor's view, in 1950, that " the proportion of collusive divorce cases has gone down rapidly, and is not so great today as it was twenty years ago." No statistical estimate can be made, but, if Professor Gower's assumptions are accepted as realistic, the figure which would have to be challenged could not be more than 30 per cent.

Lay readers of this evidence will learn that some academic lawyers think there are a sufficient, though unknown, number of collusive divorces to endanger public respect for law and the administration of justice; a view shared by some of their colleagues who practice as solicitors and at the bar. They will learn, too, that leading practitioners of the Divorce Bar, who were

[1] Evidence, p. 28.

[2] *ibid.*, pp. 46–47, Q. 333. Mr. Temple implied that Professor Gower had accepted the figure of 50 per cent. alleged by Lord Mancroft in the House of Lords in 1950. Mr. Latey, another representative of the Bar Council, quoted extensively from the denials, during that debate, of the President of the Probate, Divorce and Admiralty Division and of the Lord Chancellor.

largely responsible for preparing and presenting the Bar Council's evidence, emphatically reject such assertions. Laymen must infer from the hostility and rudeness to which Professor Gower was subjected by some legal members of the Commission and the deference they showed to the Bar Council's witnesses, that the Commissioners had pre-judged an issue which they felt ought never to have been raised publicly. Indeed, the tone of the examination of Professor Gower can be explained only on the assumption that Commissioners regarded him as an apostate, disloyal to his profession. As this matter is crucial to an informed judgment of the present working of the divorce law, the layman cannot keep an open mind in face of the conflict of witnesses' evidence. He will naturally be greatly influenced both by the views of the distinguished barristers who gave evidence for the Bar Council and by the evident repugnance with which the Commission heard Professor Gower. On the other hand, he must allow for four considerations. First, since the time of Blackstone, English lawyers have been more apt to praise than to criticise law and the administration of justice. Practising lawyers have never been a fertile source of legal reforms. Secondly, the Memorandum which Professor Gower submitted to the Commission had been read as a paper to the Anglo-French Legal Conference in 1949, before " a distinguished audience in which both branches of the legal profession were represented—including the then President and several members of the Council of the Law Society. In the resulting discussion no one suggested that my account of what normally occurs was not a wholly accurate description of the usual type of undefended case." [1] The author has been unable to trace a public denial of this statement by anyone present at the conference. Thirdly, solicitors are better placed than barristers to confirm or deny such assertions. Although Lord Morton invited practitioners

[1] Evidence, 1st Day, p. 15.

of the Divorce Bar to rebut Professor Gower's evidence, neither he nor any other Commissioner put it to the representatives of the Law Society, the governing body of the solicitors' profession. This seems a particularly surprising omission as the Law Society recommended the abolition of collusion as a bar to relief,[1] and this proposal was discussed at length during their oral evidence.[2] Equally surprising was Lord Morton's omission to put the issue squarely to Mr. J. H. Lawton, President of, and representing, the Association of County Court Registrars which had amongst its 126 members sixty-six registrars of the High Court exercising jurisdiction in divorce. The Association's Memorandum stated bluntly:

> In spite of legal safeguards, which are extensive, of course, it is felt that, though actual cases are seldom discovered, collusion is fairly common.[3]

Fourthly, Professor Gower's Memorandum had been written after, and made reference to, a House of Lords debate during which both the Lord Chancellor and the President of the Probate, Divorce and Admiralty Division of the High Court had emphatically denied that collusive cases were a serious or significant problem. This might appear dangerously irresponsible on Professor Gower's part had not the evidence before the Commission been followed by the publication in *The Modern Law Review*, one of the leading legal periodicals, of an article by Mr. C. P. Harvey, Q.C., "On the State of the Divorce Market." Mr. Harvey remarked that the present state of affairs is, "in one way, highly satisfactory for the legal profession."

[1] Evidence, 29th Day, pp. 742–743. The abolition was urged partly on the ground that it is "difficult for a solicitor to advise a lay client on the exact meaning of collusion." The Law Society wished to retain the other bars to relief.

[2] *ibid.*, pp. 753–754, Qs. 7150–7170.

[3] *ibid.*, 30th–31st Day, p. 797 and pp. 801–802, Qs. 7622–7628 and 7636–7641.

> Large incomes can be made at the Bar out of practices which consist almost entirely of undefended divorces. The hearing of an undefended suit commonly takes between ten and fifteen minutes, though much higher speeds are possible . . . Counsel are paid at an approximate rate of 12s. 6d. per minute for asking a string of leading questions. The paper work involved in settling documents, advising on evidence, and the like can be done by an experienced practitioner almost in his sleep.[1]

Such comments are commonplaces of legal discussion. Indeed, Sir Hartley Shawcross, speaking as Attorney General in 1951, did not hesitate to tell the House of Commons in 1951 :

> I remember that one used to handle these undefended cases at the rate of about one in two minutes ; " seven and one " we used to call them, and it was a very profitable morning's work, but it did not impress me at the time that there was any real principle operating in practice in the administration of our divorce laws.[2]

For the reputation of English justice this situation is, in Mr. Harvey's view, disastrous. He adds,

> To many barristers, and to some judges, the whole business seems undignified and unworthy of the talents of the profession or of the standing of the Bench. Some do not hesitate to describe it as a racket, and Lord Asquith of Bishopstone once remarked that the granting of divorces was the sort of task that Caligula would have delegated to his horse. It is the fact that undefended divorce works almost on the slot-machine principle.[3]

This is strong language for a learned legal periodical, and it is astonishing that none of the divorce practitioners who gave contrary evidence to the Commission has thought fit to challenge Mr. Harvey in subsequent numbers of

[1] *op. cit.*, p. 133.
[2] Hansard, vol. 485, col. 1001.
[3] *op. cit.*, p. 133.

The Modern Law Review. The weight of these considerations, and the impossibility of obtaining direct confirmatory or negatory evidence, must force the layman to accept the gravamen of Professor Gower's evidence, and to wonder why the Commission's Report contains no adequate discussion of this crucial aspect of the working of the divorce law.

The second important group of " abolitionists " was primarily concerned not with the damage alleged to the administration of justice, but with the injury which, they argued, the present law of divorce inflicts on the institution of marriage. The Women's Co-operative Guild, the only working-class organisation to give evidence, proposed what amounts to the irretrievable breakdown of a marriage as a ground of divorce. They prefaced their Memorandum with a statement of " the need for reform of the laws affecting marriage and divorce."

> When considering desirable changes in the law on matrimonial causes the Women's Co-operative Guild considers that the good of the community is a first priority. The sanctity of marriage must be upheld but the law as it operates at the present time frequently brings marriage into disrepute. Many people are compelled to lead lives of misery because there is no way out for them from a marriage which has completely broken up. Many others are forced to lie and perjure themselves if they want to free themselves from a situation which has become intolerable to all concerned. Some people are afraid that alteration of the law may lead to divorce for " any silly reason." The members of the Women's Co-operative Guild believe the opposite to be the case. They are putting forward proposals which, in their opinion, will uphold the sanctity of marriage and will help to make people more conscious of their responsibilities as partners to a life-long contract. They are convinced that on grounds of human need the changes implied in these proposals are necessary. Homes are broken by (many) causes and the law should be allowed to give relief where these causes are serious

> and lead to the break-up of marriage. Reasonable law, based upon human needs, is more likely to increase morality than to undermine it.[1]

This attitude is, in substance, shared by such bodies as the Ethical Union,[2] the Progressive League,[3] the Divorce Law Reform Union,[4] and the Marriage Law Reform Society.[5] The legal consequences of such an outlook were succinctly put before the Commission by the Haldane Society.

> The law cannot make people love one another, or make them live together if they do not do so of their own free will. This truism would not have to be stated were it not so often ignored in connection with divorce. To force people who do not love one another to remain together is often the apparent intention of our present divorce law when it denies divorce to couples who are unable to achieve or maintain a good marriage. The results are misery to the spouses, an unhappy home for the children, contempt for the law and a danger to society. It should be recognised that the law can only do the following things for such couples:
>
> (*a*) decide whether they should have the legal status of being married;
> (*b*) protect a party who does not desire cohabitation against the attentions of one who does;
> (*c*) make and enforce orders as to the custody of children;
> (*d*) make and enforce financial arrangements.
>
> There can be genuine disputes about (*c*) and (*d*), and such disputes can be fit subjects for decision by the court.
>
> In the case of (*a*) and (*b*), the function of the law should be mainly declaratory—to give public recognition to an already accomplished change in the private relations of the parties.[6]

[1] Evidence, 5th Day, p. 95.
[2] *ibid.*, 29th Day.
[3] *ibid.*, 36th Day.
[4] *ibid.*, 7th–8th Day.
[5] *ibid.*, 9th Day.
[6] *ibid.*, 16th–17th Day, p. 449.

On this view the law should permit divorce by consent when satisfied that the consent of both spouses is freely given. When only one spouse wishes to dissolve the marriage, divorce should be at the discretion of the court after separation for two years, and as of right after separation for three years. Problems relating to children should always be determined by the trial judge after hearing and seeing the parents and considering the report of a welfare officer, independently representing the interests of the children. Such welfare officers should be appointed to all courts of matrimonial jurisdiction and there generally perform functions similar to those of probation officers attached to magistrates courts. Maintenance orders should be made by the court after considering the responsibility for, and causes of, the divorce, and the earning capacities of both spouses.[1]

These " abolitionists " reject outright the religious concepts of marriage and the existing legal doctrine based upon them. They all share with " institutionalists " the beliefs that marriage ought normally to be a permanent and lifelong union, and that public policy should be directed to securing and strengthening the stability of the family as the basic unit of society. They differ irreconcilably from supporters of the present system by insisting that, whilst in certain respects marriage and its results are a major concern of the community, the decision to maintain or dissolve an existing marriage is essentially a private matter between husband and wife.

Not all " abolitionists " were so radical in their approach to the Commission. Many private persons,[2]

[1] Evidence, 16–17th Day, pp. 449–451.

[2] Amongst them were solicitors, Mr. H. O. Roberts and Miss M. G. Billson (10th Day, p. 285 and p. 308) ; a retired county court judge now sitting as a commissioner to hear divorce cases, His Honour W. G. Earengey, who gave evidence jointly with his wife, Mrs. Florence Earengey, a barrister and magistrate (3rd–4th Day, pp. 90–91) ; the Director of the John Hilton Bureau of the *News of the World*, Mr. T. K. P. Barrett (16th–17th Day, p. 464) ; and a metropolitan Police Magistrate and member of the House of Laity, Mr. F. J. Powell (32nd Day, p. 806).

and some organised bodies,[1] did not directly attack the principle of the matrimonial offence, but wished to add to the established exception of incurable lunacy by granting divorce to either spouse after a period of separation when there is no prospect of reconciliation. This was the purpose of Mrs. Eirene White's Bill which sought to make the breakdown of a marriage a new ground of divorce. Under Section 1 (i), the Bill provided that :

> A petition for divorce may be presented to the court either by the husband or the wife on the ground that :
>
> (*a*) the parties have lived separately for a period of not less than seven years immediately preceding the presentation of the petition ; and
>
> (*b*) there is no reasonable prospect that the cohabitation will be resumed.

Mrs. White attached great importance to two provisos. Firstly, that the husband should make good any default in paying maintenance and, secondly, that the court should be satisfied that proper provision had been made for the wife and any children of the marriage before a decree could be granted.

Mrs. White promoted her Bill because, like the Gorell Commission forty years earlier, she was anxious to

> meet the situation in which many thousands of men and women are living apart in a state which is not marriage, in any full sense of that word, but in which they are unable legally to form another union or to

[1] They included the Association of County Court Registrars (30th–31st Day, pp. 796–797) ; a group set up by the Fabian Society (18th Day, p. 498) ; and the Council of the British Medical Association (6th Day, p. 169). (The Memorandum submitted by the Council of the B.M.A. and the oral evidence of its representatives were subsequently withdrawn, although printed amongst the Commission's Minutes of Evidence.) Nine of the eleven members of a Special Committee appointed by the Law Society to draft memoranda for submission to the Commission, submitted a Memorandum (29th Day, pp. 762–764), containing proposals largely in accord with those of Mrs. White's Bill.

> establish a normal home life. The estimates of the number of those separated vary from 100,000 to a much higher figure . . . people have been so mesmerised by statistics of divorce that they have very largely disregarded this other extremely serious social problem of the marriages which are just as much broken but in which the legal tie remains. . . . There are those in their thousands who, finding that the existing law offers no relief, are taking the law into their own hands, and are bringing up children in conditions in which neither mother nor child has adequate social or financial protection . . .[1]

The Commission received abundant testimony as to the causes and consequences of the situation which Mrs. White described to the House of Commons. Legally innocent spouses may refuse to petition for divorce from their legally guilty partners for many reasons ranging from moral or religious principle to mere spite. On the other hand, divorce may be impossible because neither party is guilty of a matrimonial offence and, though both wish to dissolve their marriage, neither is prepared to commit one. The results, whether conceived in terms of personal frustration, extra-marital unions, or illegitimate children, are extensive and socially damaging. Mrs. White's supporters would, therefore, all accept "the broad principle" which Sir Sydney Littlewood, then President of the Law Society, urged upon the Commission,

> that in any case where the real fabric of the marriage had irretrievably been destroyed, it was better in the interests of the community, and civilisation being what it is, that the marriage should be put to an end, and

[1] Hansard, vol. 485, cols. 927–928. The difficulties of obtaining statistical information have already been explained. It is certain, however, that the figure of 100,000 for the number of those married but separated is a serious underestimate. In 1951, 70,000 married women, living apart from their husbands, were receiving national assistance (Hansard [H. of L.], vol. 176, col. 744). This group alone would account for 140,000 people separated but not divorced.

> that it was time we moved towards the idea that there was no longer an absolute guilt or absolute innocence in matrimonial affairs. The lesser of the evils was to say, " This marriage can never subsist, it is bad from the point of view of the children, it is bad from the point of view of the community, and therefore it should be dissolved," and that it should not be a matter of guilt or innocence on anybody's part.[1]

On this view, an extension of the grounds of divorce, even though it would weaken the doctrine of the matrimonial offence, is a lesser evil than the present prohibition of normal life to those large numbers of married persons who are separated but not divorced.

Many private persons,[2] and some organised bodies[3] share the anxieties of proponents of change concerning the undesirable consequences of separation, but insist that the suggested remedy will intensify rather than mitigate the harm to society. The first, " institutionalist " objection to the principle of Mrs. White's Bill was

[1] Evidence, 29th Day, p. 758, Q. 7229.

[2] Amongst them were the President of the Probate, Divorce and Admiralty Division of the High Court, Lord Merriman (14th–15th Day, pp. 418–419); a Lord Justice of Appeal, Sir Francis Hodson (30th–31st Day, p. 771); the Queen's Proctor, Sir Thomas Barnes (36th Day, pp. 887–888, Qs. 8573–8577); a Metropolitan Police Magistrate, Mr. T. F. Davis, and a lay magistrate, Mrs. Holt Wilson (37th Day, pp. 910–911 and 937–938); and barristers, Mr. Arthur Macmillan (5th Day, p. 126) and Mrs. Helena Normanton, Q.C. (34th Day, p. 867).

[3] They included the Bar Council (2nd Day, pp. 29–30); the Mothers' Union (3rd–4th Day, p. 81); the Association of Headmistresses (12th–13th Day, p. 376); and all the Churches. The Church of England and the Modern Churchmen's Union (6th Day, p. 141 and 19th Day, p. 509); the Church of Scotland (22nd Day, p. 568–569); and the Catholic Union of Great Britain (16th–17th Day, p. 428), were unequivocal in their opposition. The view of the Methodist Church is obscure. When their representative, the Rev. E. C. Urwin, was asked by Lord Morton (3rd–4th Day, p. 75, Q. 694), if his Church would be in favour of an extension of the grounds of divorce to cover the principle of Mrs. White's Bill, he replied: " If the suggestion were that one partner could ultimately sue for divorce on the ground of the impossibility of restoring the marriage to a real marriage, we might look at it . . ." When Lord Morton asked the same question in a different phrasing (Q. 695, p. 75), Mr. Urwin appeared to retract his previous answer.

succinctly put to the Commission in the elegant Memorandum of Mr. Arthur Macmillan :

> (i) It would introduce into English jurisprudence, for the first time, the principle that a person can come before the court and plead his own wrongdoing as a ground for obtaining a remedy.
>
> (ii) It is contrary to natural justice to deprive a spouse, against whom no wrongdoing is alleged and against his will, of his status of spouse.[1]

If the criteria for judging relations between husbands and wives are the " guilt," " wrongdoing," and " innocence " of the criminal law, Mr. Macmillan's first point is an unanswerable tautology. His supplementary argument that it is unethical to permit the guilty to coerce the innocent involves the assertion, as a moral principle, of the right of the offended spouse to take revenge on the offending spouse. Secondly, it was urged that Mrs. White's Bill would permit the religious scruples of an innocent husband or wife to be overridden and individual conscience to be outraged. This view gives power to one spouse to force the other to conform to behaviour necessitated by such scruples when the beliefs of the spouses concerning the nature of marriage differ. If Mrs. White's proposals were enacted, the offended spouse who believes in indissoluble marriage would remain free, by avoiding a second marriage, to observe the requirements of conscience. Thirdly, many witnesses pointed to the serious financial consequences of involuntary divorce for women. " If you do not remain a wife," Mr. Temple explained to the Commission on behalf of the Bar Council, " you have no prospect of becoming a widow . . . and of

[1] Evidence, 5th Day, p. 128. Arguing the same point before the Commission Mr. Temple, a Bar Council representative, made the puzzling statement that : " There would be invoked, for the first time, the principle of unilateral repudiation of a contract which a great number of people in this country regard as indissoluble." (2nd Day, p. 48). It is difficult to understand why this should be thought a novelty. The indissoluble contract is unilaterally repudiated whenever an innocent spouse secures a decree against a guilty partner.

becoming entitled to anything that can properly be called a widow's pension."[1] A divorced wife loses her rights under intestacy or, if a will has been made, her rights under the Inheritance (Family Provision) Act, 1938. In addition to her possible loss under private pension schemes, a divorced wife loses her right to benefits under the National Insurance Act which derive from her husband's contributions.[2] All these real disadvantages could easily, and ought to, be removed by legislation. Their existence is not a good argument for preserving the doctrine of the matrimonial offence. Fourthly, some witnesses were impressed by the Church of England's contention that divorce after seven years' separation would weaken or remove a deterrent to extra-marital relationships.

> . . . under present conditions if a woman enters into an illicit relationship with a married man she knows that this relationship has not the sanctions of the law, and that in consequence if the wife refuses a divorce she cannot possess the security which marriage gives. This Bill . . . removes the insecurity. The national interest requires that there should be no encouragement of such irregular unions. The insecurity attached to them may in many cases be just the factor that restrains a woman from becoming attached to a married man.[3]

It is doubtful if the predatory women described by the Church would regard the delay of seven years proposed by Mrs. White, or the one of four years proposed by the Marriage Law Reform Society,[4] before they could acquire the status of wives, as removing their present insecurity. It could be as reasonably predicted that such extension of divorce would make people more careful to avoid behaviour which they knew might result in divorce. The

[1] Evidence, 2nd Day, p. 48.

[2] There is one exception to this rule. If, at the time of divorce, a woman is drawing a retirement pension by virtue of her husband's contributions, it will continue unless and until she marries again.

[3] Evidence, 6th Day, p. 141. [4] *ibid.*, 9th Day, p. 231.

likelihood of appearing in the divorce court might well be as great a deterrent as the feeling of insecurity resulting from the knowledge that the law bars divorce in these circumstances. Moreover, the estimates of the number of existing irregular unions suggest the need for some scepticism about the deterrent effect of the present law.

These objections to Mrs. White's and similar proposals have been summarily dismissed partly because they are either tautological or invalid and, importantly, because they are irrelevant to the main " institutionalist " case. The clearest statement of this position was made to the Commission by the Catholic Union of Great Britain on behalf of the Church of Rome.

> Even those who regard divorce as a necessary evil would agree that the evil should be limited as much as possible. Divorce is now obtainable by the injured party for all the main matrimonial wrongs, adultery, desertion, cruelty, etc., and any extension of the grounds for divorce would inevitably lead, step by step, to divorce by mutual consent. Any such extension would increase the number of divorces, and if a right to divorce by mutual consent were ever conceded the number of divorces would increase enormously. Such increase, though doubtless reflecting the wishes of the parties concerned, cannot be on that ground defended for the evil of divorce is contagious. The more the number of divorces increases, the more divorce comes to be regarded as a normal feature of our society, and the more will young people, even at the time of their marriage, assume, consciously or unconsciously, that if the marriage does not appear at any time to be a happy one it can readily be dissolved. Thus when friction between the parties first begins—and some friction is inevitable in every marriage—the necessary effort to compose differences is not forthcoming and matters proceed from bad to worse. It is otherwise with those whose religion teaches them the indissolubility of marriage : since the marriage cannot be dissolved they are usually resolute that it must be made to work. But such a belief cannot readily be implanted. What

> can be implanted, both by the tenor of the laws and the procedure to be adopted, is the sense that divorce is abnormal, anti-social, and a matter greatly to be deplored.[1]

This view was accepted by all the protestant churches, by the Church of England, by secular organisations, and by individuals. Such witnesses usually made an additional comment on the prevalent attitude to marriage. Most asserted with Mr. J. E. S. Simon, Q.C., M.P., the paramount importance of the stability of the family which

> involves the stability of marriages as legal relationships. Any influence which on the whole weakens the marriage tie, in turn weakens society. . . . If individual hardship could be relieved without impairing the stability of marriage and the family as institutions . . . it should be done. That it could be done was undoubtedly the belief of the legislature in granting increased facilities for divorce in 1857, 1923 and 1937 ; indeed it was hoped and claimed that marriage and family life would thereby actually be strengthened. We have now had sufficient experience to ascertain whether these beliefs and hopes and claims were well-founded. We have learnt that they were false.
>
> It is a matter difficult of direct proof, but few, I imagine, would controvert that marriage and the family as institutions are less respected or stable than they were in 1857, or that spouses are by and large individually less secure or contented in the married state.[2]

Thus a century's experience is held to confirm the wisdom of the prediction of Lord Redesdale, the only Commissioner in 1850 who opposed the establishment of a divorce court, that " once create an appetite for such licence . . . and the demand to be permitted to satisfy it will become irresistible." [3] Divorce, conceived as an element in the achievement of personal liberty in the days of Victorian

[1] Evidence, 16th–17th Day, p. 428. [2] *ibid.*, 7th–8th Day, p. 200.

[3] First Report of Royal Commission (on) Law of Divorce 1604 (1853), pp. 28–29.

optimism, has now become the widespread licence which threatens social stability. The whole population has become divorce-minded. "This state of mind," the Bar Council explained to the Commission,

> results from a number of causes such as easier divorce, quicker divorce, cheaper divorce, and a general lowering of moral, religious and social standards, following on two great wars, the fear of a third, and a consequential disruption and instability of living conditions.[1]

Divorce breeds divorce; society must attempt to tackle the fearful legacy of past error. "Institutionalists" accordingly insist that it is now all the more essential to preserve the doctrine of the matrimonial offence as the one remaining bulwark protecting the sanctity of marriage. By emphasising the misery of unhappy couples indissolubly bound, "abolitionists" ignore the fundamentals of the situation. Their concern, like Burke's for the fate of Marie-Antoinette, pities the plumage and forgets the dying bird. Mrs. White's Bill, by introducing a new principle of divorce after separation at the option of the guilty party, would necessarily grant divorce by consent. Once this was conceded the demand to reduce the length of the separation period must prove irresistible; in law, marriage would come to be a tenancy-at-will. Few "abolitionists" would attempt to deny the truth of this conclusion, though they would probably prefer the phrase tenancy-at-affection. Some "institutionalists" do not hesitate to make a further inference. "This Bill," Mr. R. M. Bell, a barrister, assured the House of Commons, "in fact, is going to abolish marriage." [2]

For these reasons "institutionalists" opposed any extension of the grounds for divorce. Mr. Simon, a leading divorce practitioner, recommended that

> . . . in the interests of society generally, and of children

[1] Evidence, 2nd Day, p. 28. [2] Hansard, vol. 485, col. 994.

in particular, facilities for divorce should be abolished or, at least, greatly restricted.[1]

Most witnesses, however, wished only to maintain the *status quo*, and agreed with the more restrained comment of the Bar Council :

> The utmost caution should be exercised in approaching any suggestion for extending the grounds for divorce or nullity so as to avoid nourishing in those who are married or contemplating marriage, the idea that divorce is to be had for the asking, or that there is nothing wrong or disadvantageous in it for themselves or their children morally or financially.[2]

Whatever financial disadvantages of increased divorce may have been suffered by the lay public, none has been inflicted on practitioners at the Divorce Bar. Perhaps with this in mind, Lord Morton underlined the selfless disinterestedness of their evidence :

> That suggestion, I suppose, is entirely contrary to the pecuniary interests of the bar?—Yes.[3]

The sincerity of those members of the Divorce Bar who gave evidence to the Commission ought not to have been impugned by this unhappy question. No doubt the evidence of the divorce bar concerning the damaging consequences of Divorce Will command all the respect that would be accorded to the views of teetotal publicans on the evils of drink. But only the simple-minded will accept Lord Morton's suggestion that the Bar's opposition to an extension of the grounds for divorce is necessarily contrary to their pecuniary interests. If divorce by consent became a general ground, and jurisdiction were transferred from the High Court, where only the Bar has right of audience, to county courts, where solicitors also have right of audience, the resulting simplification of suits and procedure would be likely to reduce the aggregate

[1] Evidence, 7th–8th Day, p. 200. [2] *ibid.*, 2nd Day, p. 28.
[3] *ibid.*, p. 45, Q. 319.

income of the Divorce Bar. The Chairman of the Commission introduced the criterion of financial interest as a test of the Bar's evidence and it is, therefore, necessary (though in the opinion of the author irrelevant and insulting) to insist that the immediate financial interest of the Divorce Bar is bound up with the retention both of the High Court's jurisdiction and of the matrimonial offence as the basis of divorce law.

"Institutionalist" views were invariably associated with a pessimistic assessment of the many changes affecting the family during the last fifty years. Many agreed with Mrs. Coombs, a voluntary social worker interested in marriage reconciliation, who told the Commission:

> I find both husbands and wives lacking in a sense of duty and responsibility to each other and to their children. It is hard to point out to them that, if love is growing cold, duty must take its place, for it is always a new thought to them . . .[1]

Mrs. Fisher, giving evidence on behalf of the Mothers' Union, offered a more comprehensive explanation of the dangers now threatening the family.

> . . . the family itself is being squeezed out in our national set-up by two great influences, the one collectivism, and the other the exact opposite, individualism. Members of families are caught up into great groupings—trade unions, educational groups, youth movements and women's movements—and these groupings demand a loyalty which very often conflicts with the loyalty to the family as a whole. We believe that that is having a detrimental effect on family life to a very marked extent. At the same time, there is individualism. Each member of the family is treated very much as an individual and claims individual attention and relief, and thereby loses a great deal of that corporate sense of unity and responsibility which used to be such a great feature of family life.[2]

[1] Evidence, 9th Day, p. 278. [2] *ibid.*, 3rd–4th Day, p. 84, Q. 780.

" Institutionalists " not only deplore attempts to extend the grounds of divorce but also the break-up of the mid-Victorian family code.

The conflict between the " abolitionist " and " institutionalist " view of the effects of the present divorce law on the administration of justice are thus reflected in their opposing judgments of its social value. For the " abolitionist," the sanctity of marriage and the stability of the family are imperilled because the law has too little regard for human need ; for " institutionalists," they are endangered because the law fails to safeguard the integrity of institutions. In the one case, the social good is held to require divorce by consent ; in the other, either the strict maintenance of present grounds for, or the total abolition of, divorce. In so far as these conflicting views derive from belief in a divinely ordained, inherent sanctity of indissoluble marriage or from an assumption of the paramount importance of earthly happiness, they cannot be reconciled by rational discussion. Fortunately, however, they were not presented to the Commission in such terms. " Abolitionist " and " institutionalist " each grounded their case on generalisations concerning the actual social consequences of divorce. Such assertions must be in accord with empirical evidence. If not, they are either false or mere conjectures. The dispute is thus reduced to one over matters of fact. The only relevant issue is the effect of divorce on attitudes to marriage and on the stability of the family.

Historical reasons for rejecting the general " institutionalist " presupposition about the changing structure and functions of the family as a misunderstanding of the past and a consequential misinterpretation of the present, have already been outlined in Chapter III. It is here necessary to examine only their more detailed conclusions about the decline in respect for marriage, the divorce-mindedness of the population, and the great increase in the number of divorces predicted as a necessary consequence of the introduction of divorce by consent.

" Respect for the sanctity of marriage " is a concept charged with different meanings for different people. For some, it means " respect for the sanctity of divinely ordained, indissoluble marriage." So defined, it is a truism that public respect for marriage has declined *pari passu* with the decay of religious beliefs during the twentieth century. The assertion of the National Marriage Guidance Council that " the existence of comparatively easy divorce does tend to lessen respect for marriage " [1] follows necessarily from its conviction that marriage is " a divine institution and not merely a social invention." [2] The Council added a supererogatory comment, representative of this point of view, to its Memorandum.

> Indeed, the modern tendency to regard marriage as nothing but a legalised physical relationship seems to us not only inadequate but destructive of its deepest realities.[2]

Nobody suggested to the Commission that marriage either is or ought to be " nothing but a legalised physical relationship," and the Memorandum fails to disclose who does hold this unusual view. Perhaps the National Marriage Guidance Council, like other witnesses, has succumbed to the modern tendency to misrepresent the opinions about marriage of those with whom it disagrees. For those who regard marriage as a secular institution, respect implies simply an acceptance of the personal and social responsibilities inherent in a voluntary relationship between adults entered into with the intention of permanency for the purpose of mutual, spiritual, and sexual comfort and the rearing of children. A declining respect for the secular institution must have resulted in a general disillusionment with marriage and a refusal to accept, even temporarily, any of its responsibilities. Some

[1] Evidence, 5th Day, p. 109. [2] *ibid.*, p. 106.

of the advantages of marriage are today easily acquired without assuming any of its responsibilities. Sexual satisfactions " in these days of lowered sexual standards, when promiscuity is rife, even amongst women of an educated and respectable class "[1] are no longer restricted to the home or the brothel. Women today face fewer difficulties in making a career or in finding a job outside marriage. In spite of these considerations which are usually cited as factors promoting the decay of respect for marriage, the institution has never been so popular. No " institutionalist " witness attempted to explain why a higher proportion of the population is now married than at any time during the last hundred years, or why the marriage rate amongst divorced persons is higher than that for any other marital condition.[2] People are undoubtedly in flight from church and chapel, but they have not become refugees from marriage. The statistical evidence, far from supporting the theory of declining respect, suggests rather that enthusiasm for marriage has increased as disillusionment with Christianity has spread.

" Institutionalists " invariably asserted, and " abolitionists " denied, that easier and cheaper divorce has resulted in a divorce-minded population. Divorce has ceased to be a matrimonial remedy available only to one social strata ; it is now generalised throughout the community. In one sense, " divorce-mindedness " is thus simply an ugly description of recent processes by which working people have come in divorce, as in other ways, to adopt the behaviour of their financial betters. But the phrase is customarily loaded with a different and deeper meaning. The Church of England was sure that

> Each divorce does nothing at all for the national life but to demonstrate once more that if troubles arise in married life, the natural thing is to get a divorce and marry again. This belief has already

[1] Evidence, 37th Day, p. 938, from the Memorandum of Mrs. Roberta Holt Wilson. [2] For the statistical evidence, see ch. IV, pp. 39–40.

> soaked deeply into the minds of our people and not least into the minds of young people and children.[1]

Many witnesses explored the minds of young people; the Church of England, however, was the only body sufficiently enterprising to extend the investigation to children's attitudes to divorce. The results of such research differed. The Women's Co-operative Guild found that

> . . . young people are becoming more marriage conscious, and there is a genuine wish on the part of young people to make their marriage lasting. . . . The very fact of the adverse publicity on unhappy marriages has made (them) more conscious of the responsibilities of marriage . . .[2]

The Bar Council thought divorce-mindedness the second most important cause of marriage breakdown and told the Commission, with the professional caution natural in those trained to sift evidence, that

> It is much more difficult to give factual evidence of (divorce-mindedness), and our opinion is more of that intuitive kind which comes from the necessary probing of great numbers of matrimonial suits.[3]

Forensic intuition is a novel technique of social investigation with some apparent limitations. The Bar Council did not explain the intuitive methods by which it assessed the attitudes of the unmarried, and the 90-odd per cent. of the married, population whose behaviour never comes to be probed in chambers as petitioners or respondents in matrimonial suits. Other witnesses similarly paraded the unverified and contradictory results of their "experience" before the Commission. They established that different "experiences" lead

[1] Evidence, 6th Day, p. 144.

[2] *ibid.*, 5th Day, pp. 100–101, Qs. 936–937.

[3] *ibid.*, 2nd Day, p. 28. Counsel's information is derived only from what the client tells him, and that usually only from the solicitor's written instructions and the proof of the client's evidence. "Probing" seems a highly coloured description of the process.

different people to differing opinions about other people's attitudes to marriage and divorce. On this point only two witnesses submitted memoranda based on factual study. The suggestive Memorandum of Mr. T. K. P. Barrett, Director of the John Hilton Bureau of the *News of the World*, analysed a thousand letters, sampled from readers' correspondence about their matrimonial problems, received by that newspaper in one week of December 1951.[1] Mr. Barrett makes one significant comment.

> I should like to draw attention to one pleasurable impression. It is the degree of tolerance and self-criticism shown by most of these invisible witnesses. These are not people reckless of social consequences, indifferent to the sufferings of others, unaware of ethical motivation. Indeed, the respect for the conventional moral code which is shown is often the most painful factor to the correspondent.[2]

Dr. Eliot Slater and Mrs. Moya Woodside summarised for the Commission the results of their joint study of marriage amongst two hundred working-class couples in London, a group of neurotics and a control group. In her Memorandum, Mrs. Woodside said,

> Young working-class people entering on marriage today are no longer content with the patterns of the past. Their standards are higher, they are better educated, new worlds of experience have been presented to them through cinema and radio.[3]

She was questioned by the Chairman :

LORD MORTON : When you say " their standards are higher," are you speaking of the standard of comfort and enjoyment which they expect from life or their standards of duty and conduct ?

[1] Evidence, 16th–17th Day. Mr. Barrett explains (pp. 459–461), the purpose and limitations of his interesting study. He deserved more thanks than he received for his laborious and public spirited research.

[2] *ibid.*, p. 461.

[3] *ibid.*, p. 437. The research was published as *Patterns of Marriage* (1951).

> Mrs. W.: I think it applies to both. That was derived from my experience when doing this interviewing. I got the picture of the life of their parents . . . and then they told me about their own lives and it was such a contrast. They would say, "That might have been all right for our parents, but we are not going to bring up our children like that." [1]

It is noteworthy that the conclusions of Mr. Geoffrey Gorer's *Exploring English Character* (1956), the only attempt to study English attitudes towards such matters as home life, love and sex, and marriage by the empirical method of questionnaires, point in the same direction as the memoranda of Mr. Barrett and Dr. Slater and Mrs. Woodside. Mr. Gorer's material yielded two comments relevant to the dispute between "abolitionist" and "institutionalist." It seems, first, that social attitudes do not reflect one of the underlying assumptions of the legal doctrine of the matrimonial offence.

> It does seem fairly certain that an English man or woman's "honour" is no longer involved in the chastity or fidelity of his or her spouse, as would appear to have been the case in the historical past, and still occurs in a number of societies today. For the English majority "honour" would appear to inhere entirely in one's own character and behaviour; and . . . there is at least as much tendency to blame oneself for a spouse's dereliction as to blame or punish the offending spouse.[2]

Secondly, Mr. Gorer concludes his two chapters on marriage by stressing

> . . . the great importance for English men and women of the institution of marriage and the seriousness with which they consider it. It is marriage itself which is important, not, I think, love or sexual gratification; and marriage is living together, making a home together, making a life together, and raising children. Perhaps even more for English men than for English

[1] Evidence, p. 438, Q. 3575.
[2] *ibid.*, pp. 154–155.

women, parenthood is the greatest joy and greatest responsibility of adult life.[1]

"Institutionalists," it seems, view their fellow citizens in the sickly light of their own censoriousness. The accusation of widespread divorce-mindedness may confidently be dismissed as an impertinent conceit.

"Abolitionists" think that divorce is a symptom not a cause of broken homes; they therefore regard the number of divorces as measuring nothing more significant than the number of divorces.[2] Once the conjectures that easy divorce warps the true conception of marriage and creates a divorce-minded population are rejected, the only relevant social consideration is the incidence of broken homes.[3] The introduction of divorce by consent and divorce after a period of separation would inevitably result in at least a temporary, and probably large, increase in the number of divorces. Such a rise in the divorce rate would neither stimulate nor reflect any change in marriage breakdowns; it would represent the *de jure* dissolution of marriages which had existed *de facto* only in text-books of theology and in legal theory. The fear that some marriages would be dissolved for frivolous reasons would certainly be justified; an alteration in the divorce laws will not reduce the number of busybodies who are always convinced of their neighbours' frivolity. On the other hand, the present system presents no obstacles to frivolous people who wish irresponsibly to dissolve their marriages. No doubt with this in mind the Church of England's statistical spokesman, Canon Hugh Warner, predicted to the Commission in 1952 "that as a

[1] Gorer, *op. cit.*, p. 161.

[2] Some "institutionalists" have attempted a statistical proof that easier divorce leads to an increase in the number of broken homes; e.g., Canon Hugh Warner, a witness for the Church of England (Evidence, 6th Day, p. 151, Q. 1191) and Mr. J. E. S. Simon (7th–8th Day, p. 200). Their conclusions have been examined and rejected on p. 54, fn. 2.

[3] The impossibility of obtaining a reliable statistical estimate of broken homes is explained on p. 50 *et seq.*

result of legal aid the divorce figures are likely to soar away up in the next few years." [1] Between 1952 and 1954 the number of petitions filed fell by 5,500. The anxieties of the serious concerning their neighbour's levity may safely be discounted.

Parents have an overriding obligation to give their children the love and security to which the young and defenceless have an irreducible right. One of the most encouraging changes in family life has been the transition from Victorian emphasis on the duties which children owed their parents to present stress on the duties of parents to children. Some parental duties can be, and are rightly, legally enforced, but legislation can no more secure parental than marital affection. Love is a function of capacity. Married people who are driven to seek personal happiness or to escape misery outside their homes may have lost their joint capacity to fulfil the exacting requirements of parenthood.[2] In such cruel

[1] Evidence, 6th Day, p. 151, Q. 1191.

[2] In 1954, the parents of some 36,000 children were divorced (The Registrar-General's *Statistical Review of England and Wales for 1954*, p. 77, Table P4.) There is no published information from which the ages of these children can be deduced, but the Report of the Morton Commission states (Cd. 9678 (1956), p. 103) that "each year in Great Britain some 20,000 children under sixteen are affected by the divorce of their parents." The Report neither discloses the source of this estimate nor states the year to which it refers, but, presumably, it is 1954. If so, some 18,800 decrees absolute, relating to marriages with children, separated the parents of some 20,000 children under sixteen. There is no apparent reason why information as to the ages of children of divorced parents should not be published. Every petition must state the number of children of the marriage sought to be dissolved and the dates of their birth. At present the Divorce Registry, the source of the Registrar-General's statistics, extracts from petitions only the number of children ; the additional labour of adding the age of birth would not seem unduly heavy. The paucity of information caused difficulties for some witness. The Professor of Child Health in the University of London, for example, told the Commission in 1953 (38th Day, p. 942), "It is very difficult to get figures that are satisfactory, but in 1947 some figures were published, although I cannot, I am sorry to say, find out now by whom." This comment is typical of many witnesses' carelessness as to matters of fact. The figures to which Professor Moncrieff referred were, and are, published in the Registrar-General's annual *Reviews*. Typical also was Professor Moncrieff's failure to suggest to the Commission that the publication of more informative statistics is important.

situations the epithets of blame and irresponsibility are as misplaced as an accusation of cowardice against a man who fails to save a drowning child because he cannot swim. Sentimental moralising is an inappropriate though popular attitude to the effects of divorce on children.

This problem poses a dilemma discussed at great length by witnesses to the Commission. Is it more or less damaging to children either to live in a home where, at best, there is no affection between the parents and, at worst, constant open friction ; or to face the consequences of a broken home in the care of one parent ? The National Association for Mental Health [1] and the British Medical Association [2] both emphasised to the Commission the complete lack of that scientific and statistical knowledge by which alone this unhappy dilemma can be resolved. Nevertheless, the absence of scientific knowledge did not deter many witnesses from affirming strong opinions. In their evidence the Churches [3] endorsed the view of the Mothers' Union.

> We are led to believe that almost any home is better than none, and that even children who come from quarrelsome homes, or homes which in other ways are not good, have a greater stability, a better life, than those who have come out of a really broken home, a home broken by divorce.[4]

Three teachers' organisations gave similar evidence. The National Union of Teachers submitted a Memorandum,

[1] Evidence, 7th–8th Day. " The Association, basing its present remarks on the evidence of child guidance workers and child psychiatrists, is unable to state authoritatively which of two alternatives is more damaging to the mental health (present or future) of children," p. 181.

[2] *ibid.*, 6th Day. Dr. Doris Odlum said : ". . . we have tried as far as we could by enquiring of child guidance clinics and other sources to get some data on it. . . . There is unfortunately no research with any kind of statistical evidence on these subjects," p. 175, Qs. 1338 and 1342.

[3] *ibid.*, For the Roman Church, 16th–17th Day, p. 429, Q. 3515 ; for the Methodist Church, 3rd–4th Day, p. 72, Q. 647. The Church of England makes no specific comment on this issue, though it must be presumed that the Mothers' Union reflects church opinion.

[4] *ibid.*, 3rd–4th Day, p. 83.

and gave oral evidence, of which a fair summary is the statement that the Union consistently maintained its approval of happy homes. The evidential value of the Union's opinions may be judged by the following paragraph from its Memorandum :

> Many children in residential schools or homes for maladjusted children are there as a result of broken homes. The following incident reported by a teacher in one of these homes is an illustration. Three fifteen-year-old girls coming to say good night saw a photograph of a wedding in a newspaper. One of them remarked, "Don't you ever get married, will you ?" When asked, "Why ?" the second replied, "Because your husband may be unfaithful to you." The third girl added, "Men are all the same—never trust them." The teacher remembered that the three were children of divorced parents.[1]

The exegesis on this baffling parable which Mr. Griffith, of the National Union of Teachers provided for Lord Walker and Lord Morton is the only amusing incident in one and a half million words of evidence.

> LORD WALKER : I was rather struck with the form of the observation, "Do not marry, your husband may be unfaithful to you." It was not, "Do not marry, your marriage may be dissolved." I am not sure what the point of that is ?
>
> MR. GRIFFITH : The girls had a distorted view of things.
>
> LORD W. : You think that is the implication of it ?
>
> MR. G. : Yes.
>
> LORD MORTON : I thought the clue lay in the last sentence : "The teacher remembered that the three were children of divorced parents." It was an illustration of what sometimes happens when children have parents who have been divorced. Is not that the point of it ?
>
> MR. G. : Yes.

[1] Evidence, 14th–15th Day, p. 401.

LORD W.: The girls are really saying: "Your husband may be unfaithful and you may have to divorce him?"

MR. G.: I think the illustration is intended to convey...[1]

The Headmasters' Conference explained that:

> Broadly speaking, and stating the principle in simple terms, we consider that a real home, even if it is not a good one, is better for a child than none.[2]

This somewhat ambiguous principle was prefaced in the Memorandum with a laconic statement which hardly inspires confidence in the Headmasters' evidence.

> We have not felt it necessary to obtain figures of the number of children of divorced parents at the schools of which we are headmasters. The size of the problem, and its gravity, are apparent without these. Nor have we compiled any statistics, such as, for example, the proportion of children whose school career seems to show evidence of moral or mental instability and who come from "broken homes," or the proportion of the children of divorced parents whose moral or mental development gives cause for concern.[3]

The Association of Headmistresses, however, did supply the Commission with the statistical evidence despised by their male colleagues.

> The Joint Committee of the Four Secondary Associations has collected evidence from which it appears that in the 283 grammar schools under review 62·7 per cent. of about 500 cases of maladjustment, severe enough to be referred to child guidance clinics, can be attributed to "difficult home relationships," ranging from subtle tensions and jealousies to clear-cut difficulties such as broken homes, a second marriage, death of one or both parents, or adoption.[4]

The Headmistresses relied on the material in the above paragraph to support their heavy emphasis on broken homes as sources of maladjustment amongst their pupils.

[1] Evidence, 14th–15th Day, p. 408, Qs. 3387–3390.
[2] *ibid.*, 12th–13th Day, p. 365. [3] *ibid.* [4] *ibid.*, p. 375.

The size and gravity of the problem became apparent under the probing of Lord Keith, the only Commissioner who consistently distinguished between fact and opinion in his questions to witnesses. Of the children in the 283 schools covered by this "survey," 0·5 per cent. were sufficiently maladjusted to be referred to child guidance clinics and 0·1 per cent. so referred were the products of broken homes.[1] Teachers' views have been considered in some detail because Lord Morton told a witness that Commissioners were "very impressed" with the experience "of teachers . . . who have come to us on the subject. It is most devastating."[2]

The experience of religious organisations and of school-teachers pointed to the desirability of keeping children even in actively quarrelsome homes. The experience of doctors and psychiatrists, who stressed the lack of firm knowledge, and of bodies like the Association of Children's Officers[3] and the National Association of Probation Officers who deal directly with the results of broken homes, suggested the wisdom of removing children from such an atmosphere. Dr. Doris Odlum, a witness on behalf of the British Medical Association was asked whether a bad home is better or worse than a broken home.

> We have come to the conclusion . . . that the quarrelsome and unhappy home, on the whole, has a worse effect on the child than the home that is broken provided the child then goes to the parent with whom it has the more happy relationship.[4]

[1] Evidence, 12th–13th Day, p. 379, Qs. 3028–3037 and especially p. 381, Q. 3085. I have re-worked Lord Keith's calculation (p. 379) in accordance with the further information contained on p. 381. It will be observed that Miss Catnach's ("our authority on this matter") replies to Commissioners' questions were frequently misleading as she appeared to misunderstand the very limited meaning of the figures she was quoting. It is comforting that the Association of Headmistresses is not above, even in evidence submitted to a Royal Commission, an error (Q. 3085) in simple arithmetic. Perhaps the Headmasters' Conference was wise to run no risks.

[2] *ibid.*, 33rd Day, p. 846, Q. 8139.

[3] *ibid.*, 14th–15th Day, p. 395, Qs. 3204–3208 and p. 397, Qs. 3235–3239.

[4] *ibid.*, 6th Day, p. 175, Q. 1338.

In reply to the same question, Mr. H. W. Bird, representing the National Association of Probation Officers, said,

> . . . from my own experience the home in which there is continual friction is in the long run much more damaging to the children than a home in which there has been an outright break. In the latter case the child has a chance to adjust himself to the fact that one of the parents has gone, but where there is continual friction his loyalties are so strained that the consequences on the child are more serious.[1]

The conflict between " institutionalists " and " abolitionists " runs through this discussion as it runs through all other aspects of divorce. " Institutionalists " are forced by their presuppositions to assert the benefits to children of maintaining homes intact whatever the relations between parents. The weight of informed opinion is against them, as is a simple consideration curiously ignored by all witnesses. As some two-thirds of all divorced persons marry again, the chances that a child of divorced parents may achieve emotional security in a new home are high. The effects of divorce on children, though grievous, are frequently exaggerated.[2]

[1] Evidence, 11th Day, p. 338, Q. 2670.

[2] The evidence of Professor Moncrieff (38th–41st Day, p. 942) provides an instructive example. " One can scarcely imagine anything worse than to live in an atmosphere where father and mother are quarrelling all the time, and it is sometimes [*sic*] said that it is better for such a marriage to break up to give the children relief from such an atmosphere. I think this is rather a dangerous question . . . because there is no guarantee whatever that if divorce then takes place the children will get such relief as is promised them. My experience is that they will go on to an even more insecure life where they are passed from pillar to post, from relative to relative, from school to school, and this suggestion that it is far better for the children for the divorce to go through because they will be happier afterwards is just not borne out, at any rate by my personal experience." The " personal experience " of a paediatrician with a long experience as Chairman of a moral welfare committee for children is likely to be biased, though his account of the experience of the children of divorced parents doubtless is true of some. It cannot, however, be regarded as representative in circumstances in which two-thirds of such parents re-marry. The problem of these unhappy children is serious and difficult but, as with other social problems, its solution or palliation depends on methodical description and accurate definition ; hyperbole obfuscates

The rehabilitation of children of broken homes depends in part on the ease with which a new home can be established. Children would have nothing to lose, and probably much to gain, from easier and speedier facilities for divorce.

There was wide agreement, even amongst witnesses who differed profoundly on other matters, that present procedures for safeguarding the interests of children involved in divorce suits is unsatisfactory. If parents have agreed (probably collusively) on the custody of the children, the court will accept their decision ; without such agreement it must make a decision, often not having seen both parents, on the basis of affidavits drawn up for the sole purpose of securing a verdict for one or other of the contending parties. There was general approval for the proposal that the court should be directly responsible for looking after children's interests in all cases. This could be achieved by extending the experiment, following the Final Report [1] of the Denning Committee, of appointing a court welfare officer to the Divorce Division of the High Court in London. This official has so far been largely concerned with interviewing parents and seeing children in cases where there have been disputes about custody or access. Many witnesses proposed the establishment of a system of trained court welfare officers attached to all courts exercising divorce jurisdiction, and charged with the duty of reporting to the court in all cases involving children. It is noteworthy that this urgent need, and the inadequacy of present conciliation machinery, were the only issues before the Commission which secured the broad assent of nearly all witnesses.

On other, major matters affecting jurisdiction and the administration of the law witnesses remained irreconcilably divided between " abolitionist " and " institutionalist " views. Since 1878 there have been two systems of matrimonial jurisdiction in England ; one in

[1] Cd. 7204, 1947.

the High Court, the other in the magistrates' courts. In 1920, Parliament provided that certain types of divorce case could be heard at a limited number of Assize towns. The London barristers and solicitors who had " a strong financial interest in centralised justice "[1] strenuously opposed attempts to make the divorce court more accessible. Such opposition was aided by, and partly rationalised into, two firmly held beliefs. On the one hand, it was held that divorce jurisdiction, being concerned with so important a matter as the dissolution of marriage, had to be restricted to a narrow circle of specialists in order to secure uniformity of principle. On the other, it was said that the discretion of the divorce court to condone the matrimonial guilt of an innocent spouse could not properly be exercised by judges primarily engaged on other work, notwithstanding the commonplace exercise of discretion in all civil and criminal courts. " Common law judges may interpret the law so that men are hanged or imprisoned or set free, trade unions may be crippled or exalted, the whole range of civil liberty may grow greater or less through precedent upon precedent, but apparently ' discretion ' in divorce was too important for the public welfare for it to be entrusted to such unreliable judges."[2] The pressure of poor suitors during and after Hitler's war began to undermine this " grotesque edifice," and a series of *ad hoc* expedients by which Queen's Counsel and county court judges sit as Special Commissioners in Divorce, have resulted in decentralisation of the divorce work of the High Court. Magistrates throughout England and Wales have, for the last eighty years, exercised a jurisdiction in matrimonial affairs in many respects similar to that of the High Court, without the benefit of a close guild to ensure uniformity of principle.[3] Magistrates

[1] R. M. Jackson, *op. cit.*, p. 50. For the substance of this paragraph, I have relied on pp. 50–51 of Dr. Jackson's admirably lucid account of the jurisdiction of the High Court.

[2] *ibid.*, p. 51.

[3] The similarities are summarised on p. 53, fn. 2.

can order a man to pay maintenance to his separated wife on the grounds of his adultery, desertion, and persistent cruelty, or by reason of finding him a habitual drunkard or drug addict. They may have to take evidence and decide upon any defence he may raise arising from his wife's matrimonial conduct, especially upon proof of her adultery. These proceedings do not break the *vinculum matrimonii*, though they frequently have the same practical, and more damaging social, consequences.

Against this background of experience many witnesses before the Commission proposed extensive changes in jurisdiction. The character of suggested reforms differed as between "institutionalist" and "abolitionist" opinion, and reflected the familiar dispute. The major premiss of "institutionalist's" insistence that divorce jurisdiction should remain exclusively with the High Court was neatly summarised by the Denning Committee.

> In our opinion the attitude of the community towards the status of marriage is much influenced by the way in which divorce is effected. If there is a careful and dignified proceeding such as obtains in the High Court for the undoing of a marriage, then quite unconsciously the people will have a more respectful view of the marriage tie and of the marriage status than they would if divorce were effected informally in an inferior court.[1]

Neither the Denning Committee nor those who accept its restatement of the Gorell Commission's view have explained the nature of the unconscious processes by which legal actions in the High Court influence the attitude to marriage of "the people." A casual visitor to the divorce court in London might feel there had been an element of exaggeration in the Committee's description of its sittings as "dignified proceedings."

The Bar Council strongly urged the retention of High

[1] Cd. 6945, 1946, p. 7.

Court jurisdiction and the speedy replacement of Special Commissioners by the appointment of additional High Court judges. There were two main considerations behind this recommendation. Firstly,

> We regard it as essential that there should be uniformity so far as possible in the high standard of judicial ability. Further, we regard it as important that the standard of presentation of cases defended or undefended should be kept uniformly high, and Bench and Bar in this respect are mutually educative.[1]

Secondly, the Council emphasised the ritual impressiveness of High Court judges.

> Dissolution of marriage is a most important step in the life of any individual. It represents the rupture of a family unit and brings new factors into play in the lives not only of husband and wife but also of children. . . . It may not always be possible for a hearing to take place in impressive surroundings, but the presence of a High Court judge does, to some extent, offset the unsuitability of the place where he may be required to sit.[1]

On this argument, High Court judges would be even more usefully employed as celebrants of marriage in Registry Offices. The Bar Council suggested only minor changes in the jurisdiction and administration of magistrates' courts. Mr. J. E. S. Simon outlined [2] another, radical approach. As an extreme " institutionalist " who would prefer to abolish all facilities for divorce, he yielded nothing to the Bar Council in the importance he attached to retaining the jurisdiction of the High Court but wished, for this reason, to strip magistrates' courts of their important powers in matrimonial matters. Under his interesting proposal a two-tier system of " family courts " would be established. The Divorce Division of the High Court would be renamed the Matrimonial (or

[1] Evidence, 2nd Day, p. 39. [2] *ibid.*, 7th–8th Day, pp. 202–203.

Family) Division, exercising its present jurisdiction in defended cases and custody, and hearing appeals. The second tier would consist of subordinate courts of matrimonial jurisdiction with the status of county courts. They would try undefended suits and take over the existing matrimonial jurisdiction of magistrates' courts. Mr. Simon wished to transfer matrimonial jurisdiction for two main reasons. First,

> It is arguable that, so far as matrimonial causes are concerned, courts of summary jurisdiction are too accessible; that it does not conduce to a proper sense of the sanctity of the married state that disputes between husband and wife are so easily brought before them. . . . It has been argued that these courts represent as against the High Court a valuable distinction between proceedings for separation and proceedings for divorce, i.e. between matters which do not affect status, which may be undertaken lightly and easily, and those which do affect status, which are to be clothed with dignity and solemnity. From the point of view of public welfare this is a false distinction; the real distinction is between a married life which is preserved and a married life which has broken down. It should be the aim of law and of the procedure of justice to preserve not merely the matrimonial status, but the matrimonial cohabitation.[1]

This is implicit in Mr. Simon's "institutionalist" premisses and, as against the Bar Council's willingness to leave the matrimonial jurisdiction of magistrates' courts untouched, has the great merit of logical consistency. His second objection was, however, shared by many "abolitionists."

> Though their decisions may have effects which may reach far beyond the immediate order of the court and may ultimately affect status, even disputed cases are tried in a summary manner. Courts vary greatly, but the cases are on the whole tried with less care . . . than

[1] Evidence, p. 202.

matrimonial causes in the High Court. In some cases orders seem automatically to be made in favour of a wife.[1]

"Abolitionists" who stressed the unsuitability for matrimonial work of courts which deal with a heterogeneous mass of minor criminal offences and other matters, also criticised the High Court. The Haldane Society, for example, thought that

(*a*) The procedure is involved and expensive.

(*b*) The divorce and assize courts are distant and unfamiliar places to most people.

(*c*) The atmosphere of the old ecclesiastical courts still lingers in the divorce courts.[2]

Thus the very reasons which lead "institutionalists" to prefer the jurisdiction of the High Court are stressed by some "abolitionists" as grounds for abolishing it. The Haldane Society proposed that the jurisdiction in matrimonial matters now exercised by the High Court and by magistrates' courts should be transferred to county courts.

> At present county court judges hear divorce cases as commissioners of the divorce court, and are proving competent and equal to the task. The next logical step is to end this compromise and to give county courts jurisdiction in all matrimonial causes thereby enabling cases to be decided under the speedy, cheap and simple county court procedure. County courts are comparatively easily accessible places to most people, and they would become very adequate matrimonial tribunals by the addition to their staffs of court welfare officers.[3]

[1] Evidence, p. 202.

[2] *ibid.*, 16th–17th Day, p. 450.

[3] *ibid.* This proposal was originally made in 1948. When the Haldane Society gave evidence in 1952 it thought the country's financial situation did not permit the cost of transferring jurisdiction at that time. The Society maintained, however, the long-term desirability of establishing the county courts as "Family Courts."

Some "abolitionists," on the other hand, were satisfied that the value of trying matrimonial cases before lay men and women more than outweighed the disadvantages of procedure in magistrates' courts. Mr. R. S. W. Pollard, Chairman of the Marriage Law Reform Society and himself chairman of a magistrates' matrimonial court, proposed the radical transfer to magistrates of all divorce jurisdiction with the exception of nullity proceedings and questions of property rights. Magistrates, he pointed out,

> now make orders which really differ from divorce only in the fact that the parties may not re-marry. Their staff has great experience of matrimonial cases and they have good machinery capable of further improvement . . . for the enforcement of their orders. More important still, they have the services of probation officers (who) . . . constantly carry out investigations for magistrates on the parties' means or on the circumstances relating to the children. Moreover, to the probation office comes a stream of applicants for advice and often for help in reconciliation.[1]

The many proposals before the Commission for changes in jurisdiction and administration ranged between, and combined different parts of, those outlined above. The essential question in this administrative debate is not the particular scaffolding which should support the law, but what law should be supported. If the matrimonial offence is retained then a system, such as that proposed by Mr. Simon, would consolidate varying jurisdictions and remove many anomalies. If the matrimonial offence is rejected, the system established a century ago must be abolished for the reasons stated by a great master of the law, Sir Frederick Pollock.

[1] Evidence, 9th Day, p. 262. The Marriage Law Reform Society did not adopt its Chairman's proposals. It suggested the transfer of divorce jurisdiction from the High Court to county courts (*ibid.*, p. 236) though in the London area to the Queen's Bench Division (pp. 245–247) and the retention of magistrates' jurisdiction (pp. 236–239).

For some time I have thought that the cause of discontent with English jurisdiction in matrimonial causes lies deeper than controversies over the grounds for divorce or separation. When our divorce court was created its method and procedure were modelled, rather as a matter of course, on those of our civil courts in matters of ordinary litigation.

The business of the court is to do justice on the claims and defences raised by the parties ; it has little power of initiation or inquiry, very little of intervention. At most it can find occasion to make suggestions for a settlement.

Such is the frame of our civil procedure, and quite a good one for dealing with men's disputes on matters of trade and property and their individual and collective relations as neighbours and fellow-citizens.

The application of that scheme to family relations and to marriage in particular is, in my humble opinion, all wrong.

A better analogy may be found in the paternal jurisdiction of the old Court of Chancery over its wards, exercised to this day by the judges of the Chancery Division, to the general satisfaction of all concerned.

A court for matrimonial causes should have conciliation for its first object, should have the carriage of the case in its own hands and should be entrusted with wide discretion. It should have power to grant a final decree of divorce when, after full inquiry and consideration, reconciliation proves impracticable, or to make a decree *nisi* with a discretionary term of anything from three to twelve months.

I see no reason why a court equipped with such powers should not have jurisdiction to allow divorce by consent, but only by decree nisi, giving a reasonable time for a last chance of reconciliation.[1]

This chapter has traced the main threads running through the evidence submitted to the Commission. The Minutes of Evidence—the ten dozen papers prepared by

[1] From a letter to the *Daily Telegraph* (14th November 1936) printed as a supplemental note to the Memorandum submitted by Mr. Claude Mullins (Evidence, 12th–13th Day, p. 384).

individuals and organisations and the transcript of forty-one days questioning of witnesses—leave one impression. There is vast and detailed testimony of witnesses' opinions about other witnesses' opinions, endless conjectures about such crucial issues as the social consequences of divorce and attitudes to marriage, but, as to matters of fact by which alone the assertions of controversialists can be tested, there is scarcely ten pages of evidence. Once a reader has discovered a witness's view concerning the doctrine of the matrimonial offence, he can predict with confidence what that witness will say on all the important matters within the Commission's terms of reference. A reader will have learnt, too, that most witnesses approached their task with the Bellman's conviction that " What I tell you three times is true." The Morton Commission's search for evidence has produced one of the most impressive collections of unsupported cliché ever subsidised by the tax-payer.

CHAPTER VI

THE MORTON COMMISSION II

THE FUNDAMENTAL POSTULATES OF THE REPORT

THIS chapter does not summarise or discuss the many detailed recommendations of the Morton Commission. Its only purpose is to define and clarify the underlying presuppositions of the Report, and thus to assess its contribution to our understanding of contemporary problems of marriage and divorce.

Royal Commissions are professedly appointed to investigate and assemble knowledge about urgent and difficult subjects of public policy.[1] "We are unanimous," reported the Balfour Committee on the Procedure of Royal Commissions, "in believing that the appointment of Royal Commissions is useful for the elucidation of difficult subjects which are attracting public attention, but in regard to which the information is not sufficiently accurate to form a preliminary to legislation."[2] Since their heyday in the middle of the nineteenth century the functions of Royal Commissions have changed. Then they were largely a practical device for providing governments with information essential for public administration in a society facing, for the first time, the manifold consequences of expanding industrialism. Today governments command a multiplicity of permanent agencies providing a continuous flow of statistical and general

[1] The useful book of H. M. Clokie and J. W. Robinson, *Royal Commissions of Inquiry* (Stanford University Press, 1937) discusses the history, formal structure and procedure of Royal Commissions. There is no adequate study of their composition and personnel.

[2] (Cd. 5235), 1910, p. 6.

intelligence. With this development, the Royal Commissions of recent years have served different purposes. Some have been appointed by Cabinets seeking expert advice on urgent, controversial issues. Others have helped to strengthen a government's hand in tackling an awkward problem by making recommendations embodying the authority of a representative group of men and women possessing special knowledge. Occasionally Ministries have resorted to Royal Commissions as panaceas for subjects which cannot be ignored and, because they arouse emotional or religious fervours cutting across party lines, are embarrassing for politicians.

The troublesome private members' Bills of Mrs. Eirene White and Lord Mancroft [1] were the immediate occasion of the Morton Commission's appointment. Lawyers

[1] The Commission's terms of reference included the duty "to consider whether any alteration should be made in the law prohibiting marriage with certain relations by kindred or affinity." The law was consolidated by the Marriage Act, 1949 which lists (First Schedule, Part I) the degrees of relationship within which marriage is prohibited and (First Schedule, Part II) the statutory exceptions from the prohibited degrees. In 1907, for example, the Deceased Wife's Sister Marriage Act swept away the old prohibition of canon law against marriage with a dead wife's sister. But this and the later statutory exceptions relate only to marriage after the death of the spouse. The Acts expressly provide that such marriage shall be void if solemnised during the lifetime of the spouse. Thus, today, a man may marry his dead wife's sister (or aunt or niece) but not his divorced wife's sister (or aunt or niece).

Lord Mancroft introduced a Private Member's Bill in the House of Lords in 1949 the purpose of which was, in effect, to treat a divorced spouse as a deceased spouse as far as the statutory exceptions from prohibited degrees of relationship are concerned. This proposal was strongly resisted by all the churches who gave evidence to the Commission. All agreed with the Church of England (Evidence, 6th Day, p. 142) that there is a distinction, for this purpose, between death which comes *ab extra* and divorce which is unnatural and can be contrived. "The possibility of marrying a divorced partner's brother or sister casts a terrible shadow backwards. The "triangle" of emotions is taken into the circle of the family. Affections in danger of being attached to the brother-in-law or sister-in-law are no longer suppressed as improper and incapable of fulfilment, may cease to be regarded as altogether improper. . . ." This view, which seems to assume a surprisingly widespread knowledge of the law of kindred and affinity amongst the lay public, did not impress the Commission. The Report recommends (p. 301), with three dissentients, Lord Morton, Sir Frederick Burrows and Mr. Flecker, the removal of the prohibition.

dominated the Commission. Of the nineteen members who signed [1] the Report, eight were lawyers representing all branches of the profession in England and Scotland. In addition, at least three lay Commissioners were Justices of the Peace, and one a barrister's wife. Amongst the others were two schoolmasters and a Director of Education, two doctors, and a retired trade union official. Three Commissioners had been associated with the National Marriage Guidance Council. The only apparent principle behind this choice appears to have been the importance of securing a preponderance of lawyers. The Commission was not representative in any general sense, save perhaps of professional lawyers, doctors and schoolmasters; in social composition it was heavily biased towards upper- and middle-class outlooks. The personnel of the Commission suggests two comments. Firstly, the absence of known opponents and advocates of changes in the divorce laws is striking. The explanation lies probably in present doctrinal schisms within the Church of England.

During recent years, religious bodies have been the most active opponents of any extension in the grounds of divorce. If any religious opinion were to have been directly represented on the Commission, the Church of England must have provided a member. But that church is sharply divided in its views on divorce and related matters; if the government had appointed a Commissioner who reflected the doctrinal opinions of the episcopate, there would have been an outcry from those who share the outlook of the Modern Churchmen's Union. If both doctrinal positions had been represented, other difficulties would have arisen. On the one hand, the schism within the church would have provided extensive and continuous newspaper copy detrimental to the establishment and, on the other, the different churches

[1] The numbers of Commissioners varied from year to year as a consequence of deaths and resignations.

in England and Scotland would have demanded parity of representation. For these reasons the government could not have appointed a Commissioner openly identified with any sectarian religious viewpoint. In such circumstances it would have been politically inexpedient to nominate an active enthusiast for change in the divorce laws. The Commission was composed, therefore, of " impartial " members who had not publicly committed themselves on questions within the terms of reference. On the first day the Commission took evidence in public, Lord Morton emphasised his colleagues' open-mindedness.

> We have formed no view as yet on any of the suggestions made. . . . We all have open minds and are only anxious to test, as far as we can, the views put before us.[1]

The possibility that the nineteen Commissioners all had open minds on a subject of current public debate about which many people hold strong views must be qualified by the experienced observation of Sidney and Beatrice Webb.

> When we are told that a particular person has been appointed on a Royal Commission . . . on the ground that he is or claims to be an " impartial party," we may rest assured that this means merely that the selector and the selected agree in their bias.[2]

The important preliminary to any social investigation is not to secure " impartial " investigators (they do not exist this side of the grave), but to accept the inevitability of bias and the need for its correction by recognition and definition. This platitude makes the second comment on the personnel of the Commission particularly significant. Mr. Attlee's government did not see fit to appoint even one professional social scientist to the Commission. This

[1] Evidence, 1st Day, p. 4.
[2] *Methods of Social Study* (1932), p. 45.

omission from a body which, as Lord Keith explained to a witness, had

> to consider, among other things, firstly a conflict of principles, and, secondly, the question of where the good of society lies in the matter of the proposals which have been put before it,[1]

goes far to explain the character of the Report. The terms of reference charged the Commission with the duty of considering the desirability of proposed changes in the law and its administration according to the criterion of

> the need to promote and maintain healthy and happy married life and to safeguard the interests and well-being of children.

This criterion imposed the inescapable obligation to consider the causes and social consequences of divorce, and to assess the implications of changing attitudes to marriage. No Commissioner possessed expert knowledge of the considerable body of modern sociological research on such topics, or was equipped with an understanding of the techniques and potentialities of social investigation developed during the last twenty years. Lacking such essential assistance, the Morton Commission joined the Jumblies and went to sea in a sieve.

Only two witnesses specifically drew the attention of the Commission to the prevailing ignorance about the social problems underlying its terms of reference.[2] The Commission's conception of social research was starkly revealed by Lord Morton's questioning of Mr. A. J. Brayshaw, General Secretary of the National Marriage Guidance Council. In its Memorandum the Council

[1] Evidence, 7th–8th Day, p. 189, Q. 1467.

[2] The National Marriage Guidance Council and the Family Discussion Bureau of the Family Welfare Association (Evidence, 30th–31st Day, p. 786). Lady Chaterjee (*ibid.*, 14th–15th Day, p. 411) emphasised the importance of improving and extending available statistical information. The need of research was implicit in the evidence of Mr. T. K. P. Barrett and Mrs. Woodside and Dr. Slater (*ibid.*, 16th–17th Day).

suggested a number of subjects for urgent research;[1] they included an investigation of the relative stability of religious and civil marriages.

LORD MORTON: The difficulty about obtaining such information as you suggest is very great. I will tell you why. If you are dealing with something that is purely factual then there is an institution known as Social Survey which does work for government departments and would undertake surveys for us. Where facts are required over a very large number of cases of course that is very valuable, though it does involve a good deal of expense and a good deal of delay. It may be that your first point of relative stability of religious and civil marriages is a practicable one for such investigation. The information might be obtained in the way you suggest, but, without wishing to be unduly critical, where do you get to if you find that either religious marriages are more stable than civil ones or civil ones more stable than religious ones? What recommendations for a change in the law do you suggest we could base on that?

MR. B.: It would naturally prompt the question as to what factors exist in that form of marriage which appears to show the greater success, and one would then be able to see whether, on the one hand, the influence of clergy and ministers is apparently having a beneficial effect or whether, on the other hand, the facilitating of the re-marriage of divorced persons appears to be having a beneficial effect on the general stability of marriage. It obviously prompts other questions which would have to be investigated.

LORD MORTON: And the investigation of these other questions may be a matter of very great practical difficulty. . . . First of all, I think you would have to ask a great number of people very intimate questions which they might resent. Secondly, it would be very difficult to obtain genuine and frank answers from these persons because they would think, "Well,

[2] Evidence, 5th Day, p. 111.

why should I tell this stranger all about the factors that operate in my married happiness or unhappiness?" So that the results you would get in matters of that kind could not, I am afraid, be a very reliable basis on which to act. Thirdly, these investigations would involve very great public expense; if they produced results commensurate with that expense no doubt nobody would grudge it. . . . You see, I would agree with you that it would be most desirable if we could find out the things you suggest but . . . the result would be a mass of information which could not really be relied upon, for the reasons I have given. Very great public expense and a very long delay in the preparation of our report would result because we should probably have to wait years for anything like a reliable survey to be carried out.

MR. B.: . . . I hope that, before any final decision is taken, the Commission will look at the research undertaken by the Royal Commission on Population. . . . They went with great detail and with great success into attitudes to family planning, methods, degree of success, and many other extremely difficult matters . . .

LORD MORTON: I appreciate that and I am not unfamiliar with the work that was done, but . . . the Commission . . .—I think I am speaking for the other Commissioners—does see the difficulties.[1]

Mr. Brayshaw's apt reference to the Royal Commission on Population, which contained social scientists amongst its members and, in addition, appointed three specialist committees,[2] points the comparison between the procedural methods of those who are trained to collect, classify and analyse social evidence and those who are unaware that scientific method can be so employed. Lord Morton and his colleagues ignored a century's development of the social sciences and they did not use any method of investigation that would have been unfamiliar to the Campbell Commission of 1850. It is

[1] Evidence, pp. 122–123, Qs. 1083–1085. [2] Cd. 7695, 1949, p. 1.

not, therefore, surprising that Lord Morton should explain to the House of Lords that " It was impossible to prove anything one way or the other ; it was just a matter of what was the best thing." [1] His insistence that up-to-date methods would involve great delay must be judged against the four and a half years that elapsed between the appointment of his Commission and the publication of its Report.[2] Mr. Gorer's study, *Exploring English Character*,[3] was undertaken and completed, with far slimmer resources than would be available to a Royal Commission, within a similar period. Lord Morton's belief that it is impossible to ask a large number of people intimate questions concerning their attitudes to marriage and divorce, and to obtain reliable answers, contradicts a great weight of evidence summarised in any elementary text-book on statistics. A brief glance at, for example, the War-time Social Survey's report on *The Campaign against Venereal Diseases*,[4] might have persuaded Lord Morton and his colleagues that a competently organised survey can secure trustworthy and unresentful answers to the most directly intimate questions. Mr. Gorer discovered that " the stereotype of the withdrawn Englishman, resenting other people's prying into his business, received a severe jolt." [5] Lord Morton's final anxiety that the expense of investigation would have been unjustified followed naturally from his view that useful investigation was impossible. The prerequisite of fruitful social investigation is the ability and willingness to formulate relevant questions. Such capacity was not to be expected of a Commission dominated by lawyers who,

[1] Hansard (H. of L.), 24th October 1956, col. 987.

[2] The warrant of appointment was dated September 1951 ; the Report was published at Easter 1956.

[3] This book is not cited as a model of the type of investigation that might have been undertaken—it is doubtful, for example, if Mr. Gorer's sample was representative—but only as an indication of what might have been comfortably attempted in the time at the Commission's disposal.

[4] New Series No. 42 (January 1944) *op. cit.* by Pixie J. Wilson and Virginia Barker.

[5] *op. cit.*, p. 8.

whilst paying lip service to the need for judging proposals by the test of the social good, are conditioned to define both social problems and the social good in legal terms. The Commission's Report is substantial evidence of its members' ignorance of the social sciences. Their hostility to suggestions that scientific methods of investigation could assist their work can be illustrated by two representative examples. Mrs. Moya Woodside, a psychiatric social worker and co-author of the book *Patterns of Marriage* one of the few empirical studies in its field, submitted a Memorandum the conclusions of which appeared to conflict with Lord Morton's open-minded outlook.

LORD MORTON: You say: "Yet another important factor is the decline of religious influence and practice (very apparent among the members of our sample) and the growth of a more tolerant public attitude to divorce." First of all, in your view, is the decline of religious influence and practice a good thing or a bad thing for the United Kingdom?

MRS. W.: That is rather a large question.

LORD MORTON: You have put this "factor" at the end of a list of things you appear to regard as being in the nature of progress. I would like to know whether you regard it as a good thing or a bad thing?

MRS. W.: I was trying to give an objective picture of what I found and the way those people lived and thought. It seemed to me that they no longer laid the emphasis on religion that their parental generation did. I have not specifically said whether it was a good thing or a bad thing.

LORD MORTON: You have not, but the object of questioning is to test the views expressed by a witness and to know on what they are based. It was for that purpose I asked the question. If you do not wish to answer it, you need not. Do you think that the decline of religious influence and practice is a good thing or a bad thing for the country? [1]

[1] Evidence, 16th–17th Day, p. 438, Qs. 3576–3577.

This extract from the evidence has not been quoted in order to demonstrate Lord Morton's courteous, forensic skill but as an example of his attitude to empirical evidence. One Commissioner, Lord Keith, remarked: "What interests me about this survey is that it is factual; . . . based . . . upon an actual investigation of human beings." [1] But the general interest shown by the Commission in the results of a factual survey was politely expressed by Mr. Mace, a solicitor, who asked as the penultimate question of an examination which had been prefaced by a statement of Mrs. Woodside's qualifications and position as a research psychiatric social worker in the Department of Psychological Medicine at Guy's Hospital: "May I ask, has Mrs. Woodside any qualifications?" [2] Another example of the same outlook is provided by the Commission's treatment of statistical evidence. It obtained, but did not publish as evidence, compilations from the Registrar General. Thirteen tables and two diagrams are printed without discussion or explanation of their meaning in a forlorn appendix to the Report which makes, significantly, hardly any reference to them. The statistics of divorce are notoriously scanty and uninformative yet the Commission made no suggestions for their improvement. Indeed, the one reference in the Report to the collection of statistics relates to the inadequacy of information about matrimonial proceedings in magistrates' courts which makes impossible any realistic assessment of the extent of broken marriages and broken homes.

> There would be some advantage in having fuller statistical information . . . if this could be readily provided. But we were informed that to collect and tabulate this information would involve a good deal of extra work, additional clerical help in many courts and considerable expense. Our conclusion is that, in

[1] Evidence, p. 440, Q. 3602.
[2] *ibid.*, Q. 3624.

> present circumstances, the value of the additional information would not be sufficient to justify the work and expense involved in obtaining it.[1]

Clearly, a Commission which hesitated to recommend the urgency of acquiring such elementary statistical data was not likely to consider equipping itself with a research secretariat,[2] or to feel embarrassed during its deliberations by the lack of such relatively sophisticated evidence as the incidence of divorce amongst town and country dwellers, or by occupational and income groups, or by social class. Yet without such information, Commissioners could not pass from the contemplation of unsupported conjectures to the study of reality. As the Commissioners decided not to collect social evidence and obtained none from witnesses, their Report is a soufflé of whipped conjectures.[3]

The Commission thus describes the background of its inquiry and the basis of its analysis.

> The large number of marriages which each year are ending in the divorce court is a matter of grave concern. . . . Weighing all the evidence [*sic*] before us, we

[1] Report, p. 297. This was one of the relatively few recommendations which received the unanimous support of Commissioners.

[2] A research secretariat could, for example, have : (*a*) analysed the available statistical data, defined its defects, and suggested means by which it could be extended and improved ; (*b*) devised and carried out empirical investigations designed to test the assertions of witnesses in regard to such matters as attitudes to marriage, attitudes towards divorce, the penetration through different social strata of knowledge about the divorce laws and the matrimonial jurisdiction of magistrates' courts, and widespread marital irresponsibility and divorce-mindedness ; (*c*) analysed samples of divorce petitions which contain, *inter alia*, information about the number of children, the residence, the occupation and, sometimes, the income of petitioner or respondent in order to make a study of the changing incidence of divorce by social class during the last half century ; (*d*) devised a method of providing socially relevant information about the use and consequences of maintenance and separation orders obtained in magistrates' courts ; (*e*) devised and carried out a factual study of the consequences of their parents' divorces for a representative sample of children.

[3] The phrase is Professor Postan's. He once described theoretical economics as " a soufflé of whipped postulates."

> are satisfied that marriages are now breaking up which in the past would have held together.[1]

" This disturbing situation " is attributed to several factors. First,

> The complexity of modern life multiplies the potential causes of disagreement and the possibilities of friction between husband and wife. And the conditions of life today are such as to subject many marriages to additional strain. The scarcity of houses, for instance, prevents many young couples from starting their married life in a home of their own.[2]

This argument is very puzzling. The complexity of modern life comprises those factors which have raised working-class living standards to the point at which starting married life in a home of one's own has become a widespread and reasonable aspiration. The apparent belief that scarcity of housing only became a social problem after Hitler's war, serves to illustrate the Commissioners' unhistorical approach and upper-class myopia. Secondly, the Report stresses factors which, " in their other aspects," benefit the community. " Greater demands are now made of marriage," largely as a result of the social and economic emancipation of women.

> Women are no longer content to endure the treatment which in past times their inferior position obliged them to suffer. They expect of marriage that it shall be an equal partnership ; and rightly so. But the working out of this ideal exposes marriage to new strains.[3]

The Report does not explain why the growing realisation of the ideal of equal partnership ought not to be judged a new source of strength, rather than weakness, for the institution of marriage. Similarly, it is claimed that changes in sexual behaviour during the last fifty years " may have produced in the popular mind an undue

[1] Report, p. 8. [2] *ibid.*, p. 9. [3] *ibid.*

emphasis on the over-riding importance of a satisfactory sex relationship " with a resulting weakening of other factors promoting marital stability. Finally, the Report gives special prominence to the influence, " dangerous " and " insidious " in its effects, which " we believe lies at the root of the problem."

> There is a tendency to take the duties and responsibilities of marriage less seriously than formerly. Yet if, as we have said, more is now asked of marriage, it follows that more, not less, should be put into it. The result of this outlook is that there is less disposition to overcome difficulties and to put up with the rubs of daily life and, in consequence, there is an increasing disposition to regard divorce, not as the last resort, but as the obvious way out when things begin to go wrong. In other words, remedies which are intended for the relief of real hardship are used in cases where relief should be unnecessary if a proper view of their marriage obligations were taken by husband and wife.
>
> The change in the community's attitude to divorce has some share in responsibility for this situation . . .
>
> We do not wish to suggest that this outlook has spread throughout the community ; the majority of people are still ready to work hard to make their marriage a success. But its growth is insidious and endangers the whole stability of marriage.[1]

This and similar passages, from which no Commissioner dissented, accept as self-evident truths the unverified conjectures of many " institutionalist " witnesses, and indicate the prevalent bias of the Report. There is no doubt that the Commission regards the break-up of the middle-class mid-Victorian family code as leading to the disintegration of the family. The " dangers " and " insidious weaknesses " of a democratic family unit are continuously emphasised ; its potentialities for free men and women whose loyalties are those of choice, are ignored.

[1] Report, pp. 9–10.

The central issue confronting the Commission was the retention or abolition of the matrimonial offence as the basis of divorce law at a time when there is equality of access to the court and general disillusionment with the theological presuppositions which underlie that doctrine. Commissioners agreed, with one exception,[1] that "the present law based on the doctrine of the matrimonial offence should be retained."[2] Surprisingly, however, in view of this declaration, the Commissioners divided into two main groups according to their attitudes to proposals for extending the grounds of divorce. The first[3] logically resisted any extension which would admit the principle of Mrs. Eirene White's Bill.

> That would introduce into the law a principle which would have even more damaging consequences than divorce for the institution of marriage than divorce by consent, since it would mean that either spouse would be free to terminate the marriage at pleasure . . .
> . . . no married person would ever be sure that he would not be divorced. The introduction into marriage of this sense of insecurity and uncertainty would have a most disturbing effect on family life, which would ultimately react on all members of the community.[4]

[1] Lord Walker. His approach was different from that of his colleagues. He wished divorce law to be based on sound principle, and held that the doctrine of the matrimonial offence was only appropriate as defining the circumstances in which spouses should be entitled to lesser remedies such as judicial separation. The changing attitudes to divorce and the scope which present law gives for collusion have resulted, Lord Walker argued, in the matrimonial offence becoming "a technical cause of action without a real cause of complaint . . ." and, if it remains the basis of divorce law, "may well prove seriously harmful to marriage as an institution" (Report, p. 341). Lord Walker therefore urged the abandonment of the matrimonial offence and the substitution of the principle of irretrievable breakdown of marriage defined as "one where the facts and circumstances affecting the lives of the parties adversely to one another are such as to make it improbable that an ordinary husband and wife would ever resume cohabitation" (*ibid.*, p. 340).

[2] *ibid.*, p. 13.

[3] Lord Morton, Mr. Beloe, Lady Bragg, Sir Russell Brain, Sir Frederick Burrows, Mr. Flecker, Mr. Lawrence, Mr. Mace, and Mr. Justice Pearce.

[4] Report, p. 17.

The second group [1] of Commissioners wished to introduce a new ground of divorce when spouses have lived separately for seven years or more, provided that the other spouse does not object.

> We see no danger to the stability of marriage in allowing what is in effect divorce by consent under the stringent safeguard that husband and wife have lived apart for seven years . . . (it will not) . . . lessen respect for marriage and undermine it as an institution. On the contrary, by basing dissolution of marriage on a complete breakdown . . . we are, we think, heightening the respect for true marriage.[2]

Four members [3] of this group recommended the extension of this principle to meet some of the requirements of Mrs. White's Bill by allowing dissolution of marriage notwithstanding the objections of one spouse, provided the petitioner satisfies the court that the separation resulted partly from the unreasonable conduct of the objecting spouse.

> We see no benefit to society, to the individual or to the State in maintaining marriages in name which are no longer, and on all foreseeable estimates will never be, marriages in fact . . .[4]

The four Commissioners were impressed by the large number of illicit unions which, they thought, are real marriages in fact, though excluded from social and legal recognition as such by a pre-existing, broken marriage. They wished to remove the fear and frustration suffered by adults in such unions, and to protect children from the insecurity of an irregular home and from the stigma of illegitimacy. The members of these unions cannot, they argued, exercise their full capacities as citizens.

[1] Mrs. Allen, Dr. Baird, Mrs. Brace, Mr. Brown, Mrs. Jones-Roberts, Lord Keith, Mr. Maddocks, Lady Portal, and Mr. Young.

[2] Report, p. 24.

[3] Dr. Baird, Mr. Brown, Mrs. Jones-Roberts, and Lord Keith.

[4] Report, p. 25.

> . . . they are unlikely to take part in social work, political work and other ordinary activities. In particular, many of them are religious people, but it may be doubted whether there is any church in the country where two people living in adultery would feel at home . . .[1]

Even under this proposed ground of divorce, separation must have lasted at least seven years, and those whom it seeks to relieve would not therefore escape a lengthy experience of all the social and religious disadvantages of the present system.

These Commissioners never explain how they reconciled their proposals to allow divorce after long separation with their desire to retain the doctrine of the matrimonial offence. Their new ground would preserve the shell but destroy the substance of the existing law. By seeking both to meet "abolitionist" criticisms of the social consequences of present arrangements and to retain "institutionalist" principles, they would turn English divorce law from anomaly into absurdity.

The Commission was thus irreconcilably divided on the crucial issue. All members said they wished to retain the matrimonial offence as the basis of divorce law. Nine resisted any weakening of the established principle, and nine recommended a destructive exception. Each group claimed its proposal as essential for the maintenance of the community's well-being. But in the absence of actual knowledge as to the types of divorce law most likely to promote marital and familial stability, Commissioners' justifications of their views amount to no more than an identification of the social good with their personal presuppositions. Even if they had shared the same prejudices, this would still seem an inadequate basis for advising on the evils or benefits of changes in the law.

This conflict between differing and unverified conjectures runs through the whole Report. Mr. Attlee's

[1] Report, p. 26.

government did not appoint a Commission competent to investigate and, for reasons of expediency, selected as members men and women who were not publicly committed to either " abolitionist " or " institutionalist " views. The Report consequently contributes nothing to our knowledge, and fails even to clarify and define opposing viewpoints or to facilitate public discussion. Instead of the traditional division into majority and minority Reports, the Commission presented its readers with a luxuriant confusion of footnotes indicating the agreement or disagreement of different Commissioners with this or that proposition or paragraph. It is a matter of opinion whether the Morton Commission is intellectually the worst Royal Commission of the twentieth century, but there can be no dispute that its Report is the most unreadable and confused. Fifty years ago, in a social atmosphere less favourable to clear thinking on such problems, the Gorell Commission served as an agent of clarification. The Morton Commission has proved a device for obfuscating a socially urgent but politically inconvenient issue.

CONCLUSION

THIS book has attempted to assemble the materials essential for an informed understanding of the problem of divorce. It has not offered ready-made solutions or advocated this or that legislative change. In essence, it is a polemic against prejudice and ignorance written in the conviction that recent, bitter controversies can be resolved only if disputants are willing to discriminate between matters of fact and matters of opinion. The paucity of actual knowledge concerning prevailing attitudes towards marriage and the causes and the social consequences of divorce has been repeatedly emphasised. The appointment of the Morton Commission provided an opportunity to substitute increased knowledge for irreconcilable dogmas. Lord Morton and his colleagues were hostile to the social sciences and consequently unable to penetrate to the heart of the problems set before them. Hence the continuing vitality of unreason in this crucial area of human behaviour.

Every society has regulated sexual relations and provided for the nurture and rearing of children. Although the diversity the world over of such social arrangements may seem bewildering, the fact of regulation is universal. There are many marriage systems with varying religious and social sanctions and differing provisions for the dissolution of marriage. This clearly suggests that any claim to inevitable or compulsory authority for one species of this universal genus is unrealistic. In so far as divisions of opinion on divorce reflect a dispute about the nature of marriage between Christians and agnostics, reconciliation by rational argument is impossible. On the other hand, it must equally be remembered that Christianity pronounces about divorce, as it pronounces about the morality of war or the functions of private property, in many contradictory voices; and disagreements between Christians are as sharp as those between Christians and unbelievers. All Christians agree that God intended marriage as a monogamous, indissoluble union but Christians also differ irreconcilably concerning the rules of behaviour imposed by this general principle. The concept of "Christian marriage" is so variable as between different churches that it provides criteria for personal behaviour and public control only to those who adhere to particular dogmas. These present-day confusions are only aggravated by the claim, common to Christians and agnostics alike, that their particular rules will ensure the stability of the family and thus embody the good of society.

There is, beyond all dispute, a widespread rejection in the country of religious and therefore denominational interpretations of marriage and divorce, and legal rules based on them no longer command general respect. Despite this, marriage has not lost its hold as a secular institution. Indeed, the new democratic family unit of the mid-twentieth century exhibits a far healthier vitality than its Victorian counterpart. This is the social reality behind the understandable anxieties and confused polemics with which the contemporary problems of marriage, divorce and the family have been surrounded. Accordingly, one reconciliation only is possible in a democratic community between those who regard marriage as a divine institution and those who regard it as a secular contract of the greatest social importance. It was defined in the tolerant and mature comment of the late Archbishop Lang on Mr. A. P. Herbert's Bill in 1937. ". . . I came to the conclusion that it was no longer possible to impose the full Christian standard by law on a largely non-Christian population, but that the witness to that standard, and consequent disciplinary action towards its own members or persons who sought to be married by its rites, must be left to the Church, I was put in a very painful position as a result. . . . I could not as a citizen vote against the Bill, but I could not bring myself as a Churchman to vote for it; and I announced that I would not vote."[1] Here the leader of the Anglican Church recognised the essential foundations of public policy in a democracy. The religious sects must be free to impose their rules and beliefs about marriage and divorce upon their members who voluntarily accept such discipline. Civil divorce, legally ordained on terms widely accepted as rational, must be freely and easily available to all others. The continued maintenance of legal rules based on religious concepts which no longer command widespread assent is bringing the law into disrepute. It is of outstanding importance that, in this field, the rule of law should be understood, respected and reasonable. The present system with its accumulating dishonesties and perjuries is damaging to the law and hence detrimental to public morality.

Clear thinking on one further aspect of the present situation is urgently necessary. Divorce precipitates many difficult questions concerning the rights of spouses to maintenance and the principles of matrimonial property law.[2] An air of legal unreality characterises the Morton Commission's discussion of these issues and their Report does not face squarely the fundamental consideration which was stressed in a written memorandum of evidence by Lord Justice Hodson.

> There is one practical difficulty which is already assuming prominence now that divorce is comparatively rife among couples who are dependent on the weekly wage of the husband. According to our law a man has

[1] Quoted J. G. Lockhart, *Cosmo Gordon Lang* (1949), p. 235.

[2] Discussion of the technical aspects of maintenance and matrimonial property law is beyond the scope of this book. The conclusions of the Morton Commission are set out in the Report, Part VII, pp. 129–195. The article of O. Kahn-Freund, "Matrimonial Property Law in England" in W. Friedmann (ed.), *Matrimonial Property Law* (1955) is indispensable.

to maintain his wife and if she divorces him by reason of his fault the wife still in theory retains this right. I say in theory because it is practically impossible for her to enforce her rights in a large number of cases. The wage-earner (if he is divorced) is free to marry again and his wife, that is, the particular woman to whom he is at the time married, has herself a right to be maintained by him. . . . If she has a child or children and his wage is in the neighbourhood of £6 or £7 a week . . . the financial prospects of any earlier wives or their children by this man are not very good. There is simply not enough money to go round.

This problem is not noticeable among well-to-do people. A super-tax payer may and quite frequently does have a number of wives living at the same time and since after divorce his ex-wives are not treated as one with him for tax purposes he can manage quite nicely, since he is permitted to deduct all his wives' maintenance allowances from his gross income for tax purposes leaving his net income comparatively slightly affected.[1]

Thus a man may be faced with the legal obligation to maintain both a wife from whom he is divorced and a wife with whom he is living. At one extreme of the income scale, the surtax payer may be able to meet his obligations with little or no sacrifice of his real income because the State relieves him of a portion of his tax liability. The Exchequer, in effect, makes a grant out of public funds for the maintenance of the surtax payer's ex-wife. At the lower end of the income scale, public funds similarly maintain the ex-wife, although the procedure is markedly different. A divorced man with a low income cannot maintain two wives and possibly two families. There is no information as to the official treatment of such persons, but their financial situation is the same as that of men who have separated from their wives and established illicit unions. This large group, neither married nor unmarried, presents the National

[1] Evidence, 30th–31st Day, p. 772.

Assistance Board with formidable moral and administrative problems.

> If (the husband's) earnings or other resources are not enough to maintain, besides himself, both his wife (with her children, if any) and the paramour (with her children, if any) the defect has got to be met at one point or other by assistance. The Board are then faced with the delicate task of deciding whether the assistance is to be given to the wife or to the paramour. Respect for the marriage tie suggests that it is the legal wife who should be the prior charge on the husband's income . . . but important practical considerations, not least the avoidance of unnecessary expenditure of public monies, lead inescapably to the other view. . . . Extracting money from husbands to maintain wives from whom they are separated is at best an uncertain business ; it is easier to enforce the maintenance of those with whom the man is living than of those from whom he is parted . . .[1]

Whether the second union is illicit or legal, the financial difficulties are the same and public funds, through the National Assistance Board, must maintain the wives from whom such men are separated or divorced. Nevertheless, despite the commonsense approach of the National Assistance Board, the husbands of its clients face hazards unknown to surtax payers. Some three or four thousand men go to prison every year for failure to observe maintenance orders ; and the possibility of prison may be a nagging anxiety for a poor man who marries again after divorce.

If the community permits divorce it must be prepared to meet the inevitable consequences of divorce. The present system of maintenance, and the methods by which it is enforced, is a jumble of *ad hoc* expedients capriciously assembled during the last hundred years. Where the needs of justice require that citizens should have sure

[1] *Report of the National Assistance Board for 1953* (Cd. 9210), pp. 18–19, (quoted Barbara Wootton, *op. cit*).

knowledge of their responsibilities and rights, there exists uncertainty and legal and administrative chaos productive of much unnecessary and futile suffering.[1] Rational reform implies modifications in attitudes towards the consequences of divorce. As marriage creates dependencies so also its dissolution may create social casualties which confront responsible people with conflicting obligations that cannot be discharged because there is insufficient money to go round. Such casualties must be accepted at least as the temporary responsibility of social policy.

The Morton Commission sadly resembles a predecessor, the Royal Commission on Kissing, whose labours have been recorded for us by Sir Alan Herbert.

> We then collected evidence, but carefully dismissed
> The opinion of anyone who actually kissed ;
> We summoned social workers from the cities of the North,
> Good magistrates from Monmouth, Nonconformists from the Forth ;
> We summoned all the Bishops who were over sixty-one
> And asked if they were kissed and, if they were, how it was done.
> They answered in the negative and said there was abundant
> Support for the opinion that the practice was redundant—
> And that took a long, long, time.[2]

[1] The admirable article of Miss O. M. Stone, " Royal Commission on Marriage and Divorce : Family Dependants and their Maintenance " (*The Modern Law Review*, vol. 19, No. 6, 1956), is a valuable summary of the present legal position and provides an indispensable commentary on it. This issue of *The Modern Law Review* was devoted to family law and is essential reading, especially the article of Professor O. Kahn-Freund, " Divorce Law Reform ? " Professor Kahn-Freund concludes his discussion of the Morton Commission's Report with the comment that they " went with great care into the particulars of matrimonial law. But no amount of attention to detail can make up for lack of vision and for the absence of a well-considered policy based on a real knowledge of the facts. One can only hope that this disappointing document may not prove to be the epitaph of divorce law reform " (p. 600). [Regrettably, this issue of *The Modern Law Review* appeared too late to be used in the writing of this book.]

[2] *Punch* (1934), vol. 186, p. 708.

It is safe prediction that divorce reform will take a long, long time. The only cold comfort in all this depressing story is the reflection that, in tackling social problems, consciousness of ignorance may be the beginning of wisdom.

APPENDIX I

MATRIMONIAL CAUSES ACT, 1950.

(14 & 15 Geo. VI, c. 25.)

ARRANGEMENT OF SECTIONS

Divorce and Nullity of Marriage

Section

1. Grounds for petition for divorce.
2. Restriction on petitions for divorce during first three years after marriage.
3. Provision as to making adulterer co-respondent.
4. Duty of court on presentation of petition.
5. Dismissal of respondent or co-respondent from proceedings.
6. Relief to respondent on petition for divorce.
7. Divorce proceedings after grant of judicial separation or other relief.
8. Additional grounds for decree of nullity.
9. Legitimacy of children of voidable marriages.
10. Duties of King's Proctor.
11. Provisions as to costs where King's Proctor intervenes or shows cause.
12. Decree nisi for divorce or nullity of marriage.
13. Re-marriage of divorced persons.

Judicial Separation and Restitution of Conjugal Rights

14. Decree for judicial separation.
15. Decree for restitution of conjugal rights.

Presumption of Death and Dissolution of Marriage

16. Proceedings for decree of presumption of death and dissolution of marriage.

Declaration of Legitimacy, &c.

17. Declaration of legitimacy, &c.

Additional Jurisdiction in proceedings by a Wife

Section

18. Additional jurisdiction in proceedings by a wife.

Alimony, Maintenance and Custody of Children

19. Alimony and maintenance in case of divorce and nullity of marriage.
20. Alimony in case of judicial separation.
21. Wife's property and necessaries supplied to wife in case of judicial separation.
22. Alimony and periodical payments in case of restitution of conjugal rights.
23. Additional power of court to make orders for maintenance.
24. Power of court to order settlement of wife's property.
25. Power of court to make orders as to application of settled property.
26. Custody and maintenance of children.
27. Payment of alimony and maintenance to trustees and persons having charge of respondent.
28. Variation and discharge of orders for alimony and maintenance.
29. Commencement of proceedings for maintenance, settlement of property, &c.

Miscellaneous

30. Damages for adultery.
31. Power to allow intervention on terms.
32. Evidence.

Interpretation, Repeal and Short Title

33. Interpretation.
34. Repeal and savings.
35. Short title, commencement and extent.

SCHEDULE.—Enactments repealed.

An Act to consolidate certain enactments relating to matrimonial causes in the High Court in England and to declarations of legitimacy and of validity of marriage and of British nationality, with such corrections and improvements as may be authorised by the Consolidation of Enactments (Procedure) Act, 1949.

Divorce and Nullity of Marriage

Grounds for petition for divorce.

1.—(1) Subject to the provisions of the next following section, a petition for divorce may be presented to the court either by the husband or the wife on the ground that the respondent—

(*a*) has since the celebration of the marriage committed adultery; or
(*b*) has deserted the petitioner without cause for a period of at least three years immediately preceding the presentation of the petition; or
(*c*) has since the celebration of the marriage treated the petitioner with cruelty; or
(*d*) is incurably of unsound mind and has been continuously under care and treatment for a period of at least five years immediately preceding the presentation of the petition;

and by the wife on the ground that her husband has, since the celebration of the marriage, been guilty of rape, sodomy or bestiality.

(2) For the purpose of this section a person of unsound mind shall be deemed to be under care and treatment—

(*a*) while he is detained in pursuance of any order or inquisition under the Lunacy and Mental Treatment Acts, 1890 to 1930, or of any order or warrant under the Army Act, the Air Force Act, the Naval Discipline Act, the Naval Enlistment Act, 1884, or the Yarmouth Naval Hospital Act, 1931, or is being detained as a Broadmoor patient or in pursuance of an order made under the Criminal Lunatics Act, 1884;
(*b*) while he is detained in pursuance of any order or warrant for his detention or custody as a lunatic under the Lunacy (Scotland) Acts, 1857 to 1919;
(*c*) while he is detained in pursuance of any order for his detention or treatment as a person of unsound mind or a person suffering from mental illness made under any law for the time being in force in Northern Ireland, the Isle of Man or any of the Channel Islands (including any such law relating to criminal lunatics);
(*d*) while he is receiving treatment as a voluntary patient under the Mental Treatment Act, 1930, or under any such law as is mentioned in paragraph (*c*) of this subsection, being treatment which follows without any interval a period during which he was detained as mentioned in paragraph (*a*), paragraph (*b*) or paragraph (*c*) of this subsection;

and not otherwise.

Restriction on petitions for divorce during first three years after marriage.

2.—(1) No petition for divorce shall be presented to the court unless at the date of the presentation of the petition three years have passed since the date of the marriage:

Provided that a judge of the court may, upon application being made to him in accordance with rules of court, allow a petition to be presented before three years have passed on the ground that the case is one of exceptional hardship suffered by the petitioner or of exceptional depravity on the part of the respondent, but if it appears to the court at the hearing of the petition that the petitioner obtained leave to present the petition by any misrepresentation or concealment of the nature of the case, the court may, if it pronounces a decree nisi, do so subject to the condition that no application to make the decree absolute shall be made until after the expiration of three years from the date of the marriage, or may dismiss the petition, without prejudice to any petition which may be brought after the expiration of the said three years upon the same, or substantially the same, facts as those proved in support of the petition so dismissed.

(2) In determining any application under this section for leave to present a petition before the expiration of three years from the date of the marriage, the judge shall have regard to the interests of any children of the marriage and to the question whether there is reasonable probability of a reconciliation between the parties before the expiration of the said three years.

(3) Nothing in this section shall be deemed to prohibit the presentation of a petition based upon matters which have occurred before the expiration of three years from the date of the marriage.

(4) This section shall not apply in the case of marriages to which section one of the Matrimonial Causes (War Marriages) Act, 1944, applies (being certain marriages celebrated on or after the third day of September, nineteen hundred and thirty-nine, and before the first day of June, nineteen hundred and fifty).

Provision as to making adulterer co-respondent.

3.—(1) On a petition for divorce presented by the husband on the ground of adultery or in the answer of a husband praying for divorce on the said ground, the petitioner or respondent, as the case may be, shall make the alleged adulterer a co-respondent unless he is excused by the court on special grounds from so doing.

(2) On a petition for divorce presented by the wife on the ground of adultery the court may, if it thinks fit, direct that the person with whom the husband is alleged to have committed adultery be made a respondent.

Duty of court on presentation of petition.

4.—(1) On a petition for divorce it shall be the duty of the court to inquire, so far as it reasonably can, into the facts alleged and whether there has been any connivance or condonation on the part of the petitioner and whether any collusion exists between the parties, and also to inquire into any countercharge which is made against the petitioner.

(2) If the court is satisfied on the evidence that—

(*a*) the case for the petition has been proved; and

(*b*) where the grounds of the petition is adultery, the petitioner has not in any manner been accessory to, or connived at, or condoned, the adultery, or, where the ground of the petition is cruelty, the petitioner has not in any manner condoned the cruelty ; and

(*c*) the petition is not presented or prosecuted in collusion with the respondent or either of the respondents ;

the court shall pronounce a decree of divorce, but if the court is not satisfied with respect to any of the aforesaid matters, it shall dismiss the petition :

Provided that the court shall not be bound to pronounce a decree of divorce and may dismiss the petition if it finds that the petitioner has during the marriage been guilty of adultery or if, in the opinion of the court, the petitioner has been guilty—

(i) of unreasonable delay in presenting or prosecuting the petition or

(ii) of cruelty towards the other party to the marriage ; or

(iii) where the ground of the petition is adultery or cruelty, of having without reasonable excuse deserted, or having without reasonable excuse wilfully separated himself or herself from, the other party before the adultery or cruelty complained of ; or

(iv) where the ground of the petition is adultery or unsoundness of mind or desertion, of such wilful neglect or misconduct as has conduced to the adultery or unsoundness of mind or desertion.

Dismissal of respondent or co-respondent from proceedings.

5.—In any case in which, on the petition of a husband for divorce on the ground of adultery, the alleged adulterer is made a co-respondent or in which on the petition of a wife for divorce on the ground of adultery, the person with whom the husband is alleged to have committed adultery is made a respondent, the court may, after the close of the evidence on the part of the petitioner, direct the co-respondent or the respondent, as the case may be, to be dismissed from the proceedings if the court is of opinion that there is not sufficient evidence against him or her.

Relief to respondent on petition or divorce

6.—If in any proceedings for divorce the respondent opposes the relief sought on the ground of the petitioner's adultery, cruelty or desertion, the court may give to the respondent the same relief to which he or she would have been entitled if he or she had presented a petition seeking such relief.

Divorce proceedings after grant of judicial separation or other relief.

7.—(1) A person shall not be prevented from presenting a petition for divorce, or the court from pronouncing a decree of divorce, by reason only that the petitioner has at any time been granted a judicial separation or an order under the Summary Jurisdiction (Separation and Maintenance) Acts, 1895 to 1949, upon the same or substantially the same facts as those proved in support of the petition for divorce.

(2) On any such petition for divorce, the court may treat the decree of judicial separation or the said order as sufficient proof of the adultery, desertion, or other ground on which it was granted, but the court shall not pronounce a decree of divorce without receiving evidence from the petitioner.

(3) For the purpose of any such petition for divorce, a period of desertion immediately preceding the institution of proceedings for a decree of judicial separation or an order under the said Acts having the effect of such a decree shall, if the parties have not resumed cohabitation and the decree or order has been continuously in force since the granting thereof, be deemed immediately to precede the presentation of the petition for divorce.

Additional grounds for decree of nullity.

8.—(1) In addition to any other grounds on which a marriage is by law void or voidable, a marriage shall be voidable on the ground—

(*a*) that the marriage has not been consummated owing to the wilful refusal of the respondent to consummate the marriage ; or

(*b*) that either party to the marriage was at the time of the marriage of unsound mind or a mental defective within the meaning of the Mental Deficiency Acts, 1913 to 1938, or subject to recurrent fits of insanity or epilepsy ; or

(*c*) that the respondent was at the time of the marriage suffering from venereal disease in a communicable form ; or

(*d*) that the respondent was at the time of the marriage pregnant by some person other than the petitioner :

Provided that, in the cases specified in paragraphs (*b*), (*c*) and (*d*) of this subsection, the court shall not grant a decree unless it is satisfied—

(i) that the petitioner was at the time of the marriage ignorant of the facts alleged ;

(ii) that proceedings were instituted within a year from the date of the marriage ; and

(iii) that marital intercourse with the consent of the petitioner has not taken place since the discovery by the petitioner of the existence of the grounds for a decree.

(2) Nothing in this section shall be construed as validating any marriage which is by law void, but with respect to which a decree of nullity has not been granted.

Legitimacy of children of voidable marriages.

9.—Where a decree of nullity is granted in respect of a voidable marriage, any child who would have been the legitimate child of the parties to the marriage if it had been dissolved, instead of being annulled, at the date of the decree shall be deemed to be their legitimate child notwithstanding the annulment.

Duties of King's Proctor.

10.—In the case of any petition for divorce or for nullity of marriage—

(1) the court may, if it thinks fit, direct all necessary papers in the matter to be sent to His Majesty's Proctor, who shall under the directions of the Attorney-General instruct counsel to argue before the court any question in relation to the matter which the court deems to be necessary or expedient to have fully argued, and His Majesty's Proctor shall be entitled to charge the costs of the proceedings as part of the expenses of his office ;

(2) any person may at any time during the progress of the proceedings or before the decree nisi is made absolute give information to His Majesty's Proctor of any matter material to the due decision of the case, and His Majesty's Proctor may thereupon take such steps as the Attorney-General considers necessary or expedient;

(3) if in consequence of any such information or otherwise His Majesty's Proctor suspects that any parties to the petition are or have been acting in collusion for the purpose of obtaining a decree contrary to the justice of the case, he may, under the direction of the Attorney-General, after obtaining the leave of the court, intervene and retain counsel and subpœna witnesses to prove the alleged collusion.

Provisions as to costs where King's Proctor intervenes or shows cause.

11.—(1) Where His Majesty's Proctor intervenes or shows cause against a decree nisi in any proceedings for divorce or for nullity of marriage, the court may make such order as to the payment by other parties to the proceedings of the costs incurred by him in so doing or as to the payment by him of any costs incurred by any of the said parties by reason of his so doing, as may seem just.

(2) So far as the reasonable costs incurred by His Majesty's Proctor in so intervening or showing cause are not fully satisfied by any order made under this section for the payment of his costs, he shall be entitled to charge the difference as part of the expenses of his office, and the Treasury may, if they think fit, order that any costs which under any order made by the court under this section His Majesty's Proctor pays to any parties shall be deemed to be part of the expenses of his office.

Decree nisi for divorce or nullity of marriage.

12.—(1) Every decree for a divorce or for nullity of marriage shall, in the first instance, be a decree nisi not to be made absolute until after the expiration of six months from the pronouncing thereof, unless the court by general or special order from time to time fixes a shorter time.

(2) After the pronouncing of the decree nisi and before the decree is made absolute, any person may, in the prescribed manner, show cause why the decree should not be made absolute by reason of the decree having been obtained by collusion or by reason of material facts not having been brought before the court, and in any such case the court may make the decree absolute, reverse the decree nisi, require further inquiry or otherwise deal with the case as the court thinks fit.

(3) Where a decree nisi has been obtained and no application for the decree to be made absolute has been made by the party who obtained the decree, then, at any time after the expiration of three months from the earliest date on which that party could have made such an application, the party against whom the decree nisi has been granted shall be at liberty to apply to the court and the court shall, on such application, have power to make the decree absolute, reverse the decree nisi, require further inquiry or otherwise deal with the case as the court thinks fit.

Re-marriage of divorced persons.

13.—(1) Where a decree of divorce has been made absolute and either there is no right of appeal against the decree absolute or, if there is such a right of appeal, the time for appealing has expired without an appeal having been presented or an appeal has been presented but has been dismissed, either party to the marriage may marry again.

(2) No clergyman of the Church of England or of the Church in Wales shall be compelled to solemnise the marriage of any person whose former marriage has been dissolved on any ground and whose former husband or wife is still living, or to permit the marriage of any such person to be solemnised in the Church or Chapel of which he is the minister.

Judicial Separation and Restitution of Conjugal Rights

Decree for judicial separation.

14.—(1) A petition for judicial separation may be presented to the court either by the husband or the wife on any grounds on which a petition for divorce might have been presented, or on the ground of failure to comply with a decree for restitution of conjugal rights, or on any ground on which a decree for divorce a mensa et thoro might have been pronounced immediately before the commencement of the Matrimonial Causes Act, 1857, and the foregoing provisions of this Act relating to the duty of the court on the presentation of a petition for divorce, and the circumstances in which such a petition shall or may be granted or dismissed, shall apply in like manner to a petition for judicial separation.

(2) Where the court in accordance with the said provisions grants a decree for judicial separation, it shall no longer be obligatory for the petitioner to cohabit with the respondent.

(3) The court may, on the application by petition of the husband or wife against whom a decree for judicial separation has been made, and on being satisfied that the allegations contained in the petition are true, reverse the decree at any time after the making thereof, on the ground that it was obtained in the absence of the person making the application, or, if desertion was the ground of the decree, that there was reasonable cause for the alleged desertion.

Decree for restitution of conjugal rights.

15.—(1) A petition for restitution of conjugal rights may be presented to the court either by the husband or the wife, and the court, on being satisfied that the allegations contained in the petition are true, and that there is no legal ground why a decree for restitution of conjugal rights should not be granted, may make the decree accordingly.

(2) A decree for restitution of conjugal rights shall not be enforced by attachment.

Presumption of Death and Dissolution of Marriage

Proceedings for decree of presumption of death and dissolution of marriage.

16.—(1) Any married person who alleges that reasonable grounds exist for supposing that the other party to the marriage is dead may, if he is domiciled in England, present a petition to the court to have it presumed that the other party is dead and to have the marriage dissolved and the court, if satisfied that such reasonable grounds exist, may make a decree of presumption of death and of dissolution of the marriage.

(2) In any such proceedings the fact that for a period of seven years or upwards the other party to the marriage has been continually absent from the petitioner, and the petitioner has no reason to believe that the other party has been living within that time, shall be evidence that he or she is dead until the contrary is proved.

(3) Sections ten to thirteen of this Act shall apply to a petition and a decree under this section as they apply to a petition for divorce and a decree of divorce respectively.

(4) In determining for the purposes of this section whether a woman is domiciled in England, her husband shall be treated as having died immediately after the last occasion on which she knew or had reason to believe him to be living.

Declaration of Legitimacy, &c.

Declaration of legitimacy, &c.

17.—(1) Any person who is a British subject, or whose right to be deemed a British subject depends wholly or in part on his legitimacy or on the validity of any marriage, may, if he is domiciled in England or Northern Ireland or claims any real or personal estate situate in England, apply by petition to the court for a decree declaring that the petitioner is the legitimate child of his parents, and that the marriage of his father and mother or of his grandfather and grandmother was a valid marriage or that his own marriage was a valid marriage.

(2) Any person claiming that he or his parent or any remoter ancestor became or has become a legitimated person may apply by petition to the court for a decree declaring that he or his parent or remoter ancestor, as the case may be, became or has become a legitimated person.

In this subsection the expression " legitimated person " means a person legitimated by the Legitimacy Act, 1926, and includes a person recognised under section eight of that Act is legitimated.

(3) A petition under the last foregoing subsection may be presented to a county court instead of to the High Court :

Provided that, where a petition is presented to a county court, the county court, if it considers that the case is one which owing to the value of the property involved or otherwise ought to be dealt with by the High Court, may, and if so ordered by the High Court shall, transfer the matter to the High Court, and on such transfer the proceeding shall be continued in the High Court as if it had been originally commenced therein.

(4) Any person who is domiciled in England or Northern Ireland or claims any real or personal estate situate in England may apply to the court for a decree declaring his right to be deemed a British subject.

(5) Applications to the court (but not to a county court) under the foregoing provisions of this section may be included in the same petition, and on any application under the foregoing provisions of this section (including an application to a county court) the court shall make such decree as the court thinks just, and the decree shall be binding on His Majesty and all other persons whatsoever :

Provided that the decree of the court shall not prejudice any person—

(*a*) if it is subsequently proved to have been obtained by fraud or collusion ; or (*b*) unless that person has been cited or made a party to the proceedings or claims through a person so cited or made a party.

(6) A copy of every petition under this section and of any affidavit accompanying the petition shall be delivered to the Attorney-General at least one month before the petition is presented, and the Attorney-General shall be a respondent on the hearing of the petition and on any subsequent proceedings relating thereto.

(7) In any application under this section such persons shall, subject to rules of court, be cited to see proceedings or otherwise summoned as the court shall think fit, and any such persons may be permitted to become parties to the proceedings and to oppose the application.

(8) No proceedings under this section shall affect any final judgment or decree already pronounced or made by any court of competent jurisdiction.

Additional Jurisdiction in Proceedings by a Wife

Additional jurisdiction in proceedings by a wife.

18.—(1) Without prejudice to any jurisdiction exercisable by the court apart from this section, the court shall by virtue of this section have jurisdiction to entertain proceedings by a wife in any of the following cases, notwithstanding that the husband is not domiciled in England, that is to say :—

(*a*) in the case of any proceedings under this Act other than proceedings for presumption of death and dissolution of marriage, if the wife has been deserted by her husband, or the husband has been deported from the United Kingdom under any law for the time being in force relating to the deportation of aliens, and the husband was immediately before the desertion or deportation domiciled in England ;

(*b*) in the case of proceedings for divorce or nullity of marriage, if the wife is resident in England and has been ordinarily resident there for a period of three years immediately preceding the commencement of the proceedings, and the husband is not domiciled in any other part of the United Kingdom or in the Channel Islands or the Isle of Man.

(2) Without prejudice to the jurisdiction of the court to entertain proceedings under section sixteen of this Act in cases where the petitioner is domiciled in England, the court shall by virtue of this section have jurisdiction to entertain any such proceedings brought by a wife, if the wife is resident in England and has been ordinarily resident there for a period of three years immediately preceding the commencement of the proceedings.

(3) In any proceedings in which the court has jurisdiction by virtue of this section, the issues shall be determined in accordance with the law which would be applicable thereto if both parties were domiciled in England at the time of the proceedings.

Alimony, Maintenance and Custody of Children

19.—(1) On any petition for divorce or nullity of marriage, the court may make such interim orders for the payment of alimony to the wife as the court thinks just.

Alimony and maintenance in case of divorce and nullity of marriage.

(2) On any decree for divorce or nullity of marriage, the court may, if it thinks fit, order that the husband shall, to the satisfaction of the court secure to the wife such gross sum of money or annual sum of money for any term, not exceeding her life, as, having regard to her fortune, if any, to the ability of her husband and to the conduct of the parties, the court may deem to be reasonable ; and the court may for that purpose order that it shall be referred to one of the conveyancing counsel of the court to settle and approve a proper deed or instrument to be executed by all the necessary parties, and may, if it thinks fit, suspend the pronouncing of the decree until the deed or instrument has been duly executed.

(3) On any decree for divorce or nullity of marriage, the court may, if it thinks fit, by order direct the husband to pay to the wife, during their joint lives, such monthly or weekly sum for the maintenance and support of the wife as the court may think reasonable, and any such order may either be in addition to or be instead of an order made under the last foregoing subsection.

(4) The foregoing provisions of this section shall have effect, in any case where a petition for divorce is presented by a wife on the ground of her husband's insanity, as if for the references to the husband there were substituted references to the wife, and for the references to the wife there were substituted references to the husband.

20.—(1) On any petition for judicial separation, the court may make such interim orders for the payment of alimony to the wife as the court thinks just.

Alimony in case of judicial separation.

(2) On any decree for judicial separation, the court may make such order for the payment of alimony to the wife as the court thinks just.

(3) The foregoing provisions of this section shall have effect, in any case where a petition for judicial separation is presented by a wife on the ground of her husband's insanity, as if for the references to the wife there were substituted references to the husband.

21.—(1) In every case of judicial separation—

Wife's property and necessaries supplied to wife in case of judicial separation.

(*a*) any property which is acquired by or devolves upon the wife on or after the date of the decree whilst the separation continues shall, if she dies intestate, devolve as if her husband had been then dead ;

(*b*) if alimony has been ordered to be paid and has not been duly paid by the husband, he shall be liable for necessaries supplied for the use of the wife.

(2) In any case where the decree for judicial separation is obtained by the wife, any property to which she is entitled for an estate in remainder or reversion at the date of the decree shall be deemed to be property to which this section applies.

Alimony and periodical payments in case of restitution of conjugal rights.

22.—(1) On any petition for restitution of conjugal rights, the court may make such interim order for the payment of alimony to the wife as the court thinks just.

(2) Where any decree for restitution of conjugal rights is made on the application of the wife, the court may make such order for the payment of alimony to the wife as the court thinks just.

(3) Where any decree for restitution of conjugal rights is made on the application of the wife, the court, at the time of the making of the decree or at any time afterwards may, in the event of the decree not being complied with within any time limited in that behalf by the court, order the respondent to make to the petitioner such periodical payments as the court thinks just, and the order may be enforced in the same manner as an order for alimony.

(4) Where the court makes an order under the last foregoing sub-section, the court may, if it thinks fit, order that the husband shall, to the satisfaction of the court, secure to the wife the periodical payments, and for that purpose may direct that it shall be referred to one of the conveyancing counsel of the court to settle and approve a proper deed or instrument to be executed by all the necessary parties.

Additional power of court to make orders for maintenance.

23.—(1) Where a husband has been guilty of wilful neglect to provide reasonable maintenance for his wife or the infant children of the marriage, the court, if it would have jurisdiction to entertain proceedings by the wife for judicial separation, may, on the application of the wife, order the husband to make to her such periodical payments as may be just; and the order may be enforced in the same manner as an order for alimony in proceedings for judicial separation.

(2) Where the court makes an order under this section for periodical payments it may, if it thinks fit, order that the husband shall, to the satisfaction of the court, secure to the wife the periodical payments, and for that purpose may direct that a proper deed or instrument to be executed by all necessary parties shall be settled and approved by one of the conveyancing counsel of the court.

Power of court to order settlement of wife's property.

24.—(1) If it appears to the court in any case in which the court pronounces a decree for divorce or for judicial separation by reason of the adultery, desertion of cruelty of the wife that the wife is entitled to any property either in possession or reversion, the court may, if it thinks fit, order such settlement as it thinks reasonable to be made of the property, or any part thereof, for the benefit of the innocent party, and of the children of the marriage or either or any of them.

(2) Where a decree for restitution of conjugal rights is made on the application of the husband, and it appears to the court that the wife is entitled to any property, either in possession or reversion, or is in receipt of any profits of trade or earnings, the court may, if it thinks fit, order a settlement to be made to the satisfaction of the court of the property or any part thereof for the benefit of the petitioner and of the children of the marriage or either or any of them, or may order such part of the profits of trade or earnings as the court thinks reasonable to be periodically paid by the respondent to the petitioner for his own benefit, or to the petitioner or any other person for the benefit of the children of the marriage or either or any of them.

25.—The court may after pronouncing a decree for divorce for nullity of marriage inquire into the existence of ante-nuptial or post-nuptial settlements made on the parties whose marriage is the subject of the decree, and may make such orders with reference to the application of the whole or any part of the property settled either for the benefit of the children of the marriage or of the parties to the marriage, as the court thinks fit, and the court may exercise the powers conferred by this section notwithstanding that there are no children of the marriage.

Power of court to make orders as to application of settled property.

26.—(1) In any proceedings for divorce or nullity of marriage or judicial separation, the court may from time to time, either before or by or after the final decree, make such provision as appears just with respect to the custody, maintenance and education of the children the marriage of whose parents is the subject of the proceedings, or, if it thinks fit, direct proper proceedings to be taken for placing the children under the protection of the court.

Custody and maintenance of children.

(2) On an application made in that behalf, the court may, in any proceedings for restitution of conjugal rights, at any time before final decree, or, if the respondent fails to comply therewith, after final decree, make from time to time all such orders and provisions with respect to the custody, maintenance and education of the children of the petitioner and respondent as might have been made by interim orders if proceedings for judicial separation had been pending between the same parties.

(3) On any decree of divorce or nullity of marriage, the court shall have power to order the husband, and on a decree of divorce made on the power to order the husband, and on a decree of divorce made on the ground of the husband's insanity, shall also have power to order the wife, to secure for the benefit of the children such gross sum of money or annual sum of money as the court may deem reasonable, and the court may for that purpose order that it shall be referred to one of the conveyancing counsel of the court to settle and approve a proper deed or instrument to be executed by all necessary parties :

Provided that the term for which any sum of money is secured for the benefit of a child shall not extend beyond the date when the child will attain twenty-one years of age.

27.—(1) In any case where the court makes an order for alimony, the court may direct the alimony to be paid either to the wife or the husband, as the case may be, or to a trustee approved by the court on her or his behalf, and may impose such terms or restrictions as the court thinks expedient, and may from time to time appoint a new trustee if for any reason it appears to the court expedient so to do.

Payment of alimony and maintenance to trustees and persons having charge of respondent.

(2) In any case where—

(*a*) a petition for divorce or judicial separation is presented by a wife on the ground of her husband's insanity ; or

(*b*) a petition for divorce, nullity or judicial separation is presented by a husband on the ground of his wife's insanity or mental deficiency,

and the court orders payments of alimony or maintenance under section nineteen or section twenty of this Act in favour of the respondent, the court may order the payments to be made to such persons having charge of the respondent as the court may direct.

Variation and discharge of orders for alimony and maintenance.

28.—(1) Where the court has made an order under section nineteen, section twenty, section twenty-two, section twenty-three or subsection (2) of section twenty-four of this Act, the court shall have power to discharge or vary the order or to suspend any provision thereof temporarily and to revive the operation of any provisions so suspended:

Provided that in relation to an order made before the sixteenth day of December, nineteen hundred and forty-nine, being an order which, by virtue of subsection (2) of section thirty-four of this Act, is deemed to have been made under subsection (2) of section nineteen of this Act, the powers conferred by this section shall not be exercised unless the court is satisfied that the case is one of exceptional hardship which cannot be met by the discharge, variation or suspension of any order made, or deemed as aforesaid to have been made, under subsection (3) of the said section nineteen.

(2) The powers exercisable by the court under this section in relation to any order shall be exercisable also in relation to any deed or other instrument executed in pursuance of the order.

(3) In exercising the powers conferred by this section, the court shall have regard to all the circumstances of the case, including any increase or decrease in the means of either of the parties to the marriage.

Commencement of proceedings for maintenance, settlement of property, &c.

29.—When a petition for divorce or nullity of marriage has been presented, proceedings under section nineteen, twenty-four, twenty-five or subsection (3) of section twenty-six of this Act may, subject to and in accordance with rules of court, be commenced at any time after the presentation of the petition:

Provided that no order under any of the said sections or under the said subsection (other than an interim for the payment of alimony under section nineteen) shall be made unless and until a decree nisi has been pronounced, and no such order, save in so far as it relates to the preparation, execution, or approval of a deed or instrument, and no settlement made in pursuance of any such order, shall take effect unless and until the decree is made absolute.

Miscellaneous

Damages for adultery.

30.—(1) A husband may, on a petition for divorce or for judicial separation or for damages only, claim damages from any person on the ground of adultery with the wife of the petitioner.

(2) A claim for damages on the ground of adultery shall, subject to the provisions of any enactment relating to trial by jury in the court, be tried on the same principles and in the same manner as actions for criminal conversation were tried immediately before the commencement of the Matrimonial Causes Act, 1857, and the provisions of this Act with reference to the hearing and decision of petitions shall so far as may be necessary apply to the hearing and decision of petitions on which damages are claimed.

(3) The court may direct in what manner the damages recovered on any such petition are to be paid or applied, and may direct the whole or any part of the damages to be settled for the benefit of the children, if any, of the marriage, or as a provision for the maintenance of the wife.

31.—In every case in which any person is charged with adultery with any party to a suit or in which the court may consider, in the interest of any person not already a party to the suit, that that person should be made a party to the suit, the court may, if it thinks fit, allow that person to intervene upon such terms, if any, as the court thinks just.

Power to allow intervention on terms.

32.—(1) Notwithstanding any rule of law, the evidence of a husband or wife shall be admissible in any proceedings to prove that marital intercourse did or did not take place between them during any period.

Evidence.

(2) Notwithstanding anything in this section or any rule of law, a husband or wife shall not be compellable in any proceedings to give evidence of the matters aforesaid.

(3) The parties to any proceedings instituted in consequence of adultery and the husbands and wives of the parties shall be competent to give evidence in the proceedings, but no witness in any such proceedings, whether a party thereto or not, shall be liable to be asked or be bound to answer any question tending to show that he or she has been guilty of adultery unless he or she has already given evidence in the same proceedings in disproof of the alleged adultery.

(4) In any proceedings for nullity of marriage, evidence on the question of sexual capacity shall be heard in camera unless in any case the judge is satisfied that in the interests of justice any such evidence ought to be heard in open court.

Interpretation, Repeal and Short Title

33.—In this Act the expression " the court " means the High Court, except that in section seventeen, where the context so requires, it means or includes a county court, and the expression " prescribed " means prescribed by rules of court.

Interpretation.

34.—(1) The enactments set out in the Schedule to this Act are hereby repealed to the extent specified in the third column of that Schedule.

Repeal and savings.

(2) Without prejudice to the provisions of section thirty-eight of the Interpretation Act, 1889—

(*a*) nothing in this repeal shall affect any order made, direction given or thing done, under any enactment repealed by this Act or the Supreme Court of Judicature (Consolidation) Act, 1925, or deemed to have been made, given or done respectively under any such enactment, and every such order, direction or thing shall if in force at the commencement of this Act continue in force, and, so far as it could have been made, given or done under this Act, shall be deemed to have been made, given or done under the corresponding provision of this Act ;

(*b*) any other order in force at the commencement of this Act which could have been made under any provision of this Act shall be deemed to have been so made ;

(*c*) any document referring to any Act or enactment repealed by this Act or the said Act of 1925 shall be construed as referring to this Act or to the corresponding enactment in this Act;

(*d*) for the purposes of the India (Consequential Provision) Act, 1949 this Act shall be deemed to have been in force on the twenty-sixth day of January, nineteen hundred and fifty.

Short title, commencement and extent.

35.—(1) This Act may be cited as the Matrimonial Causes Act, 1950.

(2) This Act shall come into operation on the first day of January, nineteen hundred and fifty-one.

(3) This Act shall not extend to Scotland or Northern Ireland.

INDEX